JOHN GRIGG

1943

The Victory That Never Was

PENGUIN BOOKS

PENGUIN BOOKS

Published by the Penguin Group
Penguin Books Ltd, 27 Wrights Lane, London W8 5TZ, England
Penguin Putnam Inc., 375 Hudson Street, New York, New York 10014, USA
Penguin Books Australia Ltd, Ringwood, Victoria, Australia
Penguin Books Canada Ltd, 10 Alcorn Avenue, Toronto, Ontario, Canada M4V 3B2
Penguin Books (NZ) Ltd, Private Bag 102902, NSMC, Auckland, New Zealand

Penguin Books Ltd, Registered Offices: Harmondsworth, Middlesex, England

First published by Eyre Methuen 1980
Published with a new preface in Penguin Books 1999
1 3 5 7 9 10 8 6 4 2

Grateful acknowledgement is made to the following for permission to reproduce photographs:

Imperial War Museum: Roosevelt, Churchill and Mackenzie King at the 1943 Quebec
conference; Mountbatten visiting Montgomery in Normandy; Eisenhower with Marshall;
de Gaulle with Eisenhower in France; Churchill with Tedder in North Africa; Teheran
Conference (Eden, Churchill and Stalin)

Hulton Getty: Roosevelt and Churchill at Casablanca with service advisers; Roosevelt and
correspondents at Casablanca; 1943 Washington conference; Teheran conference (Roosevelt
turning to Sarah Churchill); Harris with Eaker; Brooke arriving at 10 Downing Street; Eden
with Hopkins; Alexander in Italy; Admiral Ernest King; Hitler and Mussolini;
Hitler wishing Rommel good luck

Corbis: Patton lands in Sicily

Printed in England by Clays Ltd, St Ives plc

To the memory of
my father

Contents

Preface to the 1999 Edition   ix
Preface   3

Part One   From Pearl Harbor to TORCH

I.   America In   9   /   II.   Churchill and Roosevelt   14   /   III.   How to Win?   18   /   IV.   The Tide Turns in Russia . . .   23   /   V.   . . . And in the Pacific   26   /   VI.   British Calamities   28   /   VII.   Churchill in Trouble   33   /   VIII.   The Kindling of TORCH   37   /   IX.   Hazards of TORCH   40   /   X.   Churchill's Journey   43   /   XI.   Victory at Last   47   /   XII.   Unfinished Business in North Africa   51

Part Two   Aspects of 1943

1   Emperors at Casablanca   59
2   The Price of Tunis   80
3   Italian Follies   95
4   The Captive Giant   116
5   Bombing On Regardless   136
6   Fallacies about France   158
7   The World-Sharers   175

Part Three   Questions and Arguments

I.   The Victory That Was   195   /   II.   The Wilmot Thesis   205   /   III.   "Impossible to Land in 1943"   210   /   IV.   "Atlantic Wall Too Strong"   214   /   V.   "Not Enough Landing-Craft"   218   /   VI. "Technical Resources Inadequate"   220   /   VII.   American Mistakes   223   /   VIII.   British Mistakes   227   /   IX.   Risk and Cost of Delay   231   /   X.   The Victory That Might Have Been   233

Select Bibliography   241
Index   245

Illustrations follow page 116

Maps

Russian Front, 1942–44   22

North Coast of Africa   52

West European Fronts, 1943–45   58

Preface to the 1999 Edition

Twenty years ago, when this book was written, there was an overwhelming belief that the Second World War was nobler and more just than the First, and that it was conducted by British leaders with far greater efficiency and strategic grasp. Today the prejudice persists, though to a diminishing degree. More people now are prepared to say that Britain was right to intervene in 1914, and that the nation's motives throughout the ensuing war were at least as idealistic as in 1939–45. Some, too—though fewer—are prepared to question the superiority of British leadership and performance in the second war, compared with the first. On both counts, what used to be an almost universal view of the two wars is still the majority view. Conventional wisdom dies hard.

This book is chiefly about policy and strategy from 1941 onwards. Moral issues arise, but not as the main theme. Before Churchill took over, Britain's showing in the second war was by any standards undistinguished. His conduct in 1940 was truly heroic and inspired. In the first year of his premiership he and the country captured the world's imagination (not, it must be said, standing "alone", but with vital support from the Dominions, India, the Colonial empire and an America whose president bent the rules of neutrality). Yet the epic of 1940–41 has so dazzled posterity that Britain's subsequent war effort and Churchill's leadership through the rest of the war have attracted far less critical attention than they deserve.

Of course there is still much to admire and praise in 1941–45, and in any case the war was ultimately won. But it took longer to win than the first war, even from the time (June 1941) when Russia was attacked. America was belligerent for nearly four years in the second war, compared with only seventeen months in the first, and made an immeasurably larger contribution to victory. True, Japan was a formidable enemy instead of an ally (of limited value), but on the other hand we had to contend with the Ottoman empire in the first war, whereas in the second Turkey was neutral. (The significance of Italy in both wars is complex and hard to fit into the equation.)

One point should be stressed: leaders in the second war had a huge advantage over their predecessors in the mere fact that it *was* the second. In 1914–18, world war was an entirely new experience, confronting politicians and service chiefs alike with problems that were without precedent. Leaders in the second war had the lessons of the first to guide them. Even so, it may well be thought that they made just as many mistakes, though they have so far received an invidiously "better press".

What sort of press did my book get? On the whole reviewers were very generous to it on the score of readability, and paid me the compliment of taking the arguments in it seriously. One or two indulged in some tut-tutting about my "what if ..." approach. But very soon afterwards, by coincidence, Hugh Trevor-Roper (Lord Dacre of Glanton) gave this approach to history his blessing. In his inaugural lecture as Regius Professor at Oxford he said: "History is not merely what happened: it is what happened in the context of what might have happened. Therefore it must incorporate ... the might-have-beens." Today historical hypotheses are all the rage, under the rather misleading title "counter-factual history" (misleading, because it suggests that the facts themselves are being challenged, rather than their deterministic necessity). It is right, surely, first to get the record straight, and then to argue about the past. Facts are facts, but that does not mean that they are, or ever were, inevitable.

On the substance of the book, most reviewers found reasons for dissenting from its central thesis—that a cross-Channel Allied invasion might have been mounted in 1943, with a good chance of success. Many contributory arguments are now generally accepted. For instance the Allies' crass mishandling of the Italian armistice negotiations, and its bearing on subsequent events, is now hardly a matter of dispute. The attempt to win the war by the indiscriminate terror bombing of civilians is probably more widely condemned today as a colossal mistake as well as a crime. And there is growing awareness of the enormity of Roosevelt's mistake, which Churchill after a time compounded, in being so hostile to de Gaulle and his movement. Yet the essence of what I was trying to suggest remains controversial, and still has to make its way against arguments which I believe to be fallacious.

Instead of trying to deal with a number of critics, I will concentrate here on John Keegan's review in the *Times Literary Supplement*, which seems to me the best statement of the case against mine. And I will focus on his two apparently strongest points: (i) that at the time of a cross-Channel invasion in 1943 Hitler's armoured strength, still unreduced by the great tank battle of Kursk on the Russian front, would have proved too much for the invaders, and (ii) that the available American forces, though already sufficient in numbers, would not have been adequately prepared for battle.

The first point presupposes that operations on the Russian front would have been no different in the summer of 1943 if the Allies had decided to open a proper second front then rather than a year later. But surely they *would* have been different. If the Russians had been told, after the Casablanca conference, that the Western Allies were planning to land in north-west Europe in the late spring, they would have planned an offensive to coincide with the Allied landings. They would have done this not, of course, for the Allies' *beaux yeux*, but because they could not afford to let the invasion fail. As it was, they were told after Casablanca that there would be no cross-Channel invasion in 1943, but that Anglo-American operations that year would be largely confined to the Mediterranean theatre. It is hardly surprising, therefore, that they chose to adopt a defensive posture in the spring of 1943, and that the titanic armoured battle began only when the Germans attacked in July.

If the Russians had attacked in June, the German strategic reserve would not have been free to concentrate against the Allied bridgehead, but would have been torn both ways, with the additional handicap that the two fronts would have been far more widely separated. In the spring of 1943 the Eastern front was still hundreds of miles inside the Soviet Union. Besides, Hitler was preoccupied with Russia and tended to take a cavalier view of the cross-Channel threat. Even in 1944 there was—according to Richard Overy in *Russia's War* (1997)—"no major movement of manpower westward to cope with the invasion of France". The previous year, when Hitler still had a rational hope of destroying the Red Army and achieving total victory in the East, he would surely have been at least equally reluctant to switch armoured strength from what he regarded as the vital front.

The argument about American battle-preparedness rests heavily upon the setback experienced by US troops in the Kasserine Pass engagement in Tunisia. It is true that the first impact of Rommel's attack did throw the Americans guarding the Pass into temporary disarray, just as the Germans' Ardennes offensive caused a temporary local collapse in December 1944. But on the first occasion, as on the second, the Americans soon pulled themselves together. After a few days at Kasserine, Liddell Hart tells us, Rommel became "impressed by the growing tactical skill" of the Americans.

In any case, it is quite wrong to argue from Kasserine that the American army as a whole was unfit for serious combat. Already, unseasoned American troops had shown great doggedness in the Bataan peninsula, on Corregidor and on Guadalcanal. Eight months later the US 36th division, without previous battle experience, showed conspicuous fortitude in a tight spot at Salerno. In the 1944 Normandy landings a large proportion of the American troops were new to battle, which was one reason why Hitler underrated the cross-Channel threat. I am sure that they would have done just as well in 1943 as in 1944—with the benefit of much better weather.

Other arguments will not be rehearsed here, because they are covered in the book. The text is unaltered from the original edition of 1980, because nothing that has appeared since—and of course there have been many important and fascinating additions to Second World War literature—has drawn my attention to any factual inaccuracy, or caused me to feel less confident in challenging what is still the predominant view.

John Grigg
May 1999

1943

THE VICTORY
THAT NEVER WAS

Preface

The purpose of this book is to look afresh at certain key aspects of the war in Europe during the year 1943, and to reopen a fundamental question which historians and others have been treating, almost unanimously, as closed—whether or not it was right to delay the Allied invasion of north-west Europe until 1944. The case for regarding 1944 as the earliest possible year has been asserted with overwhelming confidence, but on grounds which do not, in my view, bear close scrutiny. I have, therefore, tried to show that the conventional wisdom on this issue is blind as well as bland, and to suggest that the case for an invasion the previous year, in the spring or summer of 1943, has been wrongly dismissed.

No historical might-have-been can ever be proved, and I am not asserting positively (as others assert the contrary) that a 1943 invasion would have ended the war sooner, or at a less excruciating cost. But it seems to me that the evidence points very strongly to that conclusion, indicating too that the actual conduct of the war in 1943 was, in many ways, disastrous.

The evidence that I have considered is nearly all to be found in printed sources. I would not for a moment claim to have written a work of original research, but rather a piece of extended historical journalism, putting forward an argument about the history of the Second World War, mainly as it affected Europe. Though I believe it to be factually sound, and have done my best to ensure that it is fair, it has to be judged less as a contribution to knowledge than as a new interpretation of familiar events.

By no means all of the criticism in the book is *in itself* new. Montgomery's relative failure to exploit victories has already attracted plenty of notice, and the area bombing campaign associated with the name of Sir Arthur Harris has been much condemned. But two men with wider powers and responsibilities than either Montgomery or Harris have so far had a much "better press." They are Portal and Brooke. Portal has enjoyed an almost complete immunity from criticism; Brooke has been extravagantly admired by British writers. Both reputations seem to me inflated.

An important theme of the book, interwoven with the invasion issue, is the loss of world power by Great Britain, and the emerging ascendancy of Russia and the United States. Inevitably, the personalities of Churchill, Roosevelt, and Stalin bulk large, and I have tried to separate myth from reality in discussing the Big Three, their impact on the war, and their relations with each other. Special attention has been paid to the Churchill-Roosevelt relationship, and Churchill's role on certain major issues is, I think, shown to have been very much more complex than most people, whether fans or critics, believe.

The general effect of the book should be to bring together a number of themes which are too often considered in isolation, and so to form a view of the war as a whole which challenges the accepted view.

Part One sketches in the background to 1943—the course of the war from America's entry at the end of 1941 to the landings in French North Africa at the end of 1942. Part Two examines in some detail those aspects of 1943 which seem to have most bearing upon the central argument. Part Three begins with a brief account of how the war did, in fact, end; discusses the view of its last stages propounded early in the Cold War by Chester Wilmot; reviews the stock arguments against an invasion in 1943, endeavouring (I trust successfully) to refute them; and finally offers a tentative outline of the victory that might have been, if the Western Allies had decided to invade that year.

Readers must not expect any colourful descriptions of blasted cities or of soldiers stumbling through the smoke of battle. This is a book about high politics and grand strategy. But it should never be forgotten that in war everything is confused. At all levels it is hard to see clearly, and leaders are as likely, in their way, to stumble and make mistakes as the ordinary fighting men whose activities they seek to direct.

The errors of the great and powerful should, therefore, be treated with sympathy as well as candour, even though some of them tend to forfeit sympathy by claiming too much for themselves and showing too little charity towards their colleagues.

J.G.

April 1979

PART ONE

FROM PEARL HARBOR
TO "TORCH"

I. AMERICA IN

On 7 December 1941 Japan committed the stupendous blunder of attacking the Americans at Pearl Harbor, and four days later Hitler (and Mussolini) committed the even more stupendous one of declaring war on the United States. What had been the second great European war of the century was thus transformed into the Second World War.

The Japanese attack was not unprovoked. Of course Japan was an expansionist power, whose continuing aggression in China was a source of outrage to the United States, where a godfatherly attitude towards China was combined with fear of Japan as a naval rival and potential threat to the American West Coast. But until the autumn of 1941 the Japanese had no intention of going to war with the United States. What they wanted was a free hand in China and secure access to vital raw materials, particularly oil.

In 1940 the collapse of France and the Netherlands, and the beleaguered condition of Britain, encouraged them to seek at least economic advantages in the Far Eastern possessions of those three countries. But only the Vichy French were cooperative. The Dutch refused to give the Japanese a privileged economic position in, or guaranteed oil supplies from, the East Indies. The British agreed to close the Burma Road to China in July 1940, but only for three months, and in general showed a toughness towards Japan which bore no relation to their available forces or to any rational view of their interests.

Earlier in the century Britain and Japan had been allies, but after the First World War the alliance was allowed to lapse under pressure from the Dominions and the United States. In September 1940 Japan signed a tripartite pact with Germany and Italy, under which mutual assistance was pledged—though with some reservations on the Japanese side—in case any of the signatories was attacked "by a power at present not involved in the European war or in the Sino-Japanese conflict." But this was only a defensive arrangement, and the following year the Japanese disappointed Hitler by entering into a non-aggression pact with the Soviet Union, thus refusing to complement his invasion of Russia with any move against Soviet territory in the Far East. They could hardly have indicated more clearly that their assessment of the world balance of power was still cautious, and that Hitler's enemies were not necessarily theirs.

The Americans, meanwhile, had begun to turn the screw on Japan. At the end of 1940 stringent economic sanctions were imposed, the eventual effect of which could only be either to bring Japan to her knees or to drive her into more extensive aggression. The Japanese tried to come to terms with the United States, while showing that they would not agree to any humiliating withdrawal. To strengthen their position, in the summer of 1941, they occupied key points in southern Indo-China, but the Americans responded by freezing all Japanese assets under their control and by tightening still further their virtual blockade of Japan.

In August President Franklin D. Roosevelt spurned the suggestion of the Japanese Prime Minister, Prince Fumimaro Konoye, that they meet to discuss a settlement, despite repeated warnings from the American ambassador in Tokyo, Joseph C. Grew, that the alternative to Konoye would be a war government. In October Konoye resigned and a military regime took over, under General Hideki Tojo. There could be no reasonable doubt that the Japanese would soon take drastic action. The only questions were, precisely what and against whom?

It has been alleged that their attack on Pearl Harbor was deliberately and cold-bloodedly engineered by Roosevelt; that after trying in vain to get America into the war by goading the Germans in the Atlantic, he then turned to the Pacific and successfully goaded the Japanese. This interpretation is not supported by contemporary evidence. Roosevelt's hard line with Japan was not a thought-out consistent policy but a response to various pressures, and in fact he blundered into the Pacific war. Both he and most of his professional advisers regarded Germany as the prime, immediate threat to American security, from which a war with Japan might be a dangerous diversion. As late as 5 November 1941 he was advised in this sense by General George C. Marshall, Chief of Staff, and Admiral Harold Stark, Chief of Naval Operations.

Moreover when, towards the end of the month, Roosevelt knew from intercepts of Japanese secret messages, obtained through the code-breaking process known as "Magic," that Japan had set a time-limit for negotiations, he was prepared to agree to a *modus vivendi* which, if put forward earlier, might have averted war. But the new rulers of Japan were far less likely to be interested, and in any case were never given the chance to consider it. The Chinese were indignant at the suggested terms, and Churchill supported the Chinese, cabling Roosevelt on 26 November: "Our anxiety is about China. If they collapse our joint dangers would enormously increase. We are sure that the regard of the United States for the Chinese will govern your action. We feel that the Japanese are most unsure of themselves." From a combination of motives—including belief that a Japanese attack was now inexorable, and reluctance to incur the odium of letting China down—Roosevelt decided that the truce terms should not be presented, but that instead a ten-point note, whose terms were manifestly unacceptable, should be handed to the two Japanese special envoys in Washington.

War thus became not only certain but imminent. There could, however, be no certainty where the blow would fall, and there was no reason at all to assume that American bases or territory would be attacked. For all his hawkishness and over-optimism about deterring the Japanese, Churchill was aware that they could break the economic stranglehold to which they were being subjected merely by seizing British and Dutch possessions in the Far East, and that without American intervention the task of resisting them would be desperately hard, even if it were feasible at all. He therefore exerted himself to obtain from Roosevelt a commitment that if British territory were attacked America would intervene, though he knew very well that under the American Constitution questions of peace or war were decided ultimately not by the President but by the Senate. The most that he could hope for was a declaration which might have some moral effect, but even that proved extremely hard to extract.

Until almost the last moment Britain was in the absurd position of being pledged to go to war at once with Japan if she attacked the United States, without a reciprocal guarantee of any kind. Eventually, on 1 December, Roosevelt "threw in an aside" while talking to the British ambassador, Lord Halifax, "that in the case of a direct attack on ourselves or the Dutch, we should obviously all be together." But this was far from being a solemn or public undertaking, and, even if it had been such, would not have bound the Senate. What would have happened if the Japanese had attacked the British and Dutch without making any direct hostile move against the Americans will never be known, but it is at least possible that the Senate would have jibbed at going to war ostensibly for the sake of two European empires.

By miraculous good fortune the Japanese did not experiment with the more cunning strategy, but chose the reckless and ultimately fatal course of attacking the American fleet at Pearl Harbor—of which, by a further stroke of luck, the most important units, the aircraft-carriers, were at sea and so escaped destruction. But from Britain's point of view Pearl Harbor, though it removed one danger of which British leaders were not oblivious, actually created another to which they were blind at the time, and which even today is seldom recognised by historians and commentators. If, as Churchill says in his war memoirs, he went to bed after hearing the news of Pearl Harbor and "slept the sleep of the saved and thankful," he was in a state of complacency which the facts of the situation did not at all warrant.

America was now at war with Japan, but she was still a neutral in regard to Germany; and her neutrality might, but for Hitler, have become more rather than less genuine as a result of the Japanese attack. The common assertion that Pearl Harbor "brought America into the war" is simply not true. Pearl Harbor automatically involved Britain in war with Japan, but did not automatically involve the United States in war with Germany. On the contrary, under the shock of Pearl Harbor there was a grave danger that American public opinion might demand a concentration of effort against the Japanese, and a more correctly neutral attitude towards the Germans.

No doubt Roosevelt would have done his best to persuade the Senate to share his view of America's interest and duty, but his chances of success would have been dubious. There was much stronger public support for peace with Germany than for peace with Japan, if only because there were many fewer Americans of Japanese than of German origin, and because there was considerable racial prejudice against the Japanese; also, of course, because the Japanese had attacked without warning. But Roosevelt was spared the necessity of trying to make good his casual pledge to Halifax when, four days after Pearl Harbor, Hitler obliged him by gratuitously declaring war on the United States.

Why did Hitler do it? The step was gratuitous in that the Tripartite Pact did not require him to come to Japan's aid unless she was the victim of aggression. He had egged the Japanese on, and had given them a promise that he would act in sympathy if they took the initiative. But he was not a man to whom promises were sacrosanct, even when enshrined, as this was not, in a solemn treaty. According to all the canons of *Realpolitik* he should, in this case, have broken his informal word and stuck to the Tripartite Pact; and he could have softened the blow by assuring the Japanese that he was merely biding his time with a view to intervening at the most opportune moment. Having for so long avoided being provoked by Roosevelt's hostile measures, which in the Atlantic amounted almost to a state of undeclared war, he had every reason to extend his self-restraint into a period when the potential benefits of it were far larger.

But it seems that he suddenly lost his head, carried away by the spectacle of American discomfiture and convinced that the Americans were too soft to wage war effectively. He had never seen the United States and could not imagine what he was taking on. His decision, that of a dictator who did not have to seek the approval of any elected assembly, was perhaps the single most fateful decision of the whole war. With ample justification Churchill could have gone to bed feeling "saved" on the night of 11 December 1941, if not on the four previous nights. Pearl Harbor had threatened Britain with new and specially acute, if unacknowledged, perils. But Hitler had come to the rescue.

Euripides said that those whom the gods would destroy they first made mad, and the comment certainly applies to the behaviour of the Japanese and of Hitler in December 1941. But it cannot be said to apply to them alone, because the handling of Japan by the American and British governments was scarcely less crazy. Such, however, are the workings of Divine Providence that the folly of the Anglo-Saxon democracies was richly rewarded, while that of their enemies led to perdition.

II. CHURCHILL AND ROOSEVELT

The day after Hitler declared war on America, Winston Churchill was on his way to that country, travelling with a large retinue on board H.M.S. *Duke of York.* His destination was Washington, D.C., where he and Franklin D. Roosevelt were to meet for the first time as fellow-belligerents.

After a rough crossing, *Duke of York* reached the mouth of Chesapeake Bay on 22 December, and Churchill flew immediately to Washington. The President drove to meet him at the airport and installed him in the White House, where he stayed, on and off, for three weeks in close personal contact with his host. At the same time the two men and their advisers were engaged in a conference, code-named AR-CADIA, which set the pattern for other wartime summit meetings and established the basic machinery of Allied cooperation and decision-making. In this sense ARCADIA influenced the whole future course of the war. But above all it enabled the two leaders to get to know each other and to form what was soon being referred to as their historic friendship.

Historic it certainly was. But to what extent were they really friends? Churchill claimed in his memoirs that his fondness for Roosevelt had increased with the passage of time. "I formed a very strong affection, which grew with our years of comradeship, for this formidable politician who had imposed his will for nearly ten years upon the American scene, and whose heart seemed to respond to many of the impulses that stirred my own." The words show every sign of being carefully chosen: "formidable politician" rather than "great statesman," "imposed his will . . . upon the American scene" rather than "served the needs and aspirations of the American people." There is a suggestion of ruthlessness and of power exercised for its own sake.

All the same, Churchill's comment is unambiguous on his personal feelings for Roosevelt, and on how they developed with the shared experience of supreme command.

It would seem that in this he was deceiving himself, because the record points to a gradual, but relentless, cooling in their relations from the high level of cordiality and mutual trust apparent at AR-CADIA. When Roosevelt died in April 1945, Churchill's tribute to him in the House of Commons was markedly less glowing and convincing than that which, shortly beforehand, he had paid to Lloyd George. Though it could not be described as inadequate, or lacking in grandiloquence, there was something formal, almost distant, in his allusions to Roosevelt the man, as distinct from his achievements.

Still more to the point, Churchill did not attend Roosevelt's funeral, though most people at the time expected that he would. His excuse was that pressure had been put upon him not to leave Britain at a "most critical and difficult moment." But the moment was far less critical than others during the war when he had left the country for quite long periods, and it was not at all characteristic of him to allow his personal inclination to be overborne. Indeed it is, frankly, incredible that he would not have gone if he had truly wanted to go.

In retrospect, he owned to regretting the decision, but only on the ground that it had lost him an early chance of man-to-man discussions with the new President, Harry S. Truman, who had expressed a wish that he come over. He showed no regret about having failed to make a dramatic gesture of farewell to the President who was dead, and whose intimate, brotherly friend he was widely supposed to have been. But his absence was not overlooked, and in particular it rankled in the mind of a young admirer of F.D.R., then a mere Congressman from Texas, but later himself President of the United States; and when Churchill himself died in 1965, President Lyndon B. Johnson did not attend *his* funeral.

It would, however, be quite wrong to suggest that initial friendship between Churchill and Roosevelt turned to enmity, or even that it ceased to be friendship in any recognisable sense. Luckily for the world, there was to the end at least a modicum of goodwill and understanding between them; had it been otherwise, the war might never have been won. Besides, they were big enough to realise that history required them to get along, at least to the extent of being able to accommodate their differences on the most important problems facing the alliance. However uneasy their partnership, it could never be less than a very active partnership of convenience.

As such, it began when Roosevelt had the foresight and flair to make contact with Churchill, then First Lord of the Admiralty, at the outbreak of war, and to suggest that they should correspond personally. This they did from then onwards, and by the time Churchill became Prime Minister, they were well established as "pen friends." In August 1941 they met in Placentia Bay, Newfoundland, where they and their staff discussed the war, and where the Atlantic Charter was promulgated.

It was not their first encounter, though Churchill made the mistake of assuming that it was. Nobody reminded him that they had met once during the previous war, when he was Minister of Munitions in Lloyd George's coalition government, and Roosevelt Assistant Secretary of the Navy under Woodrow Wilson. According to John Gunther, Roosevelt was "irked" by Churchill's failure to remember the occasion. And Churchill, for his part, was clearly so anxious to forget the gaffe that he later made out that it had never occurred, recalling in his memoirs how "struck" he had been in 1918 by Roosevelt's "magnificent presence in all his youth and strength."

The incident draws attention to one fact, among others, that necessarily complicated their relations—the length of Churchill's experience of big-time politics compared with Roosevelt's. Though they were less than eight years apart in age, the difference in political seniority was much greater. When Churchill first sat in a British Cabinet, Roosevelt was not yet even a state, much less a national, politician. By the end of the First World War, Churchill had completed one career at the top and started another, whereas Roosevelt was only a junior member of the federal government. Politically, it was almost as if they belonged to different generations.

This was awkward enough, but the comparison of talents was in some respects even more invidious. Manifestly, Roosevelt had nothing like Churchill's originality of mind or command of language. Roosevelt was indeed, as Churchill said, a formidable politician, but he was not a man of genius in the sense that Churchill unquestionably was. Whereas Churchill was always bursting with ideas and did most of his own thinking—right or wrong—Roosevelt was largely dependent upon the ideas of others. As for their relative powers of utterance, Roosevelt was often able to hit upon a memorable folksy phrase, and was a master of the type of speech which reached perfection in his celebrated "fireside chats." Yet most of his statements were the work of speech-writers—as are most of the speeches nowadays of leading politicians on both sides of the Atlantic, who have become like illiterate medieval monarchs over-reliant upon the services of worldly priests. Churchill, by contrast, was not only richly capable of composing his own speeches but seemed to deliver himself of a flowing oration almost every time he opened his mouth.

The disparity of talent was, however, balanced by a disparity of power, in which it was Churchill's turn to be the underdog. As President of the United States since 1933, Roosevelt had become more powerful than Churchill had ever been or could ever hope to be. Quite apart from the disproportion in strength between the United States and even the still imperial Britain, the President, embodying the whole executive power of the Republic, had more authority within his own sphere than any British Prime Minister could possibly have within his. Churchill, for all his self-confidence and self-assertiveness, and for all the freedom of action that his unique prestige gave him, knew that in the war he was bound to be, as he himself graciously put it, Roosevelt's "lieutenant." But it was not a role that he could be expected to relish, and in fact there can be no doubt that he resented his enforced subordination to a man whom he secretly judged his inferior.

As time went on, his resentment was increased by a sense of growing alienation, as it became apparent that Roosevelt did not share his intimate, exclusive view of their partnership. Churchill dreamed— and from Britain's point of view it was perhaps the costliest illusion of his career—of a postwar world benevolently guided and guarded by the English-speaking democracies acting as a sort of condominium. In his speech to a joint session of Congress, delivered on 26 December 1941 while he was in Washington for the ARCADIA meetings, he gave eloquent expression to his dream: "It is not given to us to peer into the mysteries of the future. Still, I avow my hope and faith, sure and inviolate, that in the days to come the British and American peoples will for their own safety and for the good of all walk together side by side in majesty, in justice, and in peace." That vision of a majestic *pas de deux* ignored the realities of power and national self-interest.

Without having any such clear view of the future, Roosevelt instinctively recoiled from Churchill's vision, partly because, as an individual, he was keen to show his independence of a too conspicuous "lieutenant," and partly because, as an American, he had no taste for allowing his country's destinies to become too closely intertwined with those of the Britain that Churchill represented. He was pro-British only in two senses—that he wanted Britain to hold out against Hitler, and that he had some sentimental regard for the British people. In other ways he was distinctly anti-British. To the traditional American prejudice against the empire from which the Founding Fathers had seceded, he added his own more personal dislike of Britain's still fairly obtrusive governing class. Himself a self-conscious aristocrat, the squire of Hyde Park, he had a natural itch to cut the more splendidly endowed British aristocracy down to size.

Excelling in charm of manner and the capacity to put people at their ease, he was also a ruthless and rather feline man, whose character was at first misunderstood by the far less sensitive Churchill. Churchill's gradual disenchantment was, therefore, all the more painful. But in Washington at the end of 1941 his attitude towards his host was still that of a truly Arcadian innocence.

III. HOW TO WIN?

On his way to the Washington meetings in December 1941 Churchill prepared three papers on the future conduct of the war which were intended both to clear his own mind and to influence the Americans, particularly Roosevelt. The papers were shown to, and "generally" approved by, his professional advisers, who were travelling in the same warship. The first dealt with the Atlantic Front, the second with the Pacific Front, and the third with the "Campaign of 1943."

The argument of the first was that in 1942 the war in the West should "comprise, as its main offensive effort, the occupation and control by Great Britain and the United States of the whole of the North and West African possessions of France, and the further control by Britain of the whole North African shore from Tunis to Egypt, thus giving . . . free passage through the Mediterranean to the Levant and the Suez Canal." The French government at Vichy and its representatives in North Africa were to be offered "a blessing or a cursing." If they would cooperate in all the ways necessary "to bring France into the war again as a principal," then the Anglo-Saxon allies should promise "to re-establish France as a Great Power with her territories undiminished." But if Vichy were to persist in collaboration with Germany, in that case "the de Gaullist movement must be aided and used to the full." (General Charles de Gaulle was, of course, leader of the Free French movement.)

Churchill's second paper, on the Pacific Front, envisaged further Japanese successes in the Pacific, but not the collapse of British power in South-east Asia, which was, in fact, about to occur. The burden of the argument was that Anglo-American naval superiority over Japan should be re-asserted by May 1942, and that the Far Eastern war should not "absorb an unduly large proportion of United States forces."

The third, and most important, paper looked forward to a situation at the beginning of 1943 in which the tide would already have turned against Japan and the "whole West and North African shores from Dakar to the Suez Canal and the Levant to the Turkish frontier would be in Anglo-American hands." Turkey, "though not necessarily at war, would be definitely incorporated in the American-British-Russian front." The Russians would be in a strong position, and possibly "a footing would already have been established in Sicily and Italy, with reactions inside Italy which might be highly favourable."

But the war would not yet be over. It could be ended only "through the defeat in Europe of the German armies, *or through internal convulsions in Germany produced by the unfavourable course of the war, economic privations, and the Allied bombing offensive*" (J.G.'s italics). Preparations should be made for liberating "the captive countries of Western and Southern Europe by the landing at suitable points, successively or simultaneously, of British and American armies strong enough to enable the conquered populations to revolt." If "adequate and suitably equipped forces were landed in several of the following countries, namely, Norway, Denmark, Holland, Belgium, the French Channel coasts and the French Atlantic coasts, as well as in Italy and possibly the Balkans, the German garrisons would prove insufficient to cope both with the strength of the liberating forces and the fury of the revolting peoples." The vanguards of the various Anglo-American expeditions "should be marshalled by the spring of 1943 in Iceland, the British Isles, and, if possible, in French Morocco and Egypt." But the main body of liberating troops "would come direct across the ocean."

On the American side, neither the President nor his principal military adviser, General Marshall, needed any persuading that the correct strategy would be to beat Hitler first. This was already their settled conviction. But how to set about defeating Hitler was another matter, on which Marshall, for his part, was far from sharing Churchill's views. A whole year before Pearl Harbor he had decided that, if the United States were forced into war with Japan, Pacific operations should be restricted so as to permit concentration upon "a major offensive in the Atlantic" theatre. He never doubted that such an offensive would be necessary, or that it would have to be concentrated. At the Atlantic meeting in August 1941 he had been disturbed by Churchill's talk of defeating Hitler by bombing and blockade, without any large-scale invasion of the Continent. And at the ARCADIA conference he was no less disturbed by Churchill's alternative strategy of widely dispersed, piecemeal landings in support of local uprisings.

Roosevelt had his own reasons for being amenable at least to Churchill's ideas for action in North Africa. He wanted American land forces to be involved as soon as possible in the Atlantic theatre, to counteract the inevitable public demand for greater involvement in the Pacific. Mid-term congressional elections were due in November 1942, and Roosevelt the commander-in-chief could not be indifferent to the problems of Roosevelt the politician.

As well as all the civilian pressures for intensifying the war against Japan, he had to reckon with the political influence of the U.S. Navy, which had a very natural urge to settle accounts with the Japanese, and the potentially troublesome charisma of General Douglas

MacArthur, American land commander in the Far East, whose seniority in the Army (he was a former Chief of Staff) was matched by an addiction to high-flown rhetoric and a perceptible interest in politics. Opening a front in French North Africa might, for Roosevelt, be the only way to manage domestic opinion and at the same time do something to help the Russians, who were bearing the full weight of German military power.

In Marshall's view North Africa was a peripheral area, and he feared—rightly, as it turned out—that commitment of any substantial military effort there would detract from the build-up in north-west Europe, which alone could lead to a decision in the war with Germany. His plan, later spelled out in a memorandum bearing his name, was that British and American forces should concentrate in the United Kingdom for offensive action across the Channel. Three distinct operations were projected in this Marshall plan—BOLERO, the accumulation of men and matériel in the United Kingdom; SLEDGE-HAMMER, a possible emergency attack in the autumn of 1942, which would be launched only if the Russians seemed in imminent danger of collapse; and ROUND-UP, the decisive assault across the Channel in 1943.

The conflict between Churchill's and Marshall's ideas of Allied grand strategy was not resolved at the ARCADIA conference, though there were already indications that Roosevelt might, for political reasons, veer towards Churchill's, at any rate in the short term. But machinery was set up for running the war, in particular the Combined Chiefs of Staff Committee, with its headquarters in Washington. On this, the most important British representative was Field-Marshal Sir John Dill, recently sacked by Churchill as Chief of the Imperial General Staff (as the professional head of the British Army was then called), but known since the Atlantic meeting to enjoy the special confidence of Marshall. Dill, the disciplined, honourable, and highly professional Ulsterman, appealed to Marshall, the Virginian, who shared those qualities in full measure. Their friendship is said to have done much for Allied unity, and so it clearly did, though whether it helped to ensure the adoption of the wisest and best strategy is less certain; for Dill's special relationship with Marshall was largely used to reconcile Marshall to decisions which his judgment rejected.

The Russian Front, 1942-44

Front line, November 1942
Front line, March 1943
Front line at the end of 1943
Front line at the end of 1944

0   100   200   300 Miles
0   200   400   600 km

FINLAND

Leningrad

ESTONIA

Baltic Sea

LATVIA

LITHUANIA

EAST PRUSSIA

Vistula

Warsaw

1939 Partition

POLAND

Minsk

Smolensk

U. S. S. R.

Moscow

Tula

Kyubyshev

Orel

Kursk

Voronezh

Volga

Kiev

Dnieper

Kharkov

Stalingrad

Ukraine

Budapest

Taganrog

Don

Rostov

Odessa

ROUMANIA

Sea of Azov

Caspian Sea

Crimea

Ploesti

Bucharest

Danube

BULGARIA

YUGOSLAVIA

Black Sea

Caucasus

NSH

22

IV. THE TIDE TURNS IN RUSSIA . . .

Hitler's attack on Russia in June 1941 transformed the moral as well as the strategic character of the war. In 1939 the two great liberal democracies of Europe together challenged one of its two most dreadful tyrannies, which had just entered into a nefarious compact with the other. After the fall of France the honour of maintaining the armed struggle against Hitlerite Germany belonged for a whole year to the British Commonwealth and Empire alone, with the support of a few indomitable exiles and, of course, very active though non-belligerent assistance from the United States. The war was then still a crusade, if apparently a hopeless one.

When Russia was attacked, some grounds for rational hope once again existed, but the crusading character of the war was, to put it mildly, compromised. Churchill had no choice but to welcome the Russians as allies, though he did not retract any of his former denunciations of Bolshevism or offer any apology for having tried, twenty-odd years before, to strangle the Bolshevik revolution at birth. Privately he said that if Hitler invaded Hell he would "at least make a favourable reference to the Devil in the House of Commons."

Yet he must have known that, if the Russians put up a good resistance, he would have to go much further than that and draw a veil, for the duration, over the iniquities of the Soviet regime and its diabolical chief. In practice it was not long before British public opinion was being conditioned to regard the Soviet Union as a potential, if not yet fully evolved, democracy, and its leader as a man whose admitted toughness did not exclude at least a streak of idealism and humanity.

Moreover, pro-Russian sentiment was naturally boosted by news of the Red Army's achievements towards the end of 1941. Whereas at first it seemed that Russia might well prove to be yet another victim of German *Blitzkrieg,* and that for Britain withdrawal of the threat of invasion would be no more than temporary, after a few months it became clear that the Germans were running into serious trouble on the Eastern Front. Despite huge initial losses of men and territory, the Red Army stood firm in Leningrad and in front of Moscow, where, in December, it even launched a limited but successful counter-offensive.

Hitler had underrated the fighting spirit of the Russians, the reserves of manpower upon which Stalin could draw, and the resources of mystical patriotism that he could exploit. Since it had been assumed that the war would be as good as over before the winter, the German troops were neither equipped nor trained to deal with the intense cold. Between the end of November 1941 and the end of March 1942 they had half a million casualties from sickness alone, including nearly 230,000 cases of frostbite. During the same period Stalin was able to switch forces to the Moscow front from Siberia, where they had been standing guard against Japan. He was able to do this because he knew from a trusted spy not only that the Japanese were about to attack the United States, but also that they would not attack him. As a result, the Germans were checked and then pushed back.

Instead of blaming himself for miscalculating the odds, Hitler typically blamed his generals and assumed personal command against Russia in 1942. This was another priceless boon to his enemies, because he committed errors which deprived him of his last chance of victory. It was obvious that he needed to finish the Russians off in 1942, before the Americans had time to muster their strength and to begin to deploy it in the West. And he saw, correctly, that the prime objective had to be the Caucasus, occupation of which would deny vital oil supplies to the Soviet Union and secure them for himself. The strategy was right, but he failed to pursue it with the necessary relentlessness, avoiding all distractions. Consequently he bungled the year's campaigning and so virtually ensured his own ultimate defeat.

At first the Germans' rate of advance and depth of penetration in 1942 were as awe-inspiring as in the previous summer. Before the end of July they had captured Rostov, where the Don flows into the Sea of Azov. It seemed that the Caucasus must fall to them by the autumn. But at this critical moment Hitler diverted substantial forces to the Leningrad front and sent the Fourth Panzer Army to assist in the attack on Stalingrad, on the Volga. Neither of these moves had a decisive effect in the sector towards which it was directed. Leningrad continued to hold out, and so did Stalingrad. But the units that were moved might have enabled a decisive result to be achieved in the Caucasus. Instead, the German advance there was checked at the mountain massif, and all attempts to break through it or to outflank it were successfully resisted.

By the end of 1942 the German predicament in Russia was beginning to look grave. Hitler's forces were in full retreat from the Caucasus, and were cut off at Stalingrad. Faced with the growing power and confidence of their adversary, they were almost desperately overextended both in the length of their front line and in the distance over which their supplies had to travel. But Hitler would permit no strategic withdrawal or rationalisation of the front. He became obsessed with the need to defend every inch of conquered territory, and was particularly obsessed with the fruitless struggle for Stalingrad, no doubt partly on account of the city's symbolic name.

During the whole of the time that the fate of Russia hung in the balance, Anglo-American aid was effectively limited to the supply of war equipment and to bombing attacks on Germany. British operations in the Western Desert had no significant bearing on the titanic conflict in Russia, and it was out of the question to stage any big landing in Western Europe until the latter part of 1942—which in turn was regarded as much too soon by Churchill and the British service chiefs. Britain did, however, make considerable sacrifices for Russia. Large quantities of war matériel were sent from British factories, and what was sent from America was for the most part lost to Britain, to whom it would otherwise have been available. Above all, the burden of transporting the supplies to Russia weighed very heavily upon the Royal Navy and the British merchant marine, whose losses in the Arctic convoys are notorious. As Churchill put it: "We endured the unpleasant process of exposing our own vital security and projects for the sake of our new ally—surly, snarly, grasping, and so lately indifferent to our survival."

But Stalin's gifts as an organiser and warlord, combined with the heroic qualities of the Russian people, gave him a moral advantage which on all other grounds he deserved as little as Hitler himself. He was able, too, to benefit from the influence among rank-and-file British trade unionists of ideologues who, since June 1941, had become champions of the war effort while retaining their specially fervent devotion to the national interests of Russia. The Second Front agitation in 1942 was orchestrated by an incongruous alliance of Communist shop stewards, left-wing journalists—and Lord Beaverbrook (of whose role in the affair more later). By contrast, the established leaders of the British Labour Party were exceedingly hostile to Stalin and, as members of the Churchill coalition, did their utmost to prevent any gratuitous political concessions being made to him.

It was most unfortunate that the whole question of a Second Front became entangled with the issue of aid for Russia, instead of being judged strictly on its own merits as a strategy for winning the war in the West.

V. ... AND IN THE PACIFIC

Until 1941 the Americans' only long-sustained experience of fighting had been against each other. The operations that brought about the virtual genocide of the American Indians (in one of which the young Abraham Lincoln took part as an Army captain) were of an episodic nature, and the wars with Mexico and Spain were as brief as they were materially rewarding. Even the First World War involved the United States only for eighteen months. Since it won its independence, therefore, the only really long state of belligerence that the Republic had known was that in which it came near to destroying itself but was ultimately preserved.

As well as being relative strangers to war, the Americans were also in the habit of getting their own way. With the slightly debatable exception of the 1812 war against Britain, they had emerged victorious from all their foreign quarrels. Unlike the British, they had no disposition to glorify the memory of honourable defeats. To be beaten was, for them, a disgrace, and to lose a war—until Vietnam—more or less unthinkable. It was natural to them to assume not only that their own cause was just, but also that it would necessarily prevail.

Their reaction to Pearl Harbor and the disasters that swiftly followed was, therefore, one of shocked incredulity. For a time the news was all bad, for themselves no less than for their allies. The loss of most of their Pacific Fleet battleships would have made their position in the Philippines hard enough to hold without the further blow of losing, through incompetence, about half their military aircraft there, which despite warning were destroyed on the ground. MacArthur at first proclaimed that the whole of the Philippines must be held, but soon decided instead upon a delaying action, with most of his American forces concentrated in the Bataan peninsula and the neighbouring fortified island of Corregidor. Their resistance was stubborn. Bataan was not surrendered until March 1942, Corregidor not until May, and it was only in June that Japanese conquest of the Philippines was complete.

Meanwhile, MacArthur had moved to Australia to plan his "I shall return" strategy, and the Americans had already shown their determination to hit back, with the Doolittle air raid on Tokyo and two other Japanese cities in April. But it was in May–June that the tide turned as between America and Japan, with the decisive naval battles of the Coral Sea and Midway. The first rescued Australia from the threat of invasion, and the second marked the beginning of the end of Japan's brief naval ascendancy in the Pacific.

The Americans had the advantage of superior Intelligence, which enabled them to anticipate enemy movements. They were also most fortunate in having not lost their Pacific aircraft carriers, which were at sea while the battleships were sunk or disabled at Pearl Harbor. If it had been the other way round—i.e., if the carriers rather than the battleships had been put out of action—the struggle for supremacy in the Pacific would have lasted longer, and consequently it would have been even more difficult for Roosevelt to stick to the policy of beating Hitler first. The same would also have been true if the Japanese had outfought the Americans in either of the two crucial battles of mid-1942.

But they failed to do so. The Coral Sea was not exactly an American victory, because the losses on both sides were fairly well balanced. Yet it was beyond question a major strategic setback for the Japanese. Midway was that and more. The Japanese lost twice as many aircraft as the Americans, and four of their aircraft carriers to the Americans' one. After Midway the Hawaiian Islands were safe, and any possibility that the Japanese might be able to attack the American West Coast was effectively removed.

On land, the enemy advance was stopped in New Guinea. In particular, Australian forces with American support managed to hold the southern part of Papua (that half of the huge island that was under Australian administration), and by October 1942 had gone over to the offensive there. By the end of the year the Japanese had lost more men than the Allies in the jungle fighting, and Allied mastery in the air was undisputed.

Meanwhile, farther to the east, the U.S. Marines had been heavily engaged in the Solomon Islands. After seizing without too much difficulty the small island of Tulagi, they spent months gaining possession of its larger neighbour Guadalcanal. There, as in New Guinea, both sides had to contend with illness affecting thousands, as well as the normal hazards of war. Moreover, the need to reinforce and supply the embattled armies on the island caused a number of further important naval actions, in which both sides had serious losses. But the final outcome was on the whole favourable to the Americans, more especially in the air, and by the end of 1942 the Japanese position on Guadalcanal had become hopeless.

The year's operations in the Pacific demonstrated to all who cared to see that the United States had emerged as the world's leading maritime power, to which—rather than to Britain—Australia and New Zealand must in future look for their protection. They also showed that American troops, however deficient in battle experience, were capable of resisting well, under very adverse conditions, and of attacking equally well when the opportunity came.

VI. BRITISH CALAMITIES

While the Russians and Americans, who had entered the war neither voluntarily nor early, were fighting back with conspicuous success, the seasoned British were undergoing a series of calamities all the more galling for being in such sharp contrast with the achievements of their allies. Churchill and the British service chiefs may have felt that they knew much better than their Allied opposite numbers how the war should be fought, but the performance of the

British war machine throughout the world, resulting in many cases from faulty judgment at the top, did little to justify their self-confidence.

In the Far East, disaster followed disaster with bewildering swiftness. Between mid-December 1941 and early April 1942, at negligible cost to themselves, the Japanese seized Hong Kong, Malaya, Singapore, and most of Burma. Hong Kong resisted for eighteen days, but then surrendered with its garrison of 12,000, at a cost to the Japanese of fewer than 3,000. The conquest of mainland Malaya was accomplished in fifty-four days, with British losses of 25,000—mostly in prisoners—to the Japanese 4,600. At this point Churchill sent an instruction to the local commander, General Arthur Percival, that "the city of Singapore must be converted into a citadel and defended to the death," because Britain's "whole fighting reputation" and "the honour of the British Empire" were at stake. Nevertheless, Percival surrendered the place, with about 100,000 troops, only a week later —on 15 February 1942.

The fall of Malaya and Singapore led to the rapid conquest of the Dutch East Indies, of Thailand, and of the greater part of Burma. Thus it enabled the Japanese to threaten both Australia and India. But above all it was a most shattering psychological blow, from which the British Empire never recovered. There were good practical and humanitarian reasons for not fighting to the death in Singapore, which would soon have run out of water, because it was completely cut off —the Japanese having achieved command of the sea around Malaya with the sinking of the *Prince of Wales* and *Repulse* back in December. The troops were ill-equipped, and the island had not been fortified on the landward side. Yet there are times when a forlorn-hope resistance can not only delay the advance of an enemy, but also reduce the moral effect of his victory. It was so in the Philippines, because of the dogged, though hopeless, American defence of Bataan and Corregidor. It might also have been so in Singapore.

But whatever the military pros and cons of surrender, there can be no doubt that the political loss of face to Britain was overwhelming. In 1905 the Russians had been similarly humiliated by the Japanese, when their fleet was sunk at the battle of Tsushima. At that time the young Jawaharlal Nehru—still in India before being sent to school at

Harrow—reacted with excitement and enthusiasm to the news that an Asiatic power could so get the better of a European empire.

When Singapore fell, Nehru was one of the leaders of the Indian National Congress, by far the most important party in India, and the only one which could claim to be a comprehensive national movement. Though he had already spent half a dozen years in gaol as an agitator against the British Raj, at the time of Pearl Harbor he was at liberty—as he had been in 1939, when the war with Germany began. On that earlier occasion he was most eager to take part in a war against tyranny (he had once refused an invitation to meet Mussolini, which was more than could be said for some British politicians), but he and his colleagues were outraged when the Viceroy declared war arbitrarily on behalf of India, without seeking to associate the country's elected representatives with the declaration.

In 1942, with the Japanese at the gates of India, the British could not afford to be so high-handed, and even Churchill, though his record of hostility to Indian national aspirations was second to none, felt obliged to make some attempt to do a deal with the nationalist leaders. After the fall of Rangoon at the beginning of March, he sent Sir Stafford Cripps to India to present an offer from the British War Cabinet.

Cripps, a gifted but rather cranky Labour politician, had recently returned from the Soviet Union, after a disillusioning experience as ambassador, to be given a senior post in the Churchill coalition. Though sympathetic to India and personally known to Nehru and other Indian Congressmen, he was not quite the right man for the job, lacking political finesse and having a manner which could appear governessy. Above all, the offer itself was less than adequate. In particular, it did not go far enough towards giving Indians responsibility for the war effort.

As a result, the Cripps mission failed, and its failure precipitated a major internal crisis in India. Though Nehru was still reluctant to do anything to hinder the prosecution of the war, Gandhi (whose attitude had been equally cooperative during the First World War, without having much to show for it afterwards in political concessions to his people) decided on a non-violent campaign to force the British to "Quit India." Inevitably there was some violence, but the campaign was largely conducted in accordance with Gandhian principles, and consequently did not succeed. Even a fast "to death" by Gandhi himself did not break the authorities' nerve. The British Raj lived on for a few more years; and so did Gandhi.

On the face of it, the suppression of the "Quit India" movement was a considerable triumph for the British during a period of almost unrelieved disaster. But its longer-term effect was to destroy one of the most splendid of all British achievements, the unification of India. By the end of 1942, and until the end of the war, the Congress leaders were behind bars, and in the vacuum so created the Muslim League was given every encouragement to establish itself, working on the Muslims' fear that a united independent India would not be genuinely secular, but would enable the Hindu majority to persecute and dominate. It follows that there is a direct and fateful link between the events of 1942 and the tragic partition of India, which accompanied, and marred, that country's independence. But in the short term the Indian home front was stabilised and the Japanese were held at the eastern approaches.

For a short time, in April 1942, it seemed that the island of Ceylon might be captured. A powerful force of battleships and carriers (those used at Pearl Harbor) moved into the Indian Ocean, and aircraft from the carriers delivered severe attacks on Colombo and Trincomalee. The British naval force in the area was much inferior, but the Japanese failed to inflict a "Pearl Harbor" on it or to bring it to battle. Thereafter the threat to Ceylon was not renewed, but while it lasted it was very grave, because from Ceylon the Japanese could have struck at the British supply route to the Middle East round the Cape of Good Hope.

In the Middle East the year 1942 opened with confident hope that the Germans and Italians, having been pushed out of Cyrenaica, would soon be driven out of Tripolitania as well, and therefore out of Africa. But in late January General Erwin Rommel counterattacked and in two days advanced 100 miles. Between early February and late May he was held at Gazala, but then he attacked again, and in mid-June the British Eighth Army, commanded by General Neil Ritchie, retreated to the Egyptian frontier, leaving a large garrison to hold Tobruk. On 20 June Rommel stormed the place, and the garrison surrendered after resisting for only twenty-four hours. Thirty-five thousand men were taken prisoner. A few days later General Sir

Claude Auchinleck, the Middle East commander, took over direct command of the Eighth Army and by the end of July had halted Rommel, about fifty miles from Alexandria, in what is known as the first battle of El Alamein. So instead of clearing the enemy out of Africa the British had barely averted the loss of Egypt, and with it probably the whole Middle East, including its oil resources.

The poor showing of the British Army against the Japanese and Germans caused profound anxiety and soul-searching in high places. On the fall of Singapore Anthony Eden's private secretary, Oliver Harvey, commented in his diary: "No preparations, troops (British and Australian) refusing to fight . . . looting by troops . . . It must be hard to beat as a national disgrace. Many disturbing resemblances with the fall of France." Some months later Churchill said to his doctor, the future Lord Moran: "I cannot get over Singapore." Recording this, Moran added: "Singapore was a symptom of a malady which broke out during the war . . . from time to time. When the chance came, I asked some of the soldiers at the top how far the infection had spread. There was a discussion about the comparative merits of the soldier in the two wars that was not reassuring. I was left to turn over in my mind the social implications to a nation of a decay in its martial spirit."

After the fall of Tobruk, only four months after that of Singapore, such gloomy thoughts seem to have been shared by Churchill himself. According to Moran's diary, Churchill said at the time: "I am ashamed. I cannot understand why Tobruk gave in. More than 30,000 of our men put up their hands. If they won't fight—" He did not complete the sentence. If even Churchill could speak thus to an intimate, it is hardly surprising that unfriendly observers were beginning to conclude that the British could beat the Italians but, on land at any rate, were no longer a match for more serious adversaries.

In the war at sea, 1942 brought an intensification of the U-boat threat to Britain's survival. During the year more than 1,600 Allied ships were sunk, totalling nearly 7,800,000 tons, while no more than 7,000,000 tons of new shipping could be put into service. The Allies were having to deal with larger and more powerful U-boats, with a wider radius of action, and were not dealing with them at all effectively. America's belligerent status was for a time a positive disadvantage, because the U.S. Navy was slow to adopt the convoy system for

American merchant ships, which were no longer, of course, protected by neutrality. Another reason for the escalation of losses in the Atlantic was that, in America, a higher priority was being given to the production of landing-craft than to that of frigates. Yet another was that, in Britain, bombers were being transferred from Coastal Command to take part in the costly and essentially futile air offensive against Germany.

In February British naval prestige, recently shaken by the loss of the *Prince of Wales* and *Repulse*, suffered a further shock when a flotilla of German warships, including the big ships *Scharnhorst, Gneisenau* and *Prinz Eugen,* sailed with impunity from Brest up the English Channel and through the Straits of Dover (the only eventual damage being to *Gneisenau,* which hit a mine off the Dutch coast). As one historian of the war, Mark Arnold-Foster, has written: "For the first time since the arrival of the Spanish Armada in 1588 an enemy battle fleet had sailed the English Channel and, unlike the Armada, had got through."

VII. CHURCHILL IN TROUBLE

1942 was the only year of his wartime premiership when Churchill's position seemed less than secure. Despite his immense personal reputation, he was more vulnerable than either of his two partners in the exclusive club known as the Big Three. Roosevelt, after the 1940 Presidential election, was virtually irremovable except by death—until the completion of his unprecedented third term. And Stalin, quite simply, *was* irremovable except by death, having no elections to bother about and having either killed all possible rivals or reduced them to a state of quivering terror.

Churchill's postwar apotheosis makes it difficult now to believe that his wartime leadership could ever have been seriously at risk. But in 1942 it undoubtedly was. In the inner circles of government many important people were losing confidence in his way of running the war, while continuing to appreciate his value as a morale-booster. It was known that some of the worst disasters that had occurred were due to decisions taken by him personally, and there was a general feeling that his methods of doing business were inefficient as well as grossly inconsiderate. Men who had to be in their offices at a reasonably early hour in the morning were naturally irked by sessions with him long after midnight, in which monologue would often predominate, when they knew that he would be staying in bed until lunch the following day, and then having a nap in the afternoon.

Most of his critics wanted him to remain as Prime Minister, but either to give up being Minister of Defence or to appoint a deputy minister who would take some of the burden off him—and others. There was also a suggestion that the Chiefs of Staff should have a chairman (as, in fact, they now have) to act as a buffer between them and Churchill. But none of these proposed changes was acceptable to Churchill, who was determined not to surrender any of his power. And in the event, there was nobody with the necessary ambition or adroitness or strength of will, or with enough of a following, to force him to give way.

One who probably toyed with the idea of supplanting him was his old crony, Lord Beaverbrook, who had earned both admiration and odium as Minister of Aircraft Production in 1940–1, and who had since been Minister of Supply (military armaments). Beaverbrook, as we have seen, became the leading advocate of an early Second Front in north-west Europe, and as such tried to provide himself with mass support by appealing to militant, Soviet-orientated trade unionists. But he had no Parliamentary base, being a peer and an exceptionally isolated one at that. He owed his position in the government entirely to Churchill, of whom he was genuinely fond and towards whom he could never bring himself to behave as a single-minded rival.

He was also an inept politician. Consequently his challenge, such as it was, did not make much headway. In March 1942 he resigned, after failing to obtain the powers that he wanted as overlord of war production. Though he used his freedom to campaign openly, on both sides of the Atlantic, for a Second Front, he never presented himself to the public as an alternative to Churchill. Had he done so, his chances of success would have been negligible.

Cripps for a time seemed a rather more serious threat to the Prime Minister. He was a member of the House of Commons and of the official Labour hierarchy, from which, however, he had been estranged before the war because he had then stood for a Popular Front of left-wing parties, including the Communists. This made him potentially most attractive to left-wingers now demanding a Second Front, and his recent tour of duty as ambassador to Russia further identified him, though misleadingly, with the Soviet cause.

In fact, his Russian experiences had made him thoroughly anti-Soviet, and he did not favour an early Second Front. He was thus able to combine a popularity which largely rested upon ignorance of his attitude, with credit in high places based upon a correct understanding of it. In February 1942 Anthony Eden told an intimate that he would be willing to serve as Minister of Defence under Cripps, and a concerted move by these two men might have been decisive. But it did not occur. Churchill handled Cripps with skill, bringing him into the War Cabinet, but without an executive role. Later, when his stock had fallen (partly as a result of the failure of his Indian mission), and when Churchill's had risen again, he *was* given an executive role—but outside the War Cabinet.

As for Eden, who of all Churchill's colleagues was the best placed to coerce him, nothing could be more revealing than his willingness to serve under Cripps. He was maddened by Churchill and had long been convinced that there ought to be another Minister of Defence. He was the darling of rank-and-file Conservatives and much respected in the House of Commons, as well as in the Services. His resignation in 1938 had won him the loyalty of people who were against appeasement, while his gentlemanly restraint after resigning had prevented those who supported appeasement from being too badly antagonised.

By the new left-centre establishment that was coming into being he was regarded, unlike Churchill, as vaguely progressive and on the side of the future. Yet he lacked the resolution to strike. He wanted to be Minister of Defence, but would not make the first move. Churchill had his measure, and on the whole knew how and when to cajole him. But in 1942 Eden was perhaps the only man capable—if his temperament had been different—of leading a successful cabal against Churchill.

During the period of tension and crisis at the summit, Churchill survived two votes of confidence in the House of Commons, the first at the end of January 1942, when he had a majority of 464 to 1, and the second in July, when the vote was 476 to 25, with about forty M.P.s deliberately abstaining. These victories were less crushing than they might appear, because there was no official Opposition and the government, as a grand coalition, was able to impose discipline on nearly every Member. That so many were prepared, in July, to defy the Whips showed the extent of anxiety even among politicians only partly in the know.

Yet Churchill's standing with the general public remained very high, and it was probably this more than anything else that saved him. His many critics among those concerned with the direction of the war knew that they would have little popular backing, and much popular condemnation, for any attempt to get rid of him. In the First World War certain generals became idols in the eyes of the public, and therefore more or less unassailable. In the Second there was no such immunity for generals (except perhaps, later on, for Montgomery), but Churchill's unique contribution in 1940 enabled him to lead a charmed life until the end of the war.

Opinion polling was in its infancy, but politicians were already having to pay attention to it, however reluctantly. And throughout 1942 it pointed to the fact that people had a lot more confidence in Churchill than in his government. The percentage approving of his leadership was about twice that expressing satisfaction with the government's conduct of the war (for instance, about 80 per cent compared with 40 per cent after the fall of Tobruk—the time of the second House of Commons vote). This was scarcely logical, since the government was Churchill's, and he, by his own choice, was more responsible than the rest of the government put together for war policy and strategy. But logic seldom determines political attitudes, and in any case the British people at the time did not have enough information to go on. So far as most of them were concerned, Churchill was simply the hero of 1940, who made wonderful speeches and was by far the most impressive and colourful personality in the state, eclipsing not only his colleagues but the King as well.

All the same, nobody knew better than he that his credit even with the public was not inexhaustible. Unless he could produce results, discontent would spread, and at the next test in the House of Commons he might well be brought down. This awareness powerfully influenced his judgment of strategic issues in the second half of 1942.

VIII.   THE KINDLING OF "TORCH"

Churchill's opposition to any large-scale landing in north-west Europe during 1942 was reinforced by his private doubts about the morale and fighting quality of British troops, after the trauma of Singapore. Wherever political salvation was to be sought, it must not be across the Channel. Since the vast American Army that General Marshall was raising and training would not be ready for such an operation in 1942, the bulk of the forces involved would have to be British; and on all grounds Churchill was unwilling to expose them to the venture. He feared terrible carnage and above all, perhaps, a setback even more devastating than Singapore—and far closer to home. He therefore told the Russian Foreign Minister, V. M. Molotov, who was visiting London in May, that the British were not committed to any cross-Channel operation in 1942, and he got the War Cabinet to agree that there would be no invasion in 1942 unless *the Germans* showed signs of cracking. This effectively killed the plan, code-named SLEDGEHAMMER, for a possible major landing to draw German troops away from the Eastern Front if *the Russians'* plight seemed desperate.

Roosevelt, however, was more encouraging to Molotov, who went on to Washington after leaving London. Despite pleas for caution from his advisers, Roosevelt allowed a statement to be issued after his talks with Molotov that "full understanding was reached with regard to the urgent task of creating a Second Front in Europe in 1942." This had all the appearance of a pledge which, so far as north-west Europe was concerned, had not been, and would not be, underwritten by the British. Marshall, who wished SLEDGEHAMMER to remain on the agenda but dreaded the adoption of some "sideshow" as an alternative gesture to the Russians, could see that Roosevelt was playing into Churchill's hands. Since it now seemed that the United States was committed to a Second Front of sorts in 1942, and since the British —without whom the operation could not be mounted—would no longer contemplate SLEDGEHAMMER, the chances of a sideshow were immeasurably increased.

To work on Roosevelt, Churchill sent a special emissary who could not have been more artfully chosen for the task—Lord Louis Mountbatten, the Chief of Combined Operations. Mountbatten was barely in his forties, but had been wafted by Churchill from the command of an aircraft carrier to a post which brought him high rank in all three services and a seat on the British Chiefs of Staff Committee. This spectacular promotion was due partly to his own undoubted talents and partly to the accident of birth. As the most glamorous male member of the Royal Family since Edward VIII departed from the limelight (to become, as Duke of Windsor, a pathetic exile), he appealed strongly to Churchill, who was always a considerable royal snob. And there was probably another family reason for Churchill's interest in advancing his career. In 1914, as First Lord of the Admiralty, Churchill had allowed Mountbatten's father, Prince Louis of Battenberg, then First Sea Lord, or professional head of the Navy, to be swept into retirement by the prevailing wave of hysterical Germanophobia. Churchill cannot have felt easy in his mind about failing to put up a fight for Battenberg, and must have welcomed the opportunity, over a quarter of a century later, to make handsome amends to his son.

Mountbatten appealed to Roosevelt scarcely, if at all, less than he did to Churchill. The President, too, had rather a soft spot for royalty, despite his prejudice against the British social establishment. Even more, he had a soft spot for the Navy, and was naturally impressed by a fighting naval officer who had quite recently had a destroyer sunk under him. Roosevelt had already met Mountbatten (when his aircraft carrier, *Illustrious,* was being refitted in America in 1941) and had formed a very favourable opinion of him. Unlike Churchill, he seemed modern and progressive in the sense that F.D.R. understood those terms. Mountbatten was mildly left-wing and, though a greatgrandson of Queen Victoria, did not share Churchill's attachment to the Victorian concept of empire. Above all, as the man responsible for planning and directing commando raids on the enemy-held European coastline, he could speak with authority of the problems involved in a large cross-Channel assault.

His mission was to convince the President that any such assault would be certain to fail—and fail catastrophically—in 1942, and that even 1943 might be too soon for the full-scale invasion of north-west Europe. He was received at once by Roosevelt and their talk was strictly private, with none of the American service chiefs invited to attend or even informed of what passed between them (until a summary was provided, not by Roosevelt, but by the British Chiefs of Staff in London). The President yielded without much show of resistance to Mountbatten's arguments against a 1942 landing in France, and then suggested that American divisions might, instead, be sent to Libya or Morocco. Having done what Churchill had sent him to do, Mountbatten went out of his way to conciliate Marshall, and succeeded in making a friend of him, though not in changing his view of the strategic priorities. (Incidentally, Mountbatten's absence in America had a disastrous effect upon plans for the Dieppe raid, whose bloody failure in August was used, unjustifiably—as will be explained in Part Three—as a further argument for caution on the Second Front issue.)

After the ground had been so well prepared by his emissary, Churchill himself visited Washington again in the latter part of June. While conferring with the President, he received the stunning news that Tobruk had fallen, to which Roosevelt immediately reacted with an offer of help. As a result three hundred American tanks and one hundred American guns were sent to Egypt. Though it was obvious to him that Britain's heavy defeat in the desert would help to shift attention from north-west Europe to the Mediterranean theatre, Marshall did not cavil at the despatch of aid—on the contrary, did his utmost to expedite it—because he could see that a German breakthrough in the Middle East might be fatal to the Allied cause. At the same time, he continued to oppose any more extensive Mediterranean commitment.

Sir Alan Brooke, the British Chief of Army Staff, who was Marshall's most relentless antagonist on SLEDGEHAMMER and cross-Channel schemes generally, was nevertheless at one with him in viewing the North African project with alarm. But whereas Marshall was against it primarily because it was a "sideshow," Brooke was against it because it seemed to him too risky. The somewhat unnatural alliance of these two men was, in any case, powerless to deter their political masters.

Equally ineffective was a move by Marshall and Admiral Ernest King, the U.S. Navy chief, to demand that unless the British would give overriding priority to plans for invading the Continent the United States should concentrate upon defeating Japan. Roosevelt sensed that they were bluffing, and anyway had set his mind on North Africa. Quite apart from the apparent pledge to Molotov, he felt that the American public needed some dramatic evidence that the United States was seriously at war with the Germans.

Towards the end of July the American Chiefs of Staff, under pressure from Roosevelt, agreed with the British that SLEDGEHAMMER should be scrapped, and that TORCH should be undertaken if, by 15 September, it became clear that a cross-Channel invasion in 1943 (ROUND-UP) would be made "impracticable" by "a collapse or weakening of Russian resistance." The British Chiefs accepted this formula because it enabled their American colleagues to abandon SLEDGEHAMMER, without having to commit themselves unreservedly to TORCH. For the same reason, the British accepted the statement that TORCH would definitely imply, for 1943, "a defensive, encircling line of action for the continental European theatre, except as to air operations and blockade." These words enshrined Marshall's belief that TORCH would lead, willy-nilly, to the postponement of decisive action against Germany.

In the event, he was proved right, though Churchill did not accept the logic of his argument. Meanwhile, the agreement of the Combined Chiefs of Staff, despite its ostensible affirmation of priority for ROUND-UP—subject only to the Russians' appearing to be viable in mid-September—was in effect a decision in favour of TORCH, because that was how Roosevelt and Churchill chose to interpret it. Plans for the North African operation went ahead, and General Dwight D. Eisenhower, who since June had been U.S. Commander in the European theatre, was appointed to command the Allied expeditionary force.

IX.   HAZARDS OF "TORCH"

It was entirely rational to doubt the wisdom of the operation, even in the short term. Beyond question it was hazardous in the extreme. French North Africa was not enemy territory, but it was not friendly territory, either. It was controlled by the Vichy government, which had no intention of declaring for the Allies, or of allowing them to occupy any of those parts of the French empire whose loyalty it still retained. The men of Vichy lived in Hitler's shadow. Some of them were active Nazi sympathisers, and even those who were relatively anti-German had no sympathy for the Allies and above all wanted a quiet life.

Pétain himself aimed to restore dignity and virtue to France through the inward-looking paternalism of his regime. His name still counted for much in the armed forces, though more among officers than among other ranks. He also held the devoted or self-interested allegiance of many key civilian functionaries at home and overseas. Though ordinary French opinion was increasingly turning towards de Gaulle, there was no reason to assume that the 300,000 troops or the important naval units in French North Africa would allow the Allies to land unopposed.

Vichy's standing had been gratuitously reinforced by American diplomatic recognition, which appeared to be no mere formality, but on the contrary cordial endorsement, so long as the U.S. ambassador to Vichy was Roosevelt's confidant, Admiral William D. Leahy. Leahy was withdrawn in May 1942, after Pierre Laval had returned to power. Yet the American government remained (for reasons that will be explored in Chapter 6) hostile to General Charles de Gaulle and his movement. Washington was convinced that de Gaulle was no more than a British puppet, and a thoroughly undesirable one at that.

To the Americans it seemed that the success of TORCH would largely depend upon concealing, so far as possible, the British role in the operation, and upon altogether excluding the Fighting French. They noted the resistance offered by Vichy-controlled forces to British-cum-Gaullist action at Dakar in 1940, and in Syria the following year. They believed that the British attack, in 1940, upon the French fleet at Mers-el-Kébir had left a legacy of hatred which time and reflection had done nothing to assuage. On the other hand, they had a much exaggerated view of their own good standing with the Vichy French, and tended to assume that the local French commanders and officials in North Africa would welcome an ostensibly American expeditionary force.

It could be no more than ostensibly so, because in the circumstances

41

a large proportion of the troops involved, and nearly all the naval units, would have to be British. But an American commander was appointed in the person of Dwight D. Eisenhower, and Churchill even for a time entertained the idea of sending the British troops ashore in American uniforms. But, in fact, the Americans were not all that popular, nor the British all that unpopular. To Vichy and its creatures nothing mattered so much as preserving their own pseudo-independence, which could only mean opposing the Allies; while to the general population the Gaullist movement had a stronger appeal than "Anglo-Saxons" of any type.

As the moment for action approached, it began to dawn upon the Americans that they might need to work through some French authority other than Vichy, but their intense prejudice against de Gaulle prevented cooperation with his movement. Instead, they "discovered" another French general, Henri Giraud, to whom—they fondly imagined—pro- and anti-Vichy elements might rally. Giraud was a brave but stupid man, who in April 1942 had escaped from a German fortress to Unoccupied France. He had avoided being sent back to Germany only by signing a declaration of fulsome loyalty to Pétain —a fact of which the Americans were unaware when they started to deal with him. He was senior to de Gaulle in age and rank, but in other respects no match for him at all. The political background to TORCH was complicated enough without this further complication.

On the strategic side, American caution had the effect, paradoxically, of making the operation even riskier than it need have been. The U.S. Chiefs of Staff wished at first to land only on the Atlantic coast of Morocco and not to venture inside the Mediterranean until they had secured a firm base. They were afraid that either Franco on his own, or the Germans striking with his permission through Spain, would close the Straits of Gibraltar behind the Allied armada. Yet the only hope of occupying the whole of French North Africa swiftly, and before the Germans could intervene, lay in a bold plan to land at Oran, Algiers, and as far east as Bône. Thus there would be a chance that Tunisia as well as Algeria could be seized while the Allies still had the advantage of surprise. Landing on the Atlantic coast of Morocco would be not only a wasteful diversion of effort but also very dangerous in itself, because of the sea conditions and the presence of the new French battleship, *Jean Bart,* at Casablanca.

Whereas on the issue of cross-Channel landings the Americans had to wrestle with British doubts and fears, in the planning for TORCH it was the other way round. Eventually, at the beginning of September, the conflict of views was resolved in a compromise, under which the Americans had their way over Casablanca but agreed that landings inside the Mediterranean should include Algiers, though not Bône. This decision ensured, as things turned out, that the operation would last months rather than weeks, and so helped to frustrate plans for a cross-Channel invasion in 1943.

Yet while lacking the degree of audacity needed for total success, the TORCH project as finally agreed on was fraught with peril and might well have ended just as disastrously as a premature attempt to land in France. The initial assault force of ninety thousand men had to be transported direct from Britain or America, across seas infested with enemy submarines. It had to land in territory which might be resolutely defended by superior numbers of troops and aircraft. Its only air cover, unless and until it could gain possession of airfields, would have to come from two or three carriers and the single, desperately overcrowded strip at Gibraltar. The security risks before the landings were as daunting as the subsequent problems of supply. Only a driving sense that something had to be done in 1942 to impress the Russians and their own people could have brought the Allied leaders to embark upon such a hazardous enterprise.

The date for it was postponed from early October, which the British had favoured, to 7 November. Meanwhile, there were dramatic developments at the eastern end of the North African coast, resulting from a visit to Cairo by Churchill back in August.

X. CHURCHILL'S JOURNEY

The Prime Minister stayed in Egypt on his way to and from Russia, where he had his first encounters with Stalin. This was one of the most arduous of all his wartime journeys—an astonishing *tour de force* for a man of sixty-eight. Apart from the dangers, long-distance flying was still slow and uncomfortable, even for V.I.P.s. And the extent of German conquest made air journeys in 1942 very circuitous. To reach Cairo from London, Churchill had to fly by way of Gibraltar and Malta, a total of about twenty-three hours in the air. And from Cairo he went first to Teheran (six and a half hours), then to Moscow by way of Kuibyshev (thirteen hours).

Facing Stalin on his own ground, in the Kremlin, he gave him the news that there would be no Second Front (as the Russians understood the term) in 1942, but did his best to mollify him by talk of the bombing offensive against Germany and by outlining the plans for TORCH. Stalin was not easily mollified. At their first meeting he taunted Churchill in a quiet voice, never looking him in the eye. "A man who was not prepared to take risks could not win a war. Why were [the British] so afraid of the Germans? He could not understand. His experience showed that troops must be blooded in battle." So the Prime Minister recalled his words.

According to Alan Brooke, Churchill "crashed his fist down on the table and poured forth one of his wonderful spontaneous orations." According to Churchill himself, he "inquired whether [Stalin] had ever asked himself why Hitler did not come to England in 1940, when he was at the height of his power and we had only 20,000 trained troops, 200 guns, and 50 tanks. He did not come. The fact was that Hitler was afraid of the operation. It is not so easy to cross the Channel." Stalin "replied that this was no analogy. The landing of Hitler in England would have been resisted by the people, whereas in the case of a British landing in France the people would be on the side of the British." At length, after "an oppressive silence," they agreed to differ.

But Stalin seems to have been pleased about the air raids which "he knew . . . were having a tremendous effect in Germany." Unnecessarily, he emphasised to Churchill "the importance of striking at the morale of the German population." This was, in fact, Churchill's policy, and there was already plenty of evidence—which he did not, of course, mention to Stalin, and was anyway unwilling to accept himself—that it was proving as futile as it was bestial.

When he came to expound the case for TORCH, Churchill produced an image which has still, nearly forty years later, not lost its power to confuse and mislead. "If we could end the year in possession of North Africa we could threaten the *belly* of Hitler's Europe, and this operation should be considered in conjunction with the 1943 operation." To illustrate his point, Churchill drew a picture of a crocodile, explaining to Stalin that it was the Allies' intention "to attack *the soft belly of the crocodile as we attacked the hard snout*" (J.G.'s italics). Stalin allegedly reacted with keen interest and—forgetting for the moment his ideological position—said, "May God prosper this undertaking."

The night before he left Moscow Churchill had a long session with Stalin, unaccompanied by Brooke, at which he gave the Russian leader good reason to expect that the Allies would invade north-west Europe in 1943. This was to be a source of much acrimony later, when Churchill had been deflected from what was, at the time, a genuine hope.

In Russia his task was diplomatic, and at the end of his visit he felt that the ice was broken and some human contact established. In Egypt decisions had to be taken. Acting within his own sphere of direct power, Churchill appointed new commanders for the British forces facing Rommel. The new appointments were made before he travelled to Russia, and on his return journey he was able to observe the new men already at work.

General Auchinleck, who had stopped Rommel when he seemed to have the Nile Valley and even the oil of Persia within his grasp, had to go because he was also the man under whose general command the Eighth Army had suffered its worst defeat and Tobruk had ignominiously surrendered. Once he had taken personal command of the Army, he had won a vital defensive battle, but he paid the penalty for his earlier mistakes. Churchill unjustly condemned him for wanting time to prepare his counter-offensive against Rommel, but it was probably right that he should be replaced, because it would have been difficult for him to give the necessary boost to morale.

As commander-in-chief in the Middle East, Churchill selected a fine officer and gentleman, Harold Alexander, whose attractive personality and excellent fighting record made up for his intellectual limitations. The choice as commander of the Eighth Army was Bernard Montgomery, after the first choice, General William ("Strafer") Gott, had been shot down and killed within forty-eight hours of his appointment. Montgomery had always been Brooke's candidate for the job, but it took an intervention of Providence to obtain it for him.

His great merits are well-known—thoroughness, intense professionalism, tactical adroitness, and a flair for the sort of publicity that leadership in war requires. At a comparatively early stage in his career, when he was a major instructing at the Staff College, he had surprised and amused his audiences by lecturing on the art of high command, and by suggesting that a general in war should neglect no detail, even to the extent of wearing a distinctive hat. As Eighth Army commander he lived up to his own maxims.

But Monty also had his faults. The jaunty self-confidence that he normally possessed, and always seemed to possess, could take the form of arrogance and tactlessness. Partly for the sake of morale he cultivated a myth that everything he did went according to plan, and he was not in the habit of showing much respect for the opinions or feelings of others. In due course he earned the hearty dislike of most of the Americans with whom he came in contact, and among his own compatriots there were many who found him insufferable. This would have mattered less if his talents as a general had been quite what they were made out to be. But, in fact, his considerable ability to win battles (often at very heavy cost) was not matched by the ability to exploit victories. With anything like his resources, a commander of Rommel's adventurousness and dash would have reached Delhi in the time it took Monty to reach Tripoli.

His immediate impact, however, was formidably good, though he was even less willing than Auchinleck to be rushed into an early attack on Rommel. Within a week or so he had made himself a familiar figure to all ranks, and had achieved a psychological breakthrough which was the prelude to success on the battlefield. On 20 August Churchill spent a day with him and was "uplifted" by all that he saw. In the evening he wrote in Monty's diary: "May the anniversary of Blenheim, which marks the opening of the new Command, bring to the Commander-in-Chief of the Eighth Army and his troops the fame and fortune they will surely deserve."

Brooke was naturally delighted that his protégé made such a favourable impression on their political boss. He was also amazed at Churchill's own vitality and stamina. "We had been called at 6 A.M. [Churchill] had started the day with a bathe in the sea; we had then spent a very strenuous day touring the front. This had entailed motoring in clouds of sand, long walks between troops, addressing groups of troops, talks with officers, in fact, a non-stop tour of inspection. Return to camp with another bathe, contrary to his doctor's orders. He was rolled over by the waves and came up upside down doing the 'V' sign with his legs! Then followed a drive to aerodrome, and, as soon as we had emplaned, he said, 'I am now going to sleep' . . . He instantaneously went to sleep and never woke up till we had bumped half-way down the Heliopolis runway. Then followed a conference, dinner, after which he kept me up till 2 A.M. on the lawn outside the Embassy."

XI. VICTORY AT LAST

But it was not enough to be a human prodigy, as Churchill knew very well. Unless he could show before the end of the year that his dispositions were right, he would probably lose so much of his support in Parliament, and even in the country, that he would have to resign as Prime Minister or Minister of Defence, or both. In that case he would go down in history as a prodigious failure.

TORCH was a crucial test for the Allies, and therefore for him, but to an even greater extent his personal fortunes were bound up with those of the Eighth Army. It was, after all, a purely British force, and he alone was responsible for its performance, good or bad. He had acted personally, and on the spot, to give it new leadership. Whereas Roosevelt would share the blame if TORCH miscarried, there would be no—one to share the blame if the Eighth Army was beaten again. From Churchill's point of view it had to win, and it was also essential that it should win before the launching of TORCH, so that its triumph would not be eclipsed by or, worse still, attributed to the other operation.

In 1953 his doctor, Lord Moran, asked him to say which, for him, had been the two most anxious months of the war. He did not hesitate to reply that they had been September and October 1942. It is easy enough to see why. During the summer of 1940 the country was in mortal danger, but apart from that his own position was unassailable. In the autumn of 1942 the country's position was more secure, but his own political fate hung in the balance.

Montgomery's first battle as Eighth Army commander was defensive and, as such, highly successful. At the end of August Rommel launched a panzer attack with the intention of outflanking the main British Alamein defences from the south. His line of attack was expected (thanks to the "Ultra" code-breaking process), and in principle Montgomery's plan for resisting it was one already prepared by Auchinleck. But the defence was very well conducted. The Germans were held at the Alam Halfa ridge—which has given the battle its name in the history books—and on 2 September Rommel had to order them to withdraw from the ground they had gained.

It is now widely agreed that if Montgomery had delivered a purposeful counterattack at this moment he might well (as one biographer has put it) "have ended Rommel's army for good," and so removed the necessity for the celebrated and costly final battle of Alamein, which was to follow. But he was not, by nature, quick to seize such opportunities, and in his first encounter with the legendary Rommel his reluctance to play for the highest stakes was perhaps justifiable. He moved forward slowly and gingerly, and after the week-long battle of Alam Halfa the Eighth Army had merely re-established its original line. But the troops had confidence in their new leader, felt that Rommel could be beaten, and were ready for the greater test.

Churchill (who had with difficulty been dissuaded from staying on in Egypt to witness the German attack) was now impatient for the offensive which was to restore Britain's—and his own—prestige. He wanted it to be launched in mid-September, but Montgomery would not be hustled. With full support from Alexander, he fixed the date for starting it in the third week of October, only a fortnight before TORCH was due to take place.

By then, his superiority in manpower and matériel was such that he could hardly fail to win a battle of attrition, and it was that sort of battle that he decided to fight. The numerical strength of the Eighth Army was 230,000 against Rommel's 80,000, of whom more than 50,000 were Italian. The British had at least 1,200 front-line tanks, with almost as many more in reserve, whereas Rommel had only 240

German tanks in battleworthy condition and 280 obsolete Italian tanks. Moreover, 500 Eighth Army tanks were American Grants and Shermans, for which only 30 of Rommel's (the new Panzer IVs) were a match.

The disparity of air power was equally great—1,500 aircraft in direct support of Montgomery, compared with Rommel's 350. And of course Rommel's communications were immensely extended, and subject to effective harassment by sea and air, whereas the Eighth Army was able to go into action within a short distance of its powerful and well-stocked base.

Montgomery's plan was to concentrate his attack at the northern end of the Alamein line, with only a diversionary movement at the southern end. On 23 October the battle opened with a colossal artillery bombardment, but even so the enemy did not give much ground, and Montgomery had to vary his tactics without departing from the overall plan. In the protracted struggle that ensued, British tank losses exceeded the Germans' in a ratio of nearly four to one, and when Rommel's army was still unbroken after a week of fighting, even Brooke began to feel doubt and anxiety.

But gradually the Germans were worn down. By 2 November they were reduced to thirty tanks, while the British still had twenty times that number in action. Despite a typical order from Hitler that there should be no withdrawal, Rommel decided that the time had come to withdraw. Two days later Alexander reported to Churchill that the Eighth Army had "inflicted a severe defeat on the German and Italian forces under Rommel's command," and on 6 November he suggested that victory bells be rung. Churchill chose to wait until he could be reasonably sure that TORCH, now imminent, would not be a fiasco. But he soon acted on the suggestion.

While the bells rang out for victory, there were many for whom they might have tolled. A. J. P. Taylor has written that, at Alamein, "the proportion of casualties among men actually engaged was as heavy as on the Somme." It was a cruelly expensive victory. Worse still, it was not turned into the complete and comprehensive triumph that it should have been, because Rommel was allowed to extricate what remained of his army to fight—and to cause the Allies much trouble—another day.

Alun Chalfont has described Montgomery's exploitation of Alamein as "abysmal." Ignoring the advice of more enterprising subordinates, he made no serious attempt to cut the retreating Germans off. The excuse that has been made for him is that there was rain on 7 November which, in Arthur Bryant's words, turned "the crowded desert tracks to the Libyan frontier into rivers of mud." But if mud was such an impediment to the British pursuit, why did it not also delay the German retreat? In any case, the prime opportunity to encircle the Germans had already been lost before the rain began to fall.

When Rommel stood at El Agheila, towards the end of November, there was another chance to destroy his army. But Montgomery gave him at least a fortnight to reorganise and then continue his orderly retreat. In the event, the Eighth Army did not capture Tripoli until the third week of January 1943, by which time Rommel had withdrawn into Tunisia, so providing a major reinforcement to the Axis position there.

Granted Montgomery's failure to exploit his hard-won victory, the question has to be asked: might it not have been better for the Allied cause if, instead of taking the offensive when he did, he had merely held the Alamein line against Rommel while the TORCH operation was in progress? The most dangerous German commander and his fine army would thus have been pinned in a situation remote from the campaign in French North Africa, unable to affect the issue there and with ever-diminishing hope of escape.

On the face of it, this would have been the more enlightened strategy, but—quite apart from the political need for a British victory—it was argued at the time, and can be argued still, that Alamein was psychologically necessary as a prelude to TORCH. It may be that French resistance in North Africa would have been tougher, and Franco's attitude towards the Allies less complaisant, if there had been no Alamein to create a feeling that Axis fortunes were on the wane.

The question will never be decided one way or the other, because it rests upon imponderables. But at least it can be said with certainty that what actually happened was far from being an unqualified boon to the Allies.

XII.   UNFINISHED BUSINESS IN NORTH AFRICA

News of the Alamein victory was duly followed, after a few days, by news of the TORCH landings, which were carried out by three separate expeditionary forces under Eisenhower's overall command. The one destined for the Atlantic coast of Morocco was all American and sailed direct from Virginia. Another, whose objective was Oran, consisted of American troops carried, with a British naval escort, from the Clyde. And the third, bound for Algiers, was on the military side half-British and half-American, but on the naval side again entirely British. This huge and complex movement was accomplished with rare efficiency and—amazingly—achieved total surprise.

The Germans thought that the convoys reported passing through the Straits of Gibraltar were taking troops to land behind Rommel's retreating army in Libya, and few of the French authorities in North Africa were expecting the Allies to land when or where they did. The Americans had been in touch with dissident officers, with some of whom Eisenhower's deputy, General Mark Clark, had a secret meeting near Algiers towards the end of October (taken to and from the rendezvous in a British submarine). But even these sympathisers were given only vague advance information and consequently were unable to do as much as they might have done to organise a friendly reception for the Allies.

In any case, most of the key people were loyal to Pétain and unlikely to move without his authorisation; while the strongest element of opposition was Gaullist and, therefore, shunned by the Americans. Giraud, who was brought to Gibraltar on the eve of the landings, was soon shown to count for little. De Gaulle, who counted for much—though not with the men in power—was told of the landings only after they had occurred.

Despite all the risks, the landings were remarkably successful, though by no means unopposed. Luckily for the Americans who had to land in Morocco (under General George Patton, making his flamboyant début), 8 November was one of the days—normally about one in five—when surf conditions there were not entirely prohibitive. Even so, the troops had difficulty in getting ashore and, having done

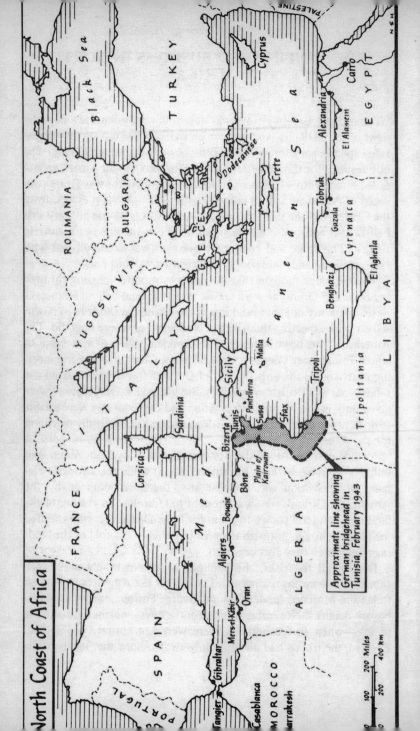

North Coast of Africa

Approximate line showing German bridgehead in Tunisia, February 1943

so, encountered resistance. There was also naval fighting off the coast. At Oran a direct assault was repulsed, but converging movements by forces landed in the neighbourhood led to the town's surrender on the morning of the tenth. In the Algiers area the troops got ashore well, but were then involved in stiff fighting which might have ended badly but for a providential development which transformed the situation.

Indeed Michael Howard judges (in the official British history) that nothing might have saved TORCH from being "if not a failure, then at best an incomplete, expensive and, in terms of Grand Strategy, unimportant success had equal good fortune not attended the political aspects of the expedition." The political fluke referred to was the presence in Algiers at the critical moment of the man who, next to Pétain himself, carried most weight with the French officer corps. This was Admiral Darlan, the Vichy commander-in-chief, who happened to be in Algiers visiting his son who had been stricken with poliomyelitis.

Darlan had been in touch with the Americans for some time, but even they had come to regard him as untrustworthy, with the result that they had shifted their support, unrealistically, to Giraud. The Germans, too, had lost confidence in him, and in April 1942 had forced Pétain to replace him as head of the government by Pierre Laval. Darlan had been an active collaborator who, when America came into the war, became sceptical of a German victory and saw the necessity for varying his collaboration. He was anti-British even before Mers-el-Kébir had turned him into a violent Anglophobe, but he had always promised that the French Fleet would not be allowed to fall into German hands, and there is reason to believe that in this, at least, he was sincere. In other respects the best that can be said for him is that he was an intelligent opportunist, but there are circumstances in which such a man can do more than any number of starry-eyed idealists to promote a good cause.

Though it was not by pre-arrangement that he was in Algiers, nothing could have been more convenient. Pétain, who had publicly denounced the Allied landings, secretly gave Darlan a free hand. The Americans, for their part, soon realised that he was the man to deal with, and by a mixture of cajolery and intimidation he was persuaded to give orders, in the Marshal's name, that resistance to the Allies should cease and that, instead, the French civilian and military authorities in North Africa should cooperate with them. As a result, Morocco and Algeria were soon effectively in the Allied camp, with the French forces there fighting alongside, rather than against, the "Anglo-Saxons."

In return for his most helpful services Darlan was made High Commissioner and naval commander-in-chief, while Giraud—who had at first expected, in his vain innocence, to be supreme commander of the whole Allied operation—had to be content with nominal command of the French ground and air forces in North Africa. This arrangement was endorsed by Eisenhower, showing the political touch and flair which were later to bring him to the U.S. Presidency. It was also approved by Roosevelt, rather more reluctantly by Churchill, and off the record by Stalin. But it provoked the understandable fury of de Gaulle and the Fighting French, and caused something of a public outcry in Britain and the United States. It was, therefore, no occasion for regret to the Allied leaders when Darlan was assassinated on Christmas Eve by a young royalist and fanatical opponent of Vichy. The scheming admiral had served his turn and become an embarrassment. (Incidentally, his assassin was tried and executed with indecent haste.)

Meanwhile, the Germans had moved into Unoccupied France—on 11 November—depriving the Pétain regime of its spurious independence and easing the consciences of French officers and officials who were defecting to the Allies. But the French Army inside France, which had been making clandestine preparations for resistance, was taken by surprise, and anyway given no orders to resist. The French Fleet at Toulon, though it disappointed the Allies by not sailing to North Africa, was scuttled in the nick of time, before the Germans could take it over. Darlan's guarantee that it would never fall into their hands was thus fulfilled.

In Tunisia the Germans acted with disconcerting speed to create a bridgehead. From 9 November onwards, they were moving in troops and aircraft, while the local French authorities were equivocal and irresolute. On 11 November the Allies landed a British force at Bougie, but even there it was three hundred miles from Tunis, and the harbour was promptly bombed by the Germans, with serious consequences for supply. Nevertheless, by 25 November British and American troops were within fifteen miles of Tunis. For a moment it seemed that TORCH might after all be an entire success, despite the mistake of not landing troops farther east at the outset.

But the moment passed. The Allies ran out of steam, the Germans brought in more reinforcements, and the advance was checked. When the Allies were ready to attack again, on 22 December, the German commander, Jürgen von Arnim, was facing them with sixty thousand men and more than two hundred tanks, including about fifty of the new Tiger model, with its 88-mm. gun. Heavy rain further assisted the defence, and within a few days Eisenhower had decided that the attempt to reach Tunis must be abandoned until the spring.

At the end of the year, therefore, the Allies could congratulate themselves upon having secured control of the whole of North Africa, from the Atlantic to the Nile, apart from Tunisia. (They had also secured French West Africa, which the Dakar expedition in 1940 had failed to wrest from Vichy. Its governor had responded to Darlan's instructions that he join the Allies.) The Italians were reeling under the impact of defeat after defeat. In Russia, the Germans had lost the battle for Stalingrad and had failed to penetrate to the oilfields of the Caucasus. In the Far East, the Japanese had been held at the approaches to India and Australia, and had already suffered major reverses at sea as well as setbacks on land.

It was time for the Allied leaders to review the progress of the war and to take crucial decisions as to its future course. Two of them, with attendant staffs, were soon to meet on the soil of French North Africa, at Casablanca, and their meeting was the first great event of the momentous, though also disastrous, year 1943.

PART TWO

ASPECTS OF 1943

West European Fronts, 1943-5

NORWAY

SWEDEN

North Sea

DENMARK

Baltic Sea

GREAT BRITAIN

Northern Ireland

EIRE

Kiel

Hamburg

Bremen

Berlin

POLAND

Vistula

London

Southampton

NETHERLANDS

Dunkirk

Brussels

BELGIUM

Cologne

GERMANY

Dresden

Plymouth

Cherbourg

Invasion beaches

Dieppe

Rouen

LUXEMBOURG

Frankfurt

Schweinfurt

Prague

Bayeux

Caen

Paris

Nuremberg

Vienna

Brest

Munich

Danube

St Nazaire

Loire

FRANCE

SWITZERLAND

Ljubljana Gap

Trieste

YUGOSLAVIA

Vichy

Lyon

Rhône

Milan

Venice

Turin

Bordeaux

1940 Partition

Genoa

Spezia

I T A L Y

Ancona

Adriatic Sea

Pisa

Florence

Marseilles

Corsica

Rome

Termoli

Bari

Anzio

Cassino

Brindisi

Naples

Salerno

Taranto

SPAIN

Tyrrhenian Sea

Sardinia

Palermo

Messina

Sicily

Mt Etna

Agrigento

Mediterranean Sea

– – – Russian front line, VE Day
——— Western Allies front line, VE Day
━━━ Allied line in Italy, Nov 1943
······· Allied line in Italy, April 1945

0   100   200   300 Miles
0   200   400 km

1   Emperors at Casablanca

In mid-January 1943 Roosevelt and Churchill, with a selection of advisers, henchmen, and hangers-on, met in a suburb of Casablanca to discuss the future of the war. This conference was of vast importance militarily, both in the decisions taken and the decisions fudged. It was also very important politically, for good and—above all—for ill. At every stage political cross-purposes and confused thinking affected strategy, and vice versa.

Roosevelt had not, at first, favoured a true summit conference. In his view, a meeting of senior staff officers, British, Russian, and American, would do. But when Churchill persuaded him that it was necessary for the principals to meet, he then merely dissented from the suggestion of Iceland as a venue, saying that he would prefer "a comfortable oasis to the raft at Tilsit." He still hoped, as the historical allusion shows, that he and Churchill would be joined by the Tsar of all the Russias, because he did not at all want to give the impression of an Anglo-American gang-up. But Stalin declined to attend, having more pressing business to attend to at home, so Casablanca became simply an Anglo-American meeting after all.

Various comfortable African "oases," including Khartoum, were considered before the choice eventually settled on Casablanca, which among other things would enable Roosevelt to allay Congressional objections to his absence by inspecting American troops. The precise site chosen was the suburb of Anfa, four or five miles to the south of Casablanca, where a luxury hotel and eighteen villas were taken over at short notice by the American Army and turned into a fortified enclave. The two best villas were allotted to the President and the Prime Minister, the others were distributed among lesser VIPs, while most of the staff officers were put up in the hotel.

This was built with wide verandahs all around, and the views from it were particularly intoxicating to men on leave, as it were, from the drabness of wartime Britain. As one of them wrote: "The dazzling blue of the water, the white of the buildings in Casablanca and the red soil dotted with green palms and bougainvillea and begonia made a beautiful picture in the sunlight." But the amenities were not merely aesthetic; more mundane tastes were provided for as well. Apart from excellent meals, cigarettes, cigars, chewing gum, sweets, soap, and even razors were freely issued.

The conference area was encircled by an exceptionally strong barbed-wire fence and guarded by "an almost solid line of military police." Beyond the fence there were numerous anti-aircraft batteries, and overhead fighter aircraft were on constant patrol. Moroccan servants were replaced by British and American soldiers, who ministered to the temporary inmates of Casablanca's "luxurious prison." Everyone, no matter how important, had to show a pass when going in or out of the compound, and was liable to be treated roughly if he failed to do so. One day Eisenhower's chief of staff, General Walter Bedell Smith, was made to walk back ten paces and lie on his stomach while his identification was checked by a suspicious military policeman. And Churchill himself once got into trouble when, returning from a walk on the sands, he was caught trying to clamber over the barbed wire.

Mystification flourished. Roosevelt was given the code-name "Admiral Q," proposed by Churchill in a cable in which he also suggested that he himself should go by the name of "Mr P." (This enabled him to add: "We must mind our P's and Q's.") But in fact the name given to him was "Air Commodore Frankland" and he arrived at the conference wearing an air commodore's uniform. Harold Macmillan substituted a code of his own, calling Churchill "the Emperor of the East," Roosevelt "the Emperor of the West." In the same spirit of classical analogy (true or false), he one day whispered to the American Robert Murphy, as Eisenhower was taking leave of the President: "Isn't he just like a Roman centurion?" And on a later occasion he remarked to some British colleagues: "These Americans represent the new Roman Empire and we Britons, like the Greeks of old, must teach them how to make it go." By such flattering conceits is impotence consoled.

Macmillan had recently been appointed Minister Resident at Eisenhower's headquarters, and it was in that capacity that he was attending the conference. Murphy had for some time been Roosevelt's special representative in North Africa, where he had been active in preparing the ground for TORCH and, subsequently, in helping to make ad hoc political arrangements with a markedly anti-Gaullist bias. His and Macmillan's role as foreign-affairs consultants to their respective "Emperors" at Casablanca was enhanced by the fact that foreign ministers proper were absent. Roosevelt was so determined that his own Secretary of State, Cordell Hull, should not come to the conference that he prevailed upon Churchill to make Eden, as well, stay at home. (The President liked to conduct foreign affairs himself, using his own men as intermediaries.)

Apart from Macmillan, the only British minister at Casablanca was Lord Leathers, Minister of War Transport, an apolitical technocrat who had attracted the Prime Minister's notice before the war when they were together on the board of the P. & O. Steamship Company (the only business directorship Churchill ever held). Roosevelt, however, was accompanied by two civilian advisers of note—Harry Hopkins and Averell Harriman. Hopkins was the President's most intimate political aide and crony, who had been living in the White House for nearly three years. Harriman was a millionaire Democrat and family friend of the Roosevelts, who had become the most influential American in wartime Britain, carrying more weight than the ambassador.

No wives were present at Casablanca, but Churchill had the company of his son, Randolph, and Roosevelt that of two of his sons, Elliott and Franklin, while Hopkins's son was brought from the front in Tunisia. Neither of the "Emperors" gave the impression of being weighed down with the cares of the world; on the contrary, both seemed to enjoy themselves like truant schoolboys. In the view of Churchill's doctor, Lord Moran, neither of them, in a way, had ever quite grown up.

Churchill arrived at Casablanca on 13 January, and that evening had a briefing session with the British Chiefs of Staff in anticipation of the first meetings of the Combined Chiefs the following day. Roosevelt arrived on the evening of the fourteenth, having flown from Miami by way of Belém in Brazil and Bathurst in Gambia—the first American President to travel by air while in office. On the twenty-third the Combined Chiefs reported the results of their work to the President and Prime Minister, and the following morning the two leaders met the press and and so brought the conference to an end.

While it was in progress, a great deal of work was done and a war of words conducted, mainly between the professionals. The Combined Chiefs met twice a day and in the evenings reported progress—or the lack of it—to their respective political masters. Masters? In a sense Roosevelt and Churchill were little more than interested bystanders at the conference. Of course no major decisions could be taken without their authority, and now and again they would bring their authority to bear. Yet it cannot be said that they dominated the strategic argument from which the big decisions emerged. To some extent, indeed, they had both lost control of events before they came to Casablanca.

Their insistence upon TORCH had limited their future freedom of action in a way that neither had grasped at the time. One consequence, which Roosevelt certainly did not intend, was a large switch of American fighting resources to the south-west Pacific. In their paper (dated 24 July 1942) grudgingly conceding the point about TORCH, the Combined Chiefs of Staff had noted that it would mean that the Allies had "definitely accepted [for 1943] a defensive, encircling line of action for the continental European theatre, except as to air operations and blockade." The Americans interpreted this as a licence to treat the Pacific war as a first charge on manpower, arms, aircraft and shipping, once the requirements for TORCH had been met. The American build-up in Britain preparatory to a landing in northern France was thus brought more or less to a full stop.

This pleased the British Chiefs, and was their reason for agreeing to the paper. But in other respects they interpreted it differently from the Americans. Apart from their unwillingness to attack Germany by the direct route, they had no desire to adopt a purely defensive posture in 1943. Brooke, in particular, had set his heart on a Mediterranean strategy, and the relative success of TORCH (about which, before-hand, he had grave doubts) fortified his belief in further offensive operations in the Mediterranean theatre.

Contrary to legend, it was not Churchill, but rather Brooke, who first carried the banner for this strategy. Far from initiating it, Churchill was a reluctant convert to it. Of course he had been the protagonist of TORCH and a strong opponent of any Second Front in north-west Europe *in 1942*. But it was not his idea that offensive action against Germany *in 1943* should be confined to the Mediterranean theatre, and moreover he had given Stalin to understand that it would not be, during their last talk—without advisers—in Moscow.

Churchill, in fact, did not favour any specific strategy. He wanted to do more or less everything. On his way to Washington after Pearl Harbor, he had projected a state of affairs at the beginning of 1943 in which the whole of North Africa would be in Allied hands, and footholds might already have been established in Sicily and mainland Italy. On the basis of that projection, he had argued that, in 1943, there should be landings by "adequate and suitably equipped forces [in] several of the following countries, namely, Norway, Denmark, Holland, Belgium, the French Channel coasts and the French Atlantic coasts, as well as in Italy and possibly the Balkans."

The object of these landings would be "to enable the conquered populations to revolt" and then fight alongside the liberating Allied troops. But it was not only by defeating Germany in the field that the war might be won. There was also, in Churchill's view, a possibility of victory "through internal convulsions in Germany produced by the unfavourable course of the war, economic privations, and the Allied bombing offensive." These alternative ways of winning still seemed to him possible a year later; hence his continued addiction to bombing. But he also still wanted to have landings, and in more than one theatre, during 1943, though he had apparently lost faith in simultaneous effective revolt by subject peoples.

At the beginning of December 1942 he challenged the British Chiefs' view that TORCH had made ROUND-UP (the full-scale Allied landing in France) impossible in 1943. When formulated in July this view had, he said, assumed that the Russians might be so weakened in 1942 that Hitler would be able to bring large forces back from the East. In fact, the opposite had occurred. The Germans were no longer, on balance, weakening the Russians on the Eastern Front, but were themselves under such pressure there that it would be out of the question for them to transfer any substantial forces to the West.

The professionals would not be moved, arguing that Allied resources in manpower, shipping, and landing-craft would be "wholly inadequate" for carrying TORCH through to a successful conclusion and mounting "the operations which we contemplate in the Mediterranean next spring and summer," in addition to ROUND-UP in July. To guard themselves against the rejoinder that they were begging the question by mentioning further operations in the Mediterranean, they went on to say that an effective ROUND-UP against an unbroken German Army in July would be "extremely doubtful," even if TORCH were curtailed and all idea of further Mediterranean campaigning abandoned.

It was suggested, too, that unless the Axis were subjected to more attacks from the south the Germans would be able to reinforce their garrisons in the north-west. Yet at the same time the British Chiefs maintained that Hitler would not be able to move forces from France to Italy or the Balkans, for fear of having to face an attack across the Channel. The absurdity of this "heads we win, tails you lose" argument was never exposed.

Yet Churchill was slow to climb down, and at the end of December he made his final attempt to keep ROUND-UP on the agenda for 1943. Unless during the summer and autumn the enemy were engaged from the west as well as from the south, the Allies would fail to use their full strength and might even fail to keep the enemy pinned down in the west. But the Chiefs of Staff got their way, with only an empty gesture to Churchill (and Marshall) in the form of a statement that, subject to all the higher priorities, there should be "the greatest possible concentration of forces in the United Kingdom with a view to re-entry on the Continent in August or September 1943."

The higher priorities were to be defeating the U-boat menace, expanding the Anglo-American bomber offensive against Germany and Italy, exploiting the Allied position in the Mediterranean, maintaining the flow of supplies to Russia, offensive operations in the Pacific "on a scale sufficient to contain the bulk of Japanese forces in that area," and operations to re-open the Burma Road. The Mediterranean position was to be exploited, it was said, by "knocking Italy out of the war, bringing Turkey into the war, and giving the Axis no respite for recuperation." Such was the programme that Churchill felt obliged to accept before he set off for Casablanca.

True, at his meeting with the British Chiefs on the evening of 13 January, he still mentioned a "preliminary" invasion of France in 1943 as one objective to be discussed, and if possible agreed on, with the Americans. But it was to rank, with the reconquest of Burma, as a secondary aim. The prime tasks on which agreement was to be sought were clearing the whole North African shore and capturing Sicily. *This order of priorities was tantamount to postponing cross-Channel action until 1944.*

Among the Combined Chiefs of Staff four men stood out, two Americans and two British. The dominant figures on the American side were General George C. Marshall, (Army) Chief of Staff since 1939, and Admiral Ernest J. King, who had succeeded Admiral Harold Stark as Chief of Naval Operations in 1942. The British stars were Air Chief Marshal Sir Charles (known to his friends as "Peter") Portal, Chief of Air Staff since the autumn of 1940, and General Sir Alan Brooke, Chief of the Imperial General Staff (professional head of the Army) since November 1941, and chairman of the British Chiefs of Staff committee since March 1942.

A fifth name should perhaps be included, that of Field Marshal Sir John Dill, though his gift was for diplomacy rather than domination. His friendship with Marshall, which enhanced beyond measure the importance of his role as head of the British joint staff mission in Washington, has already been mentioned. He was also unusual in being a man whom Brooke looked up to rather than down on—a fellow-Ulsterman, and his predecessor as C.I.G.S. At Casablanca, Dill's services as a mediator were of special value.

The less potent Chiefs at the conference were the British First Sea Lord, Admiral Sir Dudley Pound, and the American General Henry H. ("Hap") Arnold, who commanded the Army Air Forces. Pound was already in failing health and would be dead before the year was out. At one particularly tense meeting he was, according to Brooke, "as usual, asleep and with no views either way." Arnold was full of vigour, but not very formidable intellectually. Moreover, he was not the head of an independent service, like the R.A.F., but subordinate to Marshall in status as well as talent.

Mountbatten sat at the top table, since he was a member of the British Chiefs of Staff committee. But his views on future strategy did not differ essentially from Brooke's, except that he regarded Sardinia as a better bet than Sicily for the next Allied landing. Even if his approach had been radically different, it would have been difficult for him to carry his senior colleagues with him, or to persuade Churchill to back him against them. General Sir Hastings ("Pug") Ismay also attended, as Churchill's personal chief of staff, but his function was to oil the works rather than to make any independent contribution. Roosevelt's personal chief of staff, Admiral William D. Leahy, should have attended as well, but was taken ill on his way to the conference and had to be left behind. (His presence would not noticeably have affected the strategic debate, though it would have been rather embarrassing politically—for a reason that will soon be evident.)

Of the Big Four professionals at Casablanca, Marshall and Brooke were the arch-antagonists, in that they were the champions of rival strategies for winning the war in Europe. Both were men of moral as well as intellectual stature, who did not allow their antagonism to take a petty form.

Marshall had an extraordinarily clear, thorough, and resourceful mind. Above all, he had a personality which imposed itself, at all stages of his career, upon young and old. On one occasion during the First World War, when he was only a captain on the staff of a division in France, he challenged the American commander-in-chief, General John J. Pershing, with such temerity that many witnesses assumed he would be broken for it. In fact, Pershing was so impressed by the young officer's knowledge and self-confidence that he later made him his aide, and never ceased to take a special interest in his advancement.

Dean Acheson, who worked closely with Marshall after the Second World War, described him thus: "The moment [he] entered a room everyone in it felt his presence. It was a striking and communicated force. His figure conveyed intensity, which his voice, low, staccato and incisive, reinforced. It compelled respect. It spread a sense of authority and of calm. There was no military glamour about him and nothing of the martinet." Near the end of his life, when he was living in retirement, an Englishman who had known him during the war visited him at his home in Virginia. Finding that food was short in the house, Marshall drove his guest to a local country club for lunch, and as they entered the dining room everyone in it stood up, as if responding to a secret word of command.

Despite his natural aptitude for leading men, Marshall's genius for administration ensured that most of his career would be spent on the staff. In the Second World War he alone of the British and American Chiefs of Staff held his post from beginning to end of the war. It was his task, and his prodigious achievement, to convert an army of thousands into one of millions, to train it, to equip it, and to provide it with worthy leaders. Eisenhower, Bradley, Clark, Patton, and others were personally picked by him, and his judgment of men seldom failed. Churchill compared him with Carnot, the French Republic's organizer of victory, and the comparison is apt.

But Brooke's comment that Marshall's thoughts revolved around the creation of forces rather than their employment does him far less than justice. Though he never had an opportunity to display his talents in the field, he was no less interested than Brooke in strategy and tactics, and no less disappointed when the supreme command of OVERLORD was denied him. (Both men were encouraged by their respective political leaders to believe that the job would be theirs.) Marshall, like Brooke, had a very definite idea how Allied forces could best be employed in the West, and although it did not prevail in 1943 —partly through his own fault—it does not at all follow that the idea was wrong in principle, or that Brooke's alternative idea was right.

One of the handicaps with which Marshall had to contend was that the American Chiefs of Staff were not, like the British, united in giving overriding priority to the war in Europe. In Admiral King's eyes the Pacific war was more important, because it was essentially a naval war. Since this view was apparently shared by a majority of Americans, Roosevelt, as commander-in-chief, was less effective than he should have been in keeping the transfer of resources to the Pacific within strict bounds. King had too much of his own way, and the fact that all landing-craft were under the Navy's control enabled him to pre-empt them on a massive scale for the Pacific theatre.

As well as having a natural preference for the theatre in which his service was most heavily involved, King had a fairly strong prejudice against Europe, and rather more than the common American anti-British sentiment. In November 1943, when returning from the Cairo conference by a circuitous route across Africa, he had to spend a night at Khartoum and, though invited to dine and sleep at the British governor-general's palace, refused to do so and stayed ostentatiously on the airfield. This led to a stand-up row between him and Lewis Douglas, War Shipping Administrator and later U.S. ambassador in London.

Roosevelt felt rather more at ease with King than with Marshall. He called King "Ernie" both to his face and behind his back, whereas Marshall he called "George" only to his face, referring to him in conversation with others as "General Marshall." Perhaps he sensed in the Chief of Staff some disapproval of his slipshod administrative methods and often shifty behaviour. In fact, Marshall respected Roosevelt, not only as any good American is conditioned to respect the President of the United States, but also because he genuinely admired his courage, intuition, and power to *animate,* if not to administer. Roosevelt, for his part, certainly respected and trusted Marshall. But between the two men there was always something of a temperamental barrier, which meant that Marshall's influence with the President was never quite what it should have been.

It was not that Marshall was always incapable of dealing with politicians. On the contrary, he had shown himself remarkably adept in putting the Army's case across to members of the Congress, and he had made it his business to establish close relations with Harry Hopkins. But Roosevelt was another matter. Partly because he kept more aloof than Churchill from the detailed processes of strategic planning, he was less easily carried along by the views of any one professional adviser. He did not exercise systematic control over his Chiefs of Staff, but none of them—not even Marshall—was able to control him.

Brooke, who did gradually achieve ascendancy over Churchill on issues of grand strategy, was similar to Marshall in having served much of his career as a staff officer. In the First World War he was, in turn, adjutant, brigade major, and on the staff of a division. In the Second, his only experience of fighting leadership was in rearguard actions and evacuations. As commander of the B.E.F.'s II Corps he distinguished himself in the retreat to Dunkirk, and then, sent back to France to command the British troops still left there, he successfully got most of them out through Brest, St. Malo, Cherbourg, and St. Nazaire. His memory of unequal combat with Hitler's Wehrmacht in France must, however, have coloured his attitude towards Allied re-entry into Europe.

Though he belonged to the Ulster squirearchy—a nephew of his was Sir Basil Brooke, for many years Prime Minister of Northern Ireland—he was born in France and had the unusual advantage of speaking French fluently. More in keeping with his background was his love of field sports and passion for bird-watching. In one early-morning walk at Casablanca he was thrilled to see "goldfinch, stonechat, warblers of all sorts, white wagtail and several kinds of waders on the seashore, such as sanderlings, ring plover, grey plover and turnstones."

But it was not ornithology or any other country pursuit that enabled him to measure up to Churchill. Nor was it his familiarity with the French language, but rather his capacity to argue forcefully in English. While recognising Churchill's genius, he was never overawed by it and was not, like many others, made tongue-tied by the flow of Churchillian eloquence. Handy with words himself, he was, as well, self-assured to the point of arrogance, firm to the point of obstinacy. Churchill could neither bully him into submission nor sway him with glorious monologues. He knew his own mind and was a match even for Churchill in verbal contests. He was good at working on the Prime Minister's hopes, as well as on his fears.

Brooke's air of knowing best did not, however, endear him to the Americans. He spoke very fast and had the rather disconcerting habit, described by Ian Jacob, of "shooting his tongue out and round his lips with the speed of a chameleon." Marshall's biographer, Forrest C. Pogue, has this to say of him: "To most Americans, as to some of his colleagues, Brooke was icy, imperturbable and condescending. Four years younger than Marshall, he was smaller in stature, delicately boned, and with large dark eyes that had a shining, impenetrable stare." Yet Marshall became aware of "a pleasanter side" to him, and anyway was grateful to him for scotching some of Churchill's wilder schemes, such as that for an expedition to Norway.

The Americans' favourite among the British Chiefs of Staff was Portal. In Marshall's view, he had "the best mind of the lot," and without being any less opinionated than Brooke, he managed to seem less contemptuous of the opinions of others. Moreover, his particular form of dogmatism—what may be termed bomber-mania—was to a large extent shared by the Americans (in principle, if not in method of execution). He and Brooke did not agree about the potential of bombing, but from their different standpoints they could agree on a Mediterranean strategy, because Portal looked forward to being able to bomb the industry of south Germany and Austria, and the oilfields of Roumania, from Mediterranean airfields.

On one political issue, Brooke was wiser than any other Allied leader. He did not believe in the necessity to appease the Russians, because there seemed to him no conceivable danger of a separate peace between Stalin and Hitler. He could not see "how any common agreement could ever be arrived at between them which would not irreparably lower the prestige of one or the other in the eyes of their own people." But unfortunately this perception merely reinforced his hostility to a Second Front in north-west Europe in 1943.

The professional debate at Casablanca was weighted in favour of the British. Though plainly junior partners in the alliance as a whole, they were not yet over-shadowed in the European theatre. An all-British-and-Commonwealth army had recently defeated Rommel in the Western Desert, and the British contribution to TORCH had been not much less than the American on land, and much greater at sea. General Alexander's appearance at Casablanca, wearing desert shorts and an open-necked shirt with rolled-up sleeves, gave his compatriots a psychological boost and reminded the Americans that they were not yet seasoned campaigners.

The British had the further advantage of coming to the conference more united and better prepared. Whatever the differences between Churchill and the British Chiefs, or among the Chiefs themselves, they were not paraded in public. So far as the Americans could see, the British had a firm and consistent line, whereas the tug-of-war between Marshall and King, and the conflicting interests that they represented, was all too apparent.

As for preparation, the British had a headquarters ship, H.M.S. *Bulolo,* which lay at Casablanca throughout the conference and supplied the principals with all the cipher and secretarial facilities they needed. They also had a full planning staff, which on occasion had to help the Americans out, because they brought only two or three planners. The American Chiefs had to work with virtually no infrastructure, while the British were almost as well supported as they would have been at home.

The previous two Allied conferences since America entered the war having been in Washington, the Americans had no experience of attending one remote from their home base, whereas the British had learnt from experience. At Casablanca the Americans were quick to learn the same lesson, and as a result they made sure that they came in large numbers, and amply equipped, to future conferences.

But even these advantages for the British, and disadvantages for the Americans, might not have been enough to lose the central argument for Marshall, had he not prejudiced it himself by allowing one vital issue to go by default. In Churchill's original concept of the operation which became known as TORCH, it had been intended that the whole of French North Africa should be in Allied hands by the end of 1942; indeed, that the whole North African shore should be clear by then, and that possibly landings might have been effected in Sicily and mainland Italy.

This time-table had, however, proved over-optimistic, partly because of the Americans' unwillingness to push the initial landings far enough to the east, partly because of Montgomery's slowness in pursuit and failure to destroy Rommel's army, and partly because of the Germans' very bold and quick reaction to TORCH. At the end of 1942 the enemy still had a bridgehead in Tunisia, which Eisenhower said he could not eliminate until the spring.

It was assumed by all the Allied leaders in conference at Casablanca that, before anything else could be done, the Tunisian bridgehead would have to be eliminated. Marshall no less than the others worked on this assumption, and seems not to have realised its disastrous implications for his larger strategy. For a delay of several months in disposing of Tunisia was surely almost bound to mean postponing the necessary switch of troops, landing-craft, etc., from North Africa to Britain until the year was too far advanced.

The pros and cons of giving top priority to the capture of Tunis will be discussed in the next chapter. But why were they not discussed at Casablanca? Why did Marshall not raise the issue at the conference, or Churchill in his earlier exchanges with Brooke? It seems strange that the need to "take Tunis first" should have been treated as self-evident.

Without questioning it Marshall could hardly hope to make a convincing case for his own rather than Brooke's strategy in 1943. All the same he tried, but by 18 February he had thrown in the towel. That day the Combined Chiefs of Staff reported to Churchill and Roosevelt that they had agreed to follow the capture of Tunis with an invasion of Sicily, which was to be code-named HUSKY. Marshall himself explained their reasons: that with the end of the campaign in North Africa the Allies would have a large number of troops available for some other task; that the capture of Sicily would give the Allies virtually free passage through the Mediterranean, and so effect an important economy in shipping; that it would increase the possibility of knocking Italy out of the war; and that this in turn would force the Germans to take over the Italians' present commitments.

The point thus settled was by no means the only point of controversy among the Chiefs of Staff, nor was its resolution the end of their work at Casablanca. But it was the key point, and when it was out of the way, nothing of comparable importance remained.

The Chiefs' final agreement, submitted to the political leaders on the twenty-second, covered every aspect of global strategy. Defeating the U-boat was confirmed as the first charge on Allied resources, and the determination to win the war against Hitler as soon as possible reasserted. Aid to Russia in the form of shipments of supplies was to be continued, provided the cost to the Western Allies did not become "prohibitive."

Sicily was to be occupied, not only for the reasons stated four days before by Marshall, but also as a further means of helping Russia and to "create a situation" in which Turkey could be "enlisted as an active ally." But apart from a reference to "intensifying the pressure on Italy" there was no mention of invading the Italian mainland. This was, in one sense, an ominous omission.

The bomber offensive from the United Kingdom was to be further escalated. Surface action was to be confined to "such limited offensive operations" as might be "practicable with the amphibious forces available." As a sop to Marshall it was, however, stated that "the strongest possible force" should be assembled in the United Kingdom "in constant readiness to re-enter the Continent as soon as German resistance [might be] weakened to the required extent." No question of opening a Second Front in France to help the Russians—only of doing so if they had, in effect, already shown that they were winning.

To ensure that the agreed action in the European theatre should not be "prejudiced by the necessity to divert forces to retrieve an adverse situation elsewhere," the Combined Chiefs advised that "adequate" forces should be allocated to the Pacific and Far Eastern theatres. This satisfied King, who had been promised that he would not have to give up any of the forces already allotted to him, and who knew that he could use the standard of "adequacy" to justify any further demands that he might make.

Another sop to Marshall was, however, the rider that Pacific and Far Eastern operations must not "jeopardise the capacity of the United Nations to take advantage of any favourable opportunity . . . for the decisive defeat of Germany in 1943." Subject to that, plans should go ahead for the recapture of Burma, "beginning in 1943," and subject to *that* for operations against the Marshalls and Carolines, after the Japanese base at Rabaul in New Britain had been captured.

The strategic pattern so outlined represented many compromises, but the central compromise between Marshall's and Brooke's ideas was overwhelmingly in Brooke's favour. And the British scored another point when it was laid down in the final report, approved by Roosevelt and Churchill, that the command structure for the last phase in Tunisia should place three Britons—Alexander, Sir Andrew Cunningham, and Sir Arthur Tedder—in control, respectively, of land, sea, and air operations under Eisenhower, who would himself assume a sublimated, politico-strategic role; and that a similar structure should apply for HUSKY.

At the end of the conference Brigadier Ian Jacob, military assistant secretary to the War Cabinet, remarked in his diary that he could never have foreseen a result so comprehensively favourable to British ideas, which had "prevailed almost throughout." The British Chiefs could, indeed, feel proud of their success at the conference table— though it is arguable, to say the least, that their victory in the war of words delayed the Allies' actual victory by quite a long period.

While the professionals had been conferring, the "Emperors" had been leading a pleasant but rather desultory existence. Since they were involved only intermittently in the debate about future operations, they might well have devoted themselves to a searching consideration of the political problems already created by the war, or likely to arise before long. In fact, their political discussions were limited and patchy.

One reason—probably the main reason—was that Roosevelt did not really want to discuss politics with Churchill, whom he regarded as an old-fashioned imperialist intent upon making large parts of the world safe for his sort of British and European hegemony. In a revealing comment to his son Elliott, Roosevelt said at Casablanca: "The English mean to maintain their hold on their colonies. They mean to help the French maintain *their* hold on *their* colonies. Winnie is a great man for the status quo. He even looks like the status quo, doesn't he?" (So at least Elliott reports in his book *A Rendezvous with Destiny,* and the words ring true.)

Whatever the President's suspicions, French affairs had to be discussed with Churchill, insofar as the immediate future in North Africa was concerned. It was a subject which could not be altogether evaded. The "Anglo-Saxon" Allies were massively present in French protected or (in the case of Algeria) sovereign territory, as an occupying power. For decency's sake, no less than for the sake of efficiency, something had to be done to make the French establishment in North Africa more representative.

Even Roosevelt could see that Giraud, who had succeeded the murdered Darlan as High Commissioner, but who was really no more than an American puppet, would never be able to fill the bill on his own. Apart from his manifest stupidity, he clearly lacked popular support. He was also considered useless by the British, whose views could not in the circumstances be ignored.

Without admitting (he would have been the last to admit it) that the popularity denied to Giraud was, in fact, enjoyed by de Gaulle, Roosevelt could hardly refuse to have some dealings with the French leader whom the British, after a fashion, supported. It was hoped, therefore, that the two generals would both come to Casablanca, and that they would agree to form a duumvirate to administer all parts of the French empire which had broken with Vichy, but to do so under Allied control and without even the dignity of a government in exile.

Until almost the last minute de Gaulle refused to come, since he resented the manner and purpose of the invitation, and the events leading up to it, no less than the implied suggestion that he was Britain's French general in the same sense that Giraud was America's. But eventually he took the prudent course of travelling to Casablanca, where he allowed himself to be photographed shaking hands with Giraud in the presence of Roosevelt and Churchill. Apart from this empty charade he gave nothing away, and the communiqué that he and Giraud signed was a brief one drafted by himself, rather than the one prepared for him by the Allies.

The incident belongs to a story which will receive proper attention in a later chapter—the tragic story of Anglo-American misunderstanding and mishandling of France during the Second World War. Here it is only necessary to record it as an example of the "Emperors'" statecraft at Casablanca.

The best-known example—and the most controversial—was, however, proclaimed to the world by Roosevelt at his press conference with Churchill on 24 January (also the occasion of the de Gaulle–Giraud photograph). Roosevelt's words proclaiming it have to be quoted in full:

Another point, I think, we had all had it in our hearts and heads before, but I don't think that it has ever been put down on paper by the Prime Minister and myself, and that is the determination that peace can come to the world only by the total elimination of German and Japanese war power.

Some of you Britishers know the old story—we had a general called U. S. Grant. His name was Ulysses Simpson Grant, but in my, and the Prime Minister's, early days he was called "Unconditional Surrender" Grant. The elimination of German, Japanese and Italian war power means the unconditional surrender by Germany, Japan and Italy. This means a reasonable assurance of future world peace. It does not mean the destruction of the population of Germany, Italy or Japan, but it does mean the destruction of the philosophies in those countries which are based on conquest and the subjugation of other peoples.

This meeting may be called the "unconditional surrender" meeting.

Churchill, who subsequently claimed to have been surprised by the President's declaration, hastened to endorse it:

Even when there is some delay there is design and purpose and, as the President has said, the unconquerable will to pursue this quality, until we have procured the unconditional surrender of the criminal forces who have plunged the world into storm and ruin.

In his memoirs, Churchill corrected the impression that he had earlier given—in an off-the-cuff remark in the House of Commons in 1949 —that the idea of unconditional surrender was entirely new to him when it fell from the President's lips at the press conference. But he maintained that it was a surprise to hear Roosevelt utter the phrase, since it was not included in the official communiqué.

Roosevelt tried to make out that the utterance was spontaneous, telling Hopkins soon afterwards: "We had so much trouble getting those two French generals together that I thought to myself that this was as difficult as arranging the meeting of Grant and Lee—and then suddenly the press conference was on, and Winston and I had had no time to prepare for it, and the thought popped into my mind that they had called Grant Old Unconditional Surrender and the next thing I knew I had said it."

In fact, Roosevelt spoke from notes at the press conference, and his notes contained the phrase "unconditional surrender" three times over. He had discussed it in Washington before coming to Casablanca, and at Casablanca had discussed it with Churchill. On 20 January Churchill sent a message to the War Cabinet, asking what his colleagues would think of "a declaration of the firm intention of the United States and the British Empire to continue the war relentlessly until we have brought about the 'unconditional surrender' of Germany and Japan." He did not include Italy, whose omission, he said, "would be to encourage a break-up there."

The War Cabinet did not normally make any difficulties for Churchill when he was, as it were, on safari (or indeed at other times). But on this occasion it chose to assert itself, and in a particularly unfortunate way, by insisting that Italy *should* be included along with Germany and Japan. So Italy was included, though not—curiously— in the first paragraph of Roosevelt's statement. The War Cabinet's hard line towards Italy probably reflected Eden's obsession with Mussolini and the Labour Party's undiscriminating view of Fascism.

In retrospect, it seems scarcely credible that a policy declaration of such importance should have been made so casually, even though its genesis was not quite so casual as Roosevelt made out to Hopkins. Why was there "no time" for him and Churchill to prepare for the press conference, and why, above all, did they not consider all the possible implications of unconditional surrender before making it their policy?

Michael Howard has written, in the official British history of the war: " . . . it must be noted that at Casablanca the question as to whether it would soften the enemy will to resist or stiffen it does not appear to have been seriously considered at all. Neither experts on political warfare nor specialists on Axis internal affairs were present. Nor were the officials in Washington and London who were already drafting plans for the settlement of the post-war world. No representative of the Foreign Office or the State Department was invited to give an assessment of the policy in the wider context of international relations—particularly in the context of future relations with the Soviet Union."

Roosevelt's irresponsibility was greater than Churchill's, since it was he who set the pace. Churchill at least tried to modify the policy for Italy's benefit, only to be torpedoed by the War Cabinet at home. And it was, perhaps, reasonable for him to assume that a phrase which had been kept out of the official communiqué would not be produced, *viva voce,* at the press conference. All the same, he does not seem to have fully grasped the seriousness of the issue.

The motives for "unconditional surrender" are generally thought to have been a desire to convince Stalin that his Western allies were in earnest, and the need to reassure public opinion in Britain and the United States, shaken by the Darlan episode, that there was no cause to doubt the ideological purity of the two leaders. Whether the adoption of such a policy was necessary for either purpose is more than doubtful. In any case, the war's character as a crusade for democracy and human rights was already sufficiently compromised by the fact that Stalin's Russia was part of the grand alliance.

What of the policy's effect upon the enemy? It is often said that it made little difference, one way or the other, but this is not very plausible, and anyway impossible to prove. Beyond question it contributed to the appalling delay in negotiating an armistice with Italy, and it was a gift to Goebbels's propaganda machine. As for Japan, the surrender of that country was not, when the time came, unconditional, because the Japanese were allowed to insist that their Emperor should remain. So what price the policy?

It was clearly right that the Allies should refuse to have any dealings with the enemy dictators as such, and that they should proclaim their detestation of aggressive and oppressive regimes—hypocritical though the last point must appear, in view of the Soviet connection. It was also sensible to avoid any shopping-list of peace terms, such as Woodrow Wilson's "Fourteen Points." But "unconditional surrender" erred in the opposite direction, denying freedom of manoeuvre to the Allies themselves and to peace-inclined elements on the other side, which needed all the encouragement they could get.

Incidentally, Roosevelt's reference to General Grant suggests that he saw an analogy between the American Civil War and the war in which his country was currently engaged. If so, the analogy was false and misleading. Germany, Italy, and Japan were not states in a federation but independent states.

For Churchill, Casablanca was ostensibly a moment of triumph. Once again secure in his position as Prime Minister, he seemed also to be on easy, equal terms with the President. Their relationship could be thought to foreshadow that Anglo-American condominium which was, in fact, Churchill's dream.

But appearances were deceptive. In retrospect we can see that at Casablanca Churchill's control of events was slipping. TORCH had been his personal achievement. It was his idea, and he had imposed it upon the Americans and his own advisers. But now he was ceasing to be the architect of Allied strategy. At Casablanca the strategic design agreed to was Brooke's rather than his. And if he could no longer even dominate the British C.I.G.S., still less could he dominate the President of the United States.

His loss of power, or even influence, over Roosevelt must have been uncomfortably apparent to him before they parted. At his suggestion, Roosevelt accompanied him to Marrakesh after the press conference. It was a place that Churchill had long fancied, and he wanted to show it to his "illustrious colleague." Even more, he wanted to regain the intimacy with Roosevelt that he felt he was beginning to lose.

During the four-hour drive to Marrakesh, he was vividly reminded of America's growing power. All along the way the road was lined with American soldiers, and American aircraft patrolled overhead. The British merely provided the picnic lunch.

At Marrakesh the two leaders stayed overnight in the same villa— the property of a rich American woman, but requisitioned for the use of one of Murphy's agents. This man, Kenneth Pendar, presided over the evening's dinner party there, which was also attended by Hopkins, Harriman, and others. According to Churchill, it was "a very jolly dinner" at which songs were sung, with himself and Roosevelt joining in the choruses.

The jollity may have been more than a little forced. Harriman observed that Churchill kept looking for an opportunity to talk privately with Roosevelt, but was prevented by the seating arrangements. And "Roosevelt rather liked the idea that he did not have to go through with this talk. He always enjoyed other people's discomfort. I think [Harriman adds] it is fair to say that it never bothered him very much when other people were unhappy."

Next morning Roosevelt left by air for the United States. Churchill saw him off, wearing a dressing-gown covered with red dragons. Returning on his own to the villa, the Prime Minister climbed its tower and, Moran tells us, "gazed for a long time in silence at the Atlas mountains." He also painted a picture, the only one he painted during the war.

These aesthetic exercises may have been a welcome distraction from vaguely apprehensive thoughts.

2   The Price of Tunis

The new unified Allied command for destroying the enemy bridgehead in Tunisia was not due to come into effect until Montgomery's
army had crossed the Tunisian frontier. This it did not do until 16
February, Rommel having meanwhile been allowed to get his army
away to join forces with von Arnim's. Time and again Montgomery
missed the chance to trap Rommel's army, through the extreme caution and deliberation of his advance. He also gave Rommel time to
blow up the harbour installations at Tripoli, which resulted in a
further delay of several weeks in the Eighth Army's progress.

Eisenhower had the creditable idea of preventing the convergence
of the two German armies by means of a drive to the coast near Sfax,
about 150 miles south of Tunis. But when he reported this idea to the
Combined Chiefs at Casablanca he was told that it would be too risky.
Brooke particularly emphasised the danger of exposing raw American
troops to Rommel's veterans, and it was indeed true that Rommel,
anticipating just such a threat, detached a panzer division to meet it.

But it was not long before the same Americans had to fight Rommel's men on *his* initiative, because he could see that the best, and
probably the only, hope for the Axis bridgehead was to prevent a
junction between the Eighth Army and the Allied forces already in
Tunisia. It was therefore his plan to attack the southern part of those
forces, before Montgomery was in a position to threaten him. Having
forced the Allies to retreat into Algeria, he would then turn back to
deal with the Eighth Army.

This plan was tried, but without the crucial advantage of Rommel in sole command. Luckily for the Allies, who still had no unified command themselves when the attack began on 14 February, units sent northwards by Rommel came under von Arnim's control. And von Arnim's tactics were less audacious than Rommel's.

As a result, after little more than a week, it was clear that the onslaught had failed. The Allies had been given a serious fright and had suffered considerable losses, but had not been pushed back into Algeria. On 23 February, the day after it had been decided to abandon the offensive, Rommel heard that he had been appointed overall commander. If the appointment had been made earlier, the struggle for Tunisia might have been even more protracted and costly.

Frustrated in his first move, Rommel turned south against Montgomery at Médenine, about sixty miles inside Tunisia, opposite the Mareth Line. But by then Montgomery had had time to reinforce his advance guard and so had no difficulty in repulsing the attack. Seeing that nothing could keep the two Allied armies from joining up, Rommel recommended that the existing 400-mile Axis front be shortened to one of less than a quarter that length, defending Tunis and Bizerta. But Hitler, as usual, would not hear of any retreat.

On 9 March Rommel handed over command to von Arnim and went on sick leave. He never returned to Africa, and his departure was an incalculable boon to the Allies. Alexander, whose new command had become effective on 19 February, was more or less a match for von Arnim, and in all other respects the Allied superiority was crushing.

In early March, the Allies had a preponderance in Tunisia of at least two to one in fighting troops, and about nine to one in tanks. Even so it was not until 13 May that Axis resistance in Tunisia ceased. Church bells were then rung again in England for a victory which, in local terms, could hardly have been more comprehensive.

Only a few hundred able-bodied men escaped. The total bag of prisoners claimed by Eisenhower was 240,000, of which number about 125,000 were German. But whose was the strategic victory?

Commenting upon the Allies' failure to capture Tunis in December 1942, Liddell Hart wrote in his *History of the Second World War:* ". . . by the irony of luck, this failure turned out one of the biggest blessings in disguise that could have happened. For without such a failure Hitler and Mussolini would not have had the time or encouragement to pour very large reinforcements into Tunisia and build up the defence of that bridgehead to a strength of over a quarter of a million—who had to fight with an enemy-dominated sea at their backs, and if defeated would be trapped."

At first sight this seems a persuasive comment, but surely there is another side to the question. It can very well be argued that, since the Allies chose to treat reduction of the Tunisian bridgehead as their top priority task, from which no forces could be deflected, the German sacrifice there was economical in relation to the much larger peril that it helped to avert. Without the check before Tunis, and without the unanimous view at Casablanca that Tunis must be stormed before any other operation could be started, it would surely have been very much harder for Brooke to get his way about postponing cross-Channel action until 1944. The Germans certainly lost a big battle in Tunisia, but the alternative might have been to lose the war a year earlier.

Was it really necessary for the Allies to devote so much force and effort to reducing the bridgehead? Would it not have been far better from their point of view to treat it as an extremely vulnerable salient in which the enemy could be contained and then left to rot? Granted the Allies' sea and air mastery, the Axis position in Tunisia would have been bound to collapse in a gradual but relentless way, even if no serious attacks had been launched against it.

Already, before the Allied occupation of Morocco, Algeria, and Libya, Axis supplies to North Africa had been subject to crippling loss. British naval ascendancy in the Mediterranean, combined with Ultra Intelligence reports, had made life very dangerous for Axis shipping. But obviously the danger was immeasurably increased when the supply line was squeezed to a narrow channel and the Allies had ports and airfields within easy range of it.

Rommel and von Arnim calculated that they would need at least 140,000 tons of supplies a month if they were to have any chance of holding on in Tunisia. This figure was cut by higher authority to 120,000 tons—or rather to 80,000 tons, since it was assumed that up to a third might be sunk on the way.

In fact, only 29,000 tons got through during March, only 23,000 tons during April, and a mere 2,000 tons during the first week of May.

It is hardly surprising that von Arnim said later that *even without the Allied offensive* he would have had to capitulate by 1 June at the latest, because his men would have had no more to eat.

The heavy British losses in the 1941 Greek campaign, and in the battle for Crete, are often said to have been justified by the postponement of BARBAROSSA (the German invasion of Russia) for a period of five weeks. By the same token, it would seem that the German sacrifice in Tunisia must have been worth-while for the much longer respite that it helped to procure on the vital front in north-west Europe. Hitler's decision to stand and fight in Tunisia was even more of a trap for the Allies than it was for him. At least one of the Allied leaders, Brooke, was only too glad of an excuse to be stuck in the Mediterranean, but others, more especially Marshall, walked into the trap blindly.

After saying goodbye to Roosevelt at Marrakesh, Churchill did not return to Britain but went, with Brooke, on a fruitless mission to Turkey. Their purpose was to bring the Turks immediately to a state of active cooperation comparable with that of the United States before Pearl Harbor, in the hope that full belligerency would follow in due course.

The Americans at Casablanca had shown little interest in these pipe-dreams, but had not objected to Churchill's proposed journey. The War Cabinet at home *did* try to discourage him, but in vain, and he also ignored advice from the British representatives in Ankara. In their view, which turned out to be entirely correct, the Turks were more afraid of the Russians than of the Germans, and would be most reluctant to do anything to accelerate a Russian victory.

Insofar as they were willing to receive arms from the Allies, it was actually for the purpose of strengthening their defences against the future Soviet threat rather than for present use against the Germans. It would, moreover, be very difficult to deliver arms in quantity to the Turks so long as the enemy was occupying the Dodecanese and in a position to blockade Smyrna. Even allowing Allied planes to use Turkish airfields for raids on Ploesti and other key targets in the Balkans would be out of the question so long as the Turks had reason to doubt the Allies' power to protect them against a German counterstroke.

The Anglo-Turkish meeting took place during the last two days of January, in a train near the Turkish frontier with Syria; and it was as unrewarding for the visitors as Hitler's with Franco at Hendaye in October 1940. The "Franco" in the second case was President Ismet Inönü, former henchman of Atatürk, whose long-range encounters with Churchill had included Gallipoli and Chanak, but who had never before met him face-to-face.

The two men got on well enough, but Inönü avoided committing himself in any of the ways that Churchill would have wished. Nevertheless, Churchill formed a more optimistic impression than Hitler did at his meeting with Franco, and Brooke, in spite of finding his opposite number, Marshal Ferzi Çakmak, totally without competence, recorded in his diary that the visit had been "a tremendous success." He was sure that Turkey's neutrality would from then onwards "assume a more biased nature in favour of the Allies."

It needs to be stressed again at this point that Mediterranean strategy was more Brooke's obsession than Churchill's. As Brooke saw it, Churchill could never make up his mind which was the most important theatre—could never face the necessity for concentrating effort. His thoughts would turn to one theatre after another, or to several simultaneously. Only under relentless pressure from himself (Brooke) had the old man been forced to acquiesce in priority for the Mediterranean in 1943.

Yet history has been written largely on the assumption that Mediterranean strategy was Churchill's bright or (according to taste) baleful idea, and an almost deterministic continuity has been traced from his thoughts and actions in the First World War to his thoughts and actions in the Second. This view contains more error than truth.

It is, of course, true that Churchill's name became identified with the disastrous Gallipoli campaign in 1915, and that he subsequently devoted all his great resources of advocacy to an attempt to prove that the *idea* was right even though the *execution* was faulty. To a man of his temperament it would have been intolerably wounding to admit that his career had nearly been smashed beyond repair by a strategic venture into which he had been inveigled. He needed to claim credit for the brilliant originality of the idea, while rejecting the blame for what went wrong.

In fact, as Martin Gilbert has shown in his fascinating third volume of the official life of Churchill, the idea of a Dardanelles campaign was *not* originally his, and he was at first much less attracted by it than by his own idea of a naval and military attack on Zeebrugge, combined with seizure of the German island of Borkum. In one letter to Admiral Lord Fisher he wrote (4 January 1915): "Borkum is the key to all Northern possibilities . . . Ask that a regular division of Infantry be assigned to the capture of Borkum . . . I think we had better hear what others have to say about the Turkish plans before taking a decided line. I wd not grudge 100,000 men because of the great political effects in the Balkan peninsula: but Germany is the foe, & it is bad war to seek cheaper victories & easier antagonists . . ."

Gradually he was converted by "others" and then threw himself into the Dardanelles planning with characteristic zeal. Later, when the project failed, he was stuck with the sole responsibility for it. But it is clear from the evidence that in 1915 he would initially have preferred action across the Channel, striking more directly at German power. Certainly he wanted to escape from the deadlock of trench warfare, but it did not at first occur to him to work on the principle of the longest way round, the shortest way home.

Very similar, surely, was the manner of his involvement in a Mediterranean strategy during the Second World War. It was not his first choice for 1943, but he came round to it under pressure from his advisers, and from one adviser in particular. Having come round to it, he then tried to make the most of it, and after the war availed himself of every argument to justify it, including some arguments of an *ex post facto* character.

At Casablanca the Combined Chiefs of Staff had recommended as the suitable time for HUSKY (the invasion of Sicily) the full-moon period towards the end of July, but Churchill and Roosevelt had strongly urged that it should be not later than the June full moon. In April Churchill suggested that the Allies should land in Sicily before the Tunisian campaign was over, but Brooke was horrified by the suggestion.

He agreed, however, that another Allied meeting at the highest level was necessary to decide on the future course of operations in the Mediterranean, if and when Sicily was conquered. Churchill proposed to Roosevelt that such a conference should be held without delay in

Washington, and he travelled there by sea in early May, accompanied by the Chiefs of Staff, Beaverbrook, Leathers, Archibald Wavell, Ismay, and others, but once again not by the Foreign Secretary, Eden, or by any senior representative of the Foreign Office.

This Washington conference—generally known by its code-name, TRIDENT—lasted a fortnight, from the 11th to the 25th May. Yet it failed to resolve the major strategic and political questions that it was meant to resolve. Above all, it ended with no specific agreement for or against an invasion of the Italian mainland after the capture of Sicily.

The background to this appalling muddle needs to be looked at rather carefully. Planning for HUSKY had begun immediately after Casablanca, but Churchill was not able to keep a close eye on its early stages, because after his return from Turkey he went down with pneumonia and was out of action towards the end of February. Another adverse factor which compounded the ill effects of giving priority to the capture of Tunis was that the high commanders who were to be in charge of HUSKY were meanwhile responsible for conducting the Tunisian campaign. Inevitably they could devote only a very limited part of their thinking to the next operation.

Churchill still hoped that HUSKY would not exclude some cross-Channel activity in 1943. To avoid trouble Brooke refrained from disillusioning him on this score until mid-April, when the Prime Minister learned to his chagrin that HUSKY would demand the diversion of landing-craft from Britain. Artfully, Brooke explained that they would be needed not only for the initial landings but also to enable a quick success to be properly exploited.

Thus was Churchill's conversion to Brooke's Mediterranean strategy finally clinched, by a process not far removed from sleight-of-hand. Unfortunately, the more committed he became to that strategy, the more his imagination and pugnacity were to make of it in argument with the Americans. As a result, they became increasingly suspicious of him, mistakenly attributing his interest in the Mediterranean to British imperialism rather than to concern for the Allied cause.

At one stage his pugnacity seems to have saved HUSKY from possible abandonment, not, certainly, in favour of cross-Channel activity, but in favour of virtual inactivity. Eisenhower reported from Algiers that there would be little chance of success in Sicily if the island contained, at the time of the landings, "substantial, well-armed and fully organised German ground forces." And he defined "substantial as "more than two German divisions."

Churchill's reaction was withering: "If the presence of two German divisions is held to be decisive against any operation of an offensive or amphibious character open to the million men now in North Africa, it is difficult to see how the war can be carried on . . . I trust the Chiefs of Staff will not accept these pusillanimous and defeatist doctrines . . . What Stalin would think of this, when he has 185 German divisions on his front, I cannot imagine." Planning for HUSKY proceeded.

At TRIDENT another threat had to be reckoned with, that the pressure for increased belligerency against Japan would gravely weaken all plans for offensive action in Europe. Opinion polls in the United States were showing that the American public was more interested in beating the Japanese than either the Germans or the Italians, and the popular mood was well reflected in the Congress. Since the conference was taking place in Washington, the Pacific and Chinese lobbies were all the better able to make themselves felt.

At the conference table Generals Claire Chennault and Joseph Stilwell, though at loggerheads with each other, both after their own fashion spoke for China. Admiral King carried so much weight on behalf of the Navy that it was unnecessary for the naval supreme commander in the Pacific, Admiral Chester Nimitz, to attend. And General MacArthur had so much congressional and press support that he, too, did not need to be present.

Roosevelt was too strong a man to be swept completely off his chosen course of seeking victory in Europe first; yet he was not quite strong enough to hold to it with unwavering firmness. At the opening of the conference he insisted, indeed, that there must be a clear decision in favour of returning to the Continent in the spring of 1944. But he also said much—too much—of the importance of keeping up the pressure on Japan, and of keeping China in the war.

After a few days' hard pounding, Brooke wrote in his diary: "It is quite apparent now that we are a long way apart. What is more, the Americans are taking up the attitude that we led them down the garden path by taking them to North Africa. That at Casablanca we again misled them by inducing them to attack Sicily. And now they do not intend to be led astray again. Added to that the swing towards the Pacific is stronger than ever, and before long they will be urging that we should defeat Japan first!"

It was true that the Americans, like Churchill himself, had been misled at Casablanca into believing that the agreement to invade Sicily did not altogether rule out the possibility of a landing in north-west Europe during the summer of 1943. Brooke's technique was to push people gradually in the direction he wanted them to go, without ever being too explicit about the direction, and then to cut off their retreat.

The delay in Tunisia suited him, because it helped to create an irreversible situation. Only if the Americans had been prepared to go ahead with HUSKY without first capturing Tunis would he have been in serious danger of not getting his way. Churchill eventually became aware of the trap, but too late to escape from it. He then tried to convince himself that it was not a trap but the high road to victory, while the Americans, recognising and resenting it as a trap, were determined to escape from it as soon as possible.

These cross-purposes led to a fatal compromise at TRIDENT and to an equally fatal vagueness about the future. At an off-the-record meeting on 19 May, the Combined Chiefs of Staff agreed that operations should continue in the Mediterranean after HUSKY, though not what they should be. It was also agreed that the target date for invading France should be 1 May 1944, and that in November 1943 seven divisions should be withdrawn from the Mediterranean to prepare for the invasion, which in future was to be known as OVERLORD.

When this deal was reported to the political leaders, Churchill, after at first accepting it, then nearly undid all Brooke's disingenuous work by repudiating it and demanding more scope for action in the Mediterranean, including a move to the Italian mainland and thence to the Balkans. Churchill was a straightforward man who, once converted to an idea, however reluctantly, had a natural impulse to preach its virtues, and to practise what he preached. Brooke was horrified by his naïve and impolitic zeal.

At length the original agreement was, in substance, confirmed, though Churchill made no secret of his hope that he would be able to convert Eisenhower to a more ambitious Mediterranean strategy,

to follow HUSKY, when he visited Algiers immediately after TRI-
DENT. But, to show that he was not trying to do anything under-
hand, he persuaded Roosevelt to send Marshall with him to Algiers
as a guarantor of fair play.

Those who wanted a more vigorous war against Japan were by no
means worsted at the conference. Between their importunity and that
of the Mediterranean school the chance of an early victory over
Germany was crushed.

During TRIDENT Roosevelt continued to show Churchill every
outward mark of friendship, having him stay for most of the time at
the White House, and also taking him for a weekend to the mountain
refuge in Maryland which he (Roosevelt) called Shangri-La. But there
was much uneasiness and tension under the surface, which Churchill
was not by temperament well fitted to counteract.

On the drive to Shangri-La the car in which the two men were
travelling passed through the old town of Frederick, where Churchill
noticed roadside signs advertising Barbara Fritchie candy. Roosevelt
explained that Barbara was a semi-legendary character of the Civil
War and that Whittier had written a poem about her, from which he
could remember the lines:

> "Shoot, if you must, this old gray head,
> But spare your country's flag," she said.

No doubt he felt quite pleased with himself for being able to offer so
much explanation of an obscure name that had caught his guest's eye.

But he cannot have felt pleased with himself for long, because
Churchill's phenomenal memory was stirred by the two lines quoted
and he "proceeded to recite the entire poem, stating afterwards that
he had not thought of it in at least thirty years." Even a man with none
of the egocentricity common to potentates would have been irritated
by such an invidious display of virtuosity, and we may be sure that
Roosevelt was profoundly irritated.

With touching innocence, however, Churchill records that he "got
full marks" from his "highly select American audience," none of
whom corrected his "many misquotations." And he adds that he was
"encouraged" to discuss at length the characters of Stonewall Jackson
and Robert E. Lee. On arrival at Shangri-La Roosevelt called for his

stamp albums, which he worked on while Churchill "watched him with much interest and [surprisingly] in silence for perhaps half an hour."

Another source of annoyance to Roosevelt must have been Churchill's address to a joint session of Congress (his second), and the reflections upon himself to which it gave rise. Churchill gave the sort of *tour d'horizon* with which the House of Commons was familiar, and after it (according to Hopkins) "Congressmen were louder than ever in their complaints that: 'The only time we get to find out what's going on in the war is when the British Prime Minister visits Washington and tells us.'"

Churchill seems to have given injudicious countenance to this sort of talk, and soon afterwards criticized Roosevelt, to Marshall, for not taking Congress more completely into his confidence. Marshall replied that, while the President did not address Congress "except at the openings," he did talk privately with the leaders.

Churchill and Marshall, with Brooke and others, arrived in Algiers on 28 May, after an unprecedented direct flight from Newfoundland. (For reading on the journey Marshall had wanted something to inform him about India, and had asked the advice of the British ambassador, Lord Halifax, a former viceroy with views on the Indian question very different from Churchill's. Halifax had recommended Macaulay's essay on Warren Hastings. Churchill found Marshall reading it and treated him to a mid-air monologue on the subject.)

At Eisenhower's headquarters Churchill was known as "the Man Who Came to Dinner" because his previous visit—in February—had been prolonged for security reasons. This time he stayed for about a week, being joined after a day or two by Eden. Apart from discussing future operations, he took time off to inspect troops, and one day he addressed many thousands of them in a ruined amphitheatre at Carthage.

The strategic discussions, though friendly, merely led to further misunderstanding. Eisenhower was keen to exploit a quick victory in Sicily, but did not want a firm commitment to cross to the mainland unless and until such a victory had been won. Marshall remained as anxious as ever to curtail activity in the Mediterranean and to concentrate upon what he always regarded as the vital theatre. But, his biographer tells us, he "had decided not to continue arguing with Churchill," so Churchill formed the impression that he had won him round.

Back in London, Churchill said to Moran: "Marshall doesn't, for the moment, want to make up his mind what we ought to do when Sicily is taken. But he is ready to accept my plan. He is not opposed to the invasion of Italy now." But Marshall was, in fact, still opposed to it, and later explained to Moran his failure to have it out with Churchill there and then: "I did not think that the moment had come for a decision. It would be better, I said to the Prime Minister, to decide what to do when the attack on Sicily was well under way . . . I wanted more facts. I wanted to ask Winston a dozen questions, but he gave me no chance. He kept telling me what was going to happen . . . When I did get a question in, the Prime Minister brushed it aside . . . I tried to argue that we must exercise great discretion . . . I said . . . that I would be content if Sardinia were taken before the invasion of France. He replied that the difference between taking southern Italy and Sardinia was the difference between a glorious campaign and a mere convenience."

Ike's aide, Captain Harry Butcher, noted in his diary that Churchill was "so persistent in his desire to knock out Italy that he said that the British people would be proud to halve their already short rations for a month if the shipping thus released would contribute to cure the supply difficulty inherent in the conquest of Italy." Churchill himself does not quite admit to having suggested that British rations should be *halved,* but does say that he would "gladly" have asked his compatriots "to cut their rations again . . . rather than throw away a campaign which had possibilities of great success."

Churchill was thinking of the very large number of British combatant troops—more than a quarter of a million—still available in Middle East command even after the transfer of Eighth Army to Ike's command. Now that the threat to the Nile Valley, and to the oil resources of the region, was no more, it was indeed ridiculous that these men should stand idle. But if the British were to be starved to provide the shipping space to move them, it could be argued that Italy was not the most appropriate destination. In any case, the scheme was never attempted, so British enthusiasm for conquering Italy was never tested in that rather drastic way.

The net result of Churchill's efforts in Algiers was that whether or not HUSKY would be followed by an Allied invasion of the mainland would depend upon the *ad hoc* judgment of Eisenhower, subject to ratification by the Combined Chiefs of Staff. This was hardly, if at all, an improvement on the indecision of TRIDENT.

Because the commanders for HUSKY were involved in the long battle for Tunis, it was not until mid-May that plans for the next operation were complete and approved by the Combined Chiefs. The date for it had been advanced slightly—from the end of July to the tenth of that month—and for that Churchill deserves much of the credit, though probably the main reason for the change was that it suited the needs of the airborne forces. But the delay undoubtedly enabled the enemy to make some preparations in Sicily, which would otherwise have been virtually defenceless.

Fortunately, the scale of the preparations was limited by shortage of troops and by uncertainty as to where the Allied blow would fall. Though the Italians thought Sicily or Sardinia the most likely objective, Hitler was convinced that the Allies would go for the Balkan peninsula, seeing that it was both more vulnerable and a far greater prize than Italy. Moreover, he was encouraged in this faulty assessment by an outstandingly successful piece of deception—the floating ashore in Spain of a dead body in British officer's uniform ("The Man Who Never Was" of Ewen Montagu's book), bearing plans for HUSKY indicating that its objective would be Greece.

There can be no doubt that Churchill, once converted *malgré lui* to a Mediterranean strategy, saw many attractions to intervening in the Balkans as well as to invading Italy. But he was not a single-minded Balkanist, as Field Marshal Jan Smuts—alone among Western leaders—was. In any case, even the outspoken Churchill had learned in Washington that it was expedient for the time being to keep any Balkan dreams that he might have to himself, and when discussing post-HUSKY options in Algiers he went out of his way to assure the Americans that he "was not advocating sending an army into the Balkans now or in the near future."

Stalin had to be told not only that there would be no Second Front, of the kind he had been led to expect, in 1943, but also that the shipping demands for Sicily precluded any convoys to Russia during the spring and summer. His reaction to these confessions was predictably disagreeable, and in June, according to Eden, his messages "reached such a pitch of acrimony that for several weeks Mr. Churchill dropped all personal correspondence with him."

On strategic grounds Stalin certainly had a case. As we now know, the Allies' North African campaign was of no benefit to him, so far as the balance of land forces was concerned. Between November 1942 and February 1943 the Germans were able to transfer seventeen divisions from Western Europe to the Eastern Front, whereas only three divisions were brought back from the East to take part in the fight for Tunisia. Moreover, the landings in Sicily would soon convince the German high command that any cross-Channel action in 1943 could safely be discounted.

Was there also a political motive for Stalin's anger? Harriman has stated that Churchill explained, at the end of June, "his belief that Stalin's unrelenting pressure for a Second Front in 1943 sprang from his designs on the Balkans. What better way to keep the Western Allies from landing in the Balkans than to tie them down in a long and costly battle for Western Europe?" If Harriman's memory is correct, this must have been one of Churchill's earliest anticipations of what he was later to call the Iron Curtain. In general, the evidence does not suggest that such thoughts were troubling him, at any rate until the latter part of 1943, whatever Stalin's ambitions may have been.

Curiously enough, it was Marshall who showed a precocious awareness of possible postwar dangers when, in March 1943, he referred to them in support of his own cross-Channel strategy. If, he wrote to a colleague on the U.S. Army staff, the Allies "were involved at the last in Western France and the Russian Army was approaching German soil, there would be a most unfortunate diplomatic situation immediately involved with the possibility of a chaotic condition quickly following." Harriman does not claim to have used this argument in reply to Churchill in June, though he does say that he dissented from Churchill's interpretation of Stalin's pressure for a Second Front.

On the whole, it seems reasonable to assume that *all* the leaders at that time were still more exercised by the immediate and acute problems of war than by the hypothetical problems of peace. Even Stalin's interest in getting the Allies tied down in the West must, surely, have had more to do with defeating Hitlerite imperialism than with promoting his own. Though the Battle of Stalingrad was won, huge areas of Russia were still occupied and the mighty German Army still had plenty of kick in it.

Be that as it may, throughout June the Allied air forces, with a superiority of more than two to one over the enemy's in the Mediterranean theatre, prepared the ground for HUSKY. Though the attacks were widely spread to maintain deception, the fortified islands of Pantelleria and Lampedusa, which lay in the path of the invaders, were pulverised from the air and forced to surrender. By the end of the first week of July, ten of the twelve enemy airfields in southern Sicily were out of action, and the Allied command of the sky as well as the sea in the HUSKY zone was more or less complete.

It was now time for the great "sideshow" to begin, and for the incalculable price of Tunis to be exacted. On 10 July, despite a sudden storm which tested Eisenhower's nerve as it was to be tested again the following year, the invasion of Sicily went ahead. Within three days 150,000 troops had been landed, and before long the total had risen to nearly half a million. But for the hold-up in Tunisia—which had bemused even those who did not welcome it as an excuse—this huge army and the armada that transported it might have been available to cross the rather narrower channel separating Britain from France.

Two thousand ships took part in the operation. The invading forces converged on Sicily from every major port in North Africa, the Americans from west of Tunis, the British from Tunis and all ports east. One Canadian division sailed direct from the United Kingdom, and the two airborne divisions flew from the plain of Kairouan.

Those who persist in arguing that an invasion of France would have been out of the question in 1943, because the Allies did not yet have enough landing-craft for such an enterprise, should note carefully that in the first stage of HUSKY nine divisions were simultaneously afloat —*two more* than in the first stage of OVERLORD the following year.

3   Italian Follies

Sicily was soon conquered. On 17 August Alexander, Ike's deputy and operational commander for HUSKY, reported to Churchill that "the last German soldier" had been "flung out of Sicily," and that it could be assumed all the Italian forces on the island had been destroyed. The message was reminiscent of his equally bland one to Churchill reporting the victory of Alamein. And it was equally misleading, because once again the fruits of victory had been largely forfeited through a lack of audacity and initiative.

At the time of the landings, there were about 60,000 German soldiers in Sicily. Of these about 5,500 were captured during the campaign, but nearly 40,000 got away, taking with them nearly 50 tanks and 10,000 other vehicles, 94 guns, and 17,000 tons of supplies. In the circumstances the phrase "flung out" was a euphemism indeed. (The B.E.F. left most of its equipment behind when it was evacuated from Dunkirk. Yet in British folklore Dunkirk almost has the status of a victory.)

The Italians, certainly, did less well. Out of nearly 200,000 only about 60,000 reached the mainland, and most of their transport was abandoned. But the Italians had lost whatever interest they had in the war and could no longer be regarded as serious combatants. The enemy troops who mattered were the Germans, and they not only inflicted much heavier losses than they suffered in Sicily, but then managed to escape from the island to fight—and fight all too effectively—another day.

How and why was this allowed to happen? The actual campaign on the whole went very well for the Allies, only the airborne landings proving a disaster (because, in Nigel Nicolson's view, the soldiers and airmen had only three weeks' training together, despite the months of waiting). It was, however, unfortunate that the two Army commanders should both have been super-egotistical showmen, one bold to the point of rashness, the other cautious to the point of timidity. And in a situation which demanded boldness it was particularly unfortunate that their superior officer, Alexander, should have been more inclined, from force of habit, to defer to the one who was cautious.

The two Army commanders were, of course, the American George S. Patton and the British B. L. Montgomery, who were not made for smooth cooperation with their fellow-men, and least of all with each other. Alexander had acted as a sort of glorified road manager to Montgomery all the way from Egypt to Tunisia, and the relationship persisted. Since Ike left the conduct of operations largely to Alexander, and Alexander tended to endorse whatever Monty did or proposed, inevitably Monty had more than his fair share of influence over the course of HUSKY. Besides, propaganda had already made such a hero of him in the eyes of the British public that it would have been difficult for any other British general to cut him down to size.

Soon after the landings—the plan for which, incidentally, had been radically altered at his dictation—Monty ordered the Eighth Army to advance northwards along roads which had been assigned to Patton's Seventh Army. Patton was indignant, and all the more so because he believed that he could have made rapid progress along those roads towards Messina, whereas Monty's somewhat desert-weary troops were soon brought to a halt. But Alexander weakly upheld Monty's high-handed action.

For the rest of the campaign Patton tried to do his own thing without being too overtly insubordinate. He struck northwestwards to capture Agrigento and Palermo, and from there moved along the north shore of the island until he reached Messina. But even he did not move fast enough to prevent the bulk of the German Army escaping across the Straits.

It is true that the Eighth Army had to face the stiffest opposition, and that the terrain of north-eastern Sicily, dominated by Mount Etna, greatly assisted the defence. But it is therefore all the harder to understand why Monty was so slow to try an amphibious outflanking move, for which he had the resources. Patton had launched three amphibious landings behind his front before Monty attempted one behind his—just south of Messina, on the 15th–16th August, by which time it was too late for him to trap the retreating Germans. It is hard to dismiss the thought that he was goaded into his last-minute attempt only by annoyance at seeing that Patton was about to reach Messina ahead of him.

But the supreme opportunity for an amphibious operation was not strictly Monty's responsibility, and the fact that it was missed not, therefore, strictly his fault. This opportunity was for a landing in Calabria, the toe of Italy, on the far side of the Straits of Messina. The German commander in Italy, Field-Marshal Albert Kesselring, was expecting such a landing but had no means of stopping it, because until the escape of his forces from Sicily he had only two German divisions to defend the whole of southern Italy. If the Allies had put even quite a small force ashore in Calabria, the Germans would have been denied use of the Straits and the Sicilian campaign would, in Kesselring's view, have "developed into an overwhelming Allied victory."

That the chance was not taken reflects, above all, upon the politicians who had allowed the campaign to begin with no clear decision about what was to follow. The tactical requirements of HUSKY were thus, in one vital respect, sacrificed to uncertainty about the scope of future Mediterranean strategy. Eisenhower had been left, after the Algiers discussions, with a vague licence to exploit success in Sicily, but only with the approval of the Combined Chiefs of Staff, whose thoughts, as will be seen, were by the end of July ranging much further afield than Calabria.

Of course, if either he or Alexander had been a Nelson there *would* have been a landing in Calabria, whatever instructions had or had not been given by higher authority. But the Duke of Brontë's spirit, though perhaps hovering frustratedly over the battle zone, was notably absent from all the Allied land commanders except, in some measure, Patton.

As soon as it became apparent that HUSKY would turn out well, the remote-controllers in Washington and London, instead of making sure that the German Army in Sicily was cut off and destroyed, began to plan more ambitiously. And it was Marshall, of all people, who started the rot by suddenly deciding, about the middle of July, that an amphibious attack be directed at the area of Naples.

This project, code-named AVALANCHE, made the strongest possible appeal to Churchill, to whom the alternatives of a landing in Sardinia or of crawling up the leg of Italy, "like a harvest bug from the ankle upwards," seemed equally inadequate. It was, indeed, one of the ideas that Churchill had already put forward, though it would have died a natural death if Marshall had not volunteered his agreement, stressing—Michael Howard says, "in almost Churchillian terms"—the importance of "boldness and taking justifiable risks."

In fact, Marshall's motives for boldness in this instance were by no means the same as Churchill's. He was no nearer than before to sharing Churchill's dream of setting the Balkans on fire by a series of post-HUSKY operations. But there was one basic cliché of Allied planning since Casablanca that he still accepted without question or definition, and that was the insistently proclaimed need to "knock Italy out of the war." Just as he had been drawn into the Sicilian commitment through a failure to challenge the assumption that the German bridgehead in Tunisia had to be reduced, so he was drawn into a more far-reaching Italian commitment by failure to challenge the prevailing erroneous view of Italy's importance in the war.

Allied leaders never seem to have asked themselves exactly what they meant by the elimination of Italy. Did they mean that the Italian nation would cease to be belligerent, or that Italy would cease to be an obstacle to Allied victory? Was their thinking focussed upon the Italian people and *their* value, as distinct from their territory's value, to the Germans; or was it, rather, focussed upon Italy as the well-known "geographical expression"? To produce the right answer it should have been focussed upon both, with a due recognition that they might lead to opposite strategic conclusions.

Ever since Mussolini had declared war, at the time when France was falling, his participation had been, on balance, an immense burden and liability to Hitler. In North Africa the early defeat of his forces by numerically much inferior British had imposed the necessity for sending German troops to the desert. The reinforcement and supply of these troops had been a costly drain on Hitler's resources, and since they were never reinforced enough to achieve a break-through to the Nile Valley and Middle Eastern oil, the whole effort was in the long run largely wasted.

In Europe, Mussolini's invasion of Greece and subsequent discomfiture had forced Hitler to come to the rescue at a most inconvenient moment, and had upset his time-table for the invasion of Russia. Now, with the Allies controlling the whole southern shore of the Mediterranean, the Italian incubus must have seemed even heavier, because Hitler knew very well that he could rely upon his partner neither to hold down subject populations nor to defend a long and vulnerable coastline. "It would be easier to do it myself" might well have summed up his feeling—and that, in fact, was precisely what Allied policy and strategy combined to enable him to do.

The only soft feature of the so-called underbelly of Europe (a metaphor derived incidentally from looking at the Continent from a northern standpoint) was the attitude of the modern inhabitants of Italy to war. Unlike the ancient Romans, or the modern Spaniards, French, Yugoslavs, Albanians, Greeks, and Turks, they had no very conspicuous tradition of, or taste for, martial prowess. It was not that they were incapable of showing courage. In the *Risorgimento,* and at times during the First and Second World Wars, many Italians fought with heroism. But as a generalisation it is surely true that the nation which Mussolini led into the war on Hitler's side was as ill-equipped psychologically as materially for the ordeal.

In all other respects, however, the "under" part of Europe was, and is, anything but soft. Natural softness is to be found on the northern coasts of Europe, not on the southern. Indeed, the southern territories of Europe have been fashioned by nature to an exceptional degree of hardness, and few more so than Italy with its long mountainous spine. (In the present context spines are more to the point than bellies.)

Moreover, the physical hardness of southern Europe could only be enhanced by the toughness of the Germans as a fighting nation, something of its kind unsurpassed in human history. If the Allies wanted to effect landings and promote popular uprisings in southern Europe, it was clearly desirable that the enemy occupying forces should be Italian rather than German. At least, one might have *thought* that this would have been clearly desirable. In fact, the Allied leadership acted in such a way that the whole of the Balkans, and more than half of Italy, passed under Germany's exclusive control.

In a sense, Italy was not knocked out of the war, but *brought into it*—as a place where the Germans were able to engage very large Allied forces, with immensely long communications, on ground naturally favouring defence, for the best part of two more years. The root cause of this disaster was that the idea of eliminating Italy was never properly analysed before Italy was invaded. But additional reasons are to be found in the way the Allies' political and military decisions were carried out.

So far as the politics were concerned, we have seen that Casablanca offered only unconditional surrender, which Churchill tried in vain to mitigate for Italy's benefit. At TRIDENT the political mechanics of getting the Italians out of the war were hardly considered at all, despite the increased urgency of the subject.

This is scarcely credible, granted that important Italians had been making secret overtures to the Allies over the past year—one of them the very Marshal Pietro Badoglio with whom Italy's surrender was ultimately to be negotiated. Nervous of another "Darlan" incident, and hobbled by the unconditional surrender formula, the Allied leaders blundered forward with no agreed policy for Italy.

On 25 July, while the Sicilian campaign was in progress, they were confronted with a dramatic new situation and an opportunity for which they were almost totally unprepared. Mussolini was overthrown and the Fascist regime collapsed. Three days later the Badoglio government, which had taken its place, entered into clandestine communication with the Allies through agents in Lisbon and Tangier. But it was more than six weeks before the Allies were in a position to make a deal with the Italians, and then it was too late.

The Germans showed no such hesitancy. As soon as he heard the news of Mussolini's fall, Hitler ordered Rommel (who had just been posted to Greece) to assemble a force in the Alps for possible entry into Italy. Characteristically going one better than his instructions, Rommel decided at once to cross the frontier and take possession of the Alpine passes. The Italians could only protest, and were then unable to stop his further infiltration without revealing that they were about to make a separate peace. By the beginning of September he had eight divisions in north Italy, to act as a reserve for Kesselring's nine or ten divisions south of the line Pisa-Ancona.

Meanwhile, the Allied leaders had been pursuing tortuous negotiations with the Italians, and had been holding another full-dress conference—this time at Quebec, with the code-name QUADRANT. The negotiations were made more tortuous by the fact that there were two sets of Allied terms going the rounds—the so-called Long Terms, which originated in the British Foreign Office (and were marked by Eden's somewhat obsessive attitude to Italy), and the Short Terms, which had been devised by Eisenhower and his political advisers Macmillan and Murphy.

There is no need to waste any time on the details of these rival documents, though it is fair to say that Eisenhower's terms, as well as having that merit of brevity, were more politic than the Long Terms, in that they contained no explicit reference to unconditional surrender. But even if Ike the embryo politician had received immediate support for his terms from the established politicians, no swift bargain could have been struck with the Italians in the absence of swift action by Ike the military commander. Badoglio wanted not merely to surrender but to make Italy co-belligerent with the Allies. Yet he could do neither effectively unless and until the Allies were able to appear on the Italian mainland in strength.

This—because of the failure to agree on post-HUSKY strategy before Sicily was invaded—they were unable to do until precious weeks had passed. It was not until early September that the amphibious attack on the Naples area, assented to by Marshall in mid-July, could be launched. By then the Germans had had plenty of time to collect their available forces, and their thoughts.

If the Salerno landings (AVALANCHE) could have been carried out immediately after the Sicilian campaign—the German forces in Sicily having been trapped there by an Allied landing on the far side of the Straits of Messina—and if the Badoglio government had simultaneously declared Italy co-belligerent with the Allies on the basis of Ike's Short Terms, it is just possible, though still unlikely, that the Allies might have won a quick victory in Italy. As it was, they doomed themselves to a slow, painful, and expensive struggle in a country to which the enemy had much easier access than they had.

The Salerno operation was full of risks, as Brooke for one admitted (though he was prepared to accept them for the sake of his Mediterranean dream). The landings occurred at the extreme limit of fighter cover, and after a very long sea-crossing. The main British assault force sailed from Tripoli, the main American one from Oran. Even the troops that sailed from north Sicilian ports had farther to sail than the invading forces on D-Day.

Even so, it is arguable that Salerno was not risky enough, in the sense that it could not be decisive and only an amphibious operation that *could* be decisive was worth attempting. Successful landings at Salerno would lead, with luck, to the capture of Naples, but Naples was still a hundred miles south of Rome, which was the key political objective. Admiral Andrew Cunningham, the Allied naval commander—an officer who did have the Nelson touch—favoured landings in the Rome area, despite the necessary absence of fighter cover. But his view did not prevail.

There was, however, a late promise to the Italians of an airborne landing in the Rome area, when it seemed that they might not sign the armistice terms. This was only a week before AVALANCHE was due to begin. Soon afterwards, on 3 September, the Short Terms were signed, in Sicily, by the Italian General Giuseppe Castellano, who was then presented with the Long Terms, much to his astonishment. Controversy about the terms, and fear of the Germans, caused a last-minute attempt by the Italians to revoke their capitulation. At the same time, the airborne landing was cancelled at the Italians' request.

Ike was thankful enough to cancel the airborne landing, but had no intention of allowing the Italians to renege on their agreement to surrender. Thus they had the worst of both worlds, by being exposed to the Germans as having ratted without having any Allied troops to protect them. As the Allied convoys were sailing towards the Salerno beaches, on 8 September, Radio Algiers broadcast the news that Italy had been granted an armistice, and had accepted it "without reservation." After a brief interlude of agonised indecision, King Victor Emmanuel himself authorised Badoglio to bow to the *fait accompli* by broadcasting as agreed from the Rome radio station.

This he did little more than an hour after the broadcast from Algiers. Then he made his escape, as did the King and most of the other leading Italians who were in or near the capital. (Three weeks later Badoglio signed the Long Terms, under protest, on board a British battleship in Malta harbour.) The Italian forces in the Rome area, five divisions, were taken completely by surprise, and anyway had no urge to fight. In next to no time the men had given up their arms and gone home, and it was much the same throughout the whole of central and northern Italy.

The one important gain, from the Allies' point of view, was that the Italian fleet eluded the Germans, sailing from Spezia to Malta with the loss of only the flagship, *Roma,* which was sunk by a German guided bomb. In other respects the Italian surrender, though on paper to the Allies, was in reality over much of the country surrender *to the Germans.*

The paper transaction involved considerable hypocrisy and some sharp practice on the part of the Allies. While lip-service was paid to unconditional surrender, in fact a great deal of time—far too much time, indeed—was spent discussing conditions. Moreover, the discussions had to be held at a variety of places remote from the Italian government, which had to take the ultimate decision—in Lisbon, Tangier, Madrid, Algiers, and Sicily. This further delayed and complicated proceedings which were already made sufficiently difficult by the lack of coherent Allied policy.

It should not have been necessary for the negotiations to be conducted in more than one place, and that place could have been Rome itself; for the Italian capital had the unique advantage of containing a tiny neutral state, the Vatican, to which the British and American governments had accredited representatives. By a triumph of ineptitude, however, neither of them was equipped with a secure code, so the ideal channel of communication was unserviceable.

That the Italians were ever brought to surrender was very largely due to Eisenhower, who showed all the political realism and flexibility that the politicians conspicuously failed to show. The terms that the Italians at length agreed to sign were his Short Terms, and it was no fault of his that the objectionable Long Terms were subsequently thrust upon them. Later, however, and after the Long Terms had been signed, he succeeded in having them modified so that "unconditional surrender" was, in effect, edited out of the document.

News that the Italians had capitulated, heard by the Allied troops as they approached the Salerno beaches, was a bad preparation for the very stern test that lay ahead of them, because it created a false idea that the enemy was disintegrating. But the Germans were not disintegrating at all, and they were the enemy that counted.

Though heavily outnumbered, they were expecting the Allies at Salerno and gave them a hot reception—which was hotter than it need have been, because the Allied commander, the American general Mark Clark, was so convinced of being able to achieve surprise that he forbade any preliminary naval bombardment. The first landings took place on a two-corps front, on both sides of Salerno, in the small hours of 9 September. By the end of the third day, when it had been hoped that Naples might have been reached, the Allies had only two narrow beachheads and were in serious danger of being thrown back into the sea.

Meanwhile, Montgomery's Eighth Army was advancing with predictable slowness over the three hundred miles from the toe of Italy, where it had landed on 3 September, nearly a a week before AVALANCHE began. Monty was the last man to break any speed records, and his instructions were not phrased in such a way as to give him any special sense of urgency. Alexander had merely told him to seize the toe of Italy, so that Allied naval forces could operate through the Straits of Messina, and if the enemy withdrew to "follow him up with such force as [he could] make available, bearing in mind that the greater the extent to which he could engage enemy forces in the southern tip of Italy, the more assistance [he would] be giving to AVALANCHE."

Clearly the Allied high command had grossly underrated the toughness of German resistance at Salerno. Monty's advance was seen at the planning stage as little more than an optional extra, whereas in fact it became a matter of life and death to the men struggling in the Salerno beachheads. There was, at any rate, no question of having to force the Germans to withdraw from the toe of Italy. They had gone before Monty's men crossed the Straits, and the terrific preparatory barrage to which he subjected the mainland shore was a complete waste of ammunition. (It is ironic that such a barrage was not allowed at Salerno, where it was desperately needed.)

Until the sixteenth the fate of AVALANCHE hung in the balance. At one point Mark Clark was considering evacuation, but Alexander quietly vetoed the idea. The Germans had been reinforced, not least by a panzer division which had disengaged from Monty's front and moved north with all the speed that he was incapable of showing. As yet the only sign of the Eighth Army was the arrival of a group of war correspondents, who had covered the ground well ahead of the army whose exploits they were supposed to be reporting.

The Allied beachheads survived only because the Germans were pounded from the air, and by the naval guns which had, so regrettably, been silent before the landings. But it can hardly be said that AVALANCHE was a success. As originally conceived by Churchill, it was to be a "landing on the Italian west coast with the objective the port of Naples and the march on Rome, [to] cut off and leave behind all the Axis forces in Western Sicily and all ditto in the toe, ball, heel and ankle." In fact, the Germans had got away from Sicily and south Italy in good order and in substantial strength. As for the Allied objectives, it was not until 1 October that Naples was captured—at the cost of nearly twelve thousand casualties since the landings—and not until June of the following year that Rome fell.

There was, however, a remarkable Allied success on the heel of Italy, though it led to yet another missed opportunity. When post-HUSKY operations were being considered, one that was thought about but rejected was a descent upon the key port of Taranto. Only when news came through that that part of Italy was very lightly held was the idea revived, a few days before AVALANCHE.

Admiral Cunningham then offered to provide the ships for a landing force, if any troops were available. Fortunately, a British airborne division was at a loose end in Tunisia, so it was embarked on some cruisers and a minelayer, and on 9 September—the day of the Salerno landings—entered the port of Taranto, which it captured more or less intact. Within a few days Brindisi and Bari also had been seized.

Unfortunately, the initial order was merely that a base should be secured on the heel of Italy "with a view to a subsequent advance," so there was no immediate move into the vacuum beyond Bari. On the thirteenth, to make matters worse, the troops who had established such a promising position on the east coast were put under Monty's command, at a time when he was advancing ponderously up the west coast with no thought to spare for anywhere else.

It was not until more than a week after he had joined forces with Mark Clark's men that he authorised a major advance on the east coast, and by then there were Germans in the way. Soon the British forces, though now much stronger, were checked at the line of the Trigno River, just beyond Termoli. The chance of breaking right through on the eastern flank had existed for a brief period, but the daring leadership was not there to grasp it and it was irrevocably lost.

We must now return to the Allied conference at Quebec (QUADRANT), which occurred a short time before the Italian armistice and the fateful move from Sicily to the mainland. Churchill again crossed the Atlantic by sea and on 12 August went, with his daughter Mary, to spend a couple of days with Roosevelt at Hyde Park, while the Chiefs of Staff got down to business at Quebec. (Mrs. Churchill as well as Mary accompanied Churchill to QUADRANT, but she was tired on arrival in Quebec and did not go to Hyde Park.)

Roosevelt had insisted that the conference be held in Canada rather than in London, ostensibly so that he would not have to leave the Western Hemisphere while there were domestic matters requiring his attention. But there are always such matters requiring the attention of a President of the United States, and it is a striking, suggestive fact that Roosevelt contrived never to attend a meeting in London during the war. Though the demands of his work and of the American Constitution did not prevent his travelling to Casablanca, Cairo, Teheran, and Yalta, he used those demands as an excuse for never setting foot on the metropolitan territory of his principal ally.

Though Quebec was chosen for his convenience in August 1943, he did not turn up there until the seventeenth, nearly a week after the arrival of the British party. But meanwhile he had shown Churchill that he stood solidly with his advisers against any development of the Mediterranean war at the expense of OVERLORD. There was to be no repetition of Churchill's feat, on the issue of TORCH, in securing the President's support for an idea of his against strong opposition from the American service chiefs.

Roosevelt's will had been stiffened not only by Marshall but also by Marshall's friend and admirer the Secretary of War, Henry L. Stimson. Stimson was an eminent Republican, in his mid-seventies, appointed by Roosevelt in June 1940 to give his Administration an air of bi-partisanship at a time of deepening international crisis—and when a Presidential election was imminent. (Another Republican, Frank Knox, was at the same time appointed Secretary of the Navy.) Earlier in his career Stimson had been Governor-General of the Philippines during the Presidency of Calvin Coolidge, and Secretary of State under Herbert Hoover. In the War Department he was very far from being a figurehead.

Chancing to be in London the previous month, when the Sicilian campaign was in its early stages, he had seen Churchill read too much into Marshall's assent to AVALANCHE and had hastened to correct the false impression. Marshall, he explained, had agreed to a landing on the Italian mainland for no other purpose than to speed the collapse of Italy and so to clear the decks for OVERLORD. He was in no sense converted to a Mediterranean as opposed to a cross-Channel strategy.

Churchill seems to have argued very freely with Stimson, and vice versa. Indeed, the War Secretary used to say that he "could cut loose at the Englishman as he never felt free to do with his [own] chief" —interesting evidence of the distant and elusive character that underlay Roosevelt's surface affability; also, of course of the quasi-mystical reverence that Americans feel for the Presidency. According to Stimson, Churchill spoke of the Channel filled with corpses and said that if he were commander-in-chief he would not launch a cross-Channel operation. Having pledged his word, he said that he would go through with the operation loyally, and would not seek to push the advance in Italy farther north than Rome, unless there was "a complete Italian capitulation throwing open the whole of Italy as far as the northern boundary."

Stimson returned to the United States, after visiting Algiers as well as London, convinced that the President would have to take a very strong line if the priorities agreed to at TRIDENT were not to be upset by British doubts, fears, and fancies. Just before Churchill arrived at Hyde Park, he submitted a powerful memorandum to Roosevelt, in which he made four main points well calculated to appeal to the President.

First, he said, "We cannot now rationally hope to be able to cross the Channel and come to grips with our German enemy under a British commander." The Prime Minister and Chief of the Imperial General Staff were "frankly at variance with such a proposal." "The shadows of Dunquerque and Passchendaele" still hung too heavily over their imaginations. Though they paid lip-service to OVER-LORD, their hearts were not in it, and it would require "more independence, more faith and more vigour" than would be found in any British commander.

His second point he defined as "a vital difference of faith." "The American Staff still believes that only by massing the immense vigour and power of the American and British nations under the overwhelming mastery of the air which they already exercise far into the north of France . . . can Germany be really defeated and the war brought to a real victory. On the other side, the British theory (which cropped out again and again in unguarded sentences of the British leaders with whom I have just been talking) is that Germany can be beaten by a series of attritions in northern Italy, in the eastern Mediterranean, in Greece, in the Balkans, in Roumania and other satellite countries."

The President had to decide—this was Stimson's third point—"to assume the responsibility of leadership in this great final movement of the European war." And finally, it was necessary to put America's "most commanding soldier in charge of this critical operation at this critical time." Marshall, who had "a towering eminence of reputation," should be appointed overlord of OVERLORD.

These views coincided with, and reinforced, the President's inclinations, and were therefore well-timed. Churchill went to Hyde Park having promised Brooke, as recently as 7 July, that the OVERLORD command would be *his,* if he wanted it. Yet when faced with Roosevelt's request that it should go to an American, the Prime Minister did not hesitate to abandon his undertaking to Brooke. In return for conceding the prime command to an American, Churchill had the consolation of securing the Mediterranean command, and the new command in South-east Asia, for British officers. But the details of this bargain had yet to be worked out.

On the crucial issue, Mediterranean strategy versus OVERLORD, Churchill had no chance of bringing Roosevelt round to his point of view, because—quite apart from the military arguments—there was one consideration which had acted in Churchill's favour when he was putting the case for TORCH, but which now acted in the opposite sense. This was the timing of military campaigns in relation to American domestic political campaigns. 1944, like 1942, would be an election year in the United States, but whereas in 1942 the Mediterranean had been the better political bet, because a cross-Channel attack was not yet feasible, in 1944 the sort of Mediterranean operations that Churchill had in mind were likely to have less dramatic and decisive results than could be expected from OVERLORD.

Even Brooke came to QUADRANT in a somewhat defeatist spirit, so far as Mediterranean strategy was concerned. Though his commitment to OVERLORD was still, as ever, strictly limited, and his imagination much more easily excited by what he called the "strategic treasures" of the Mediterranean, he could see that an invasion of north-west Europe was more or less inevitable in 1944, and was prepared up to a point to make a virtue of necessity.

A preliminary plan had already been drawn up by COSSAC (General Frederick Morgan and his staff). This Brooke accepted in principle, though he had many criticisms to make of it in detail. He was embarrassed, therefore, not only by Churchill's extravagant and over-candid advocacy of Mediterranean strategy, which he himself now preferred to commend only as an adjunct to OVERLORD, but also by a revival of Churchill's interest in a landing in Norway as an alternative to the agreed landing in France. Again, as at TRIDENT, he feared that Churchill might arouse the Americans' suspicions without achieving any worth-while result.

If QUADRANT had not occurred exactly when it did, Mediterranean strategy might have been killed stone dead, instead of being merely checked and severely circumscribed. But at a time when the enemy position in Sicily was collapsing, and when the Italians were suing for peace, even the most anti-sideshow-minded American could hardly fail to be affected, in some degree, by euphoria, and to feel that some sort of Italian campaign had to be kept going.

Churchill certainly did not get what he wanted. The paramount claims of OVERLORD were reasserted, and the Americans insisted upon the transfer of troops and resources that had been agreed to at TRIDENT. But in the flush of a partly illusory victory, they also conceded that Rome as well as Naples should be captured, that Sardinia, Corsica, and, if possible, the Dodecanese should be occupied, and that Balkan insurgents should be supplied across the Adriatic.

This was far from being an unlimited licence to start new operations, or to pursue existing ones, in the Mediterranean theatre. But even so it was, in one respect at least, too much. Rome was to prove a very costly objective, and even Naples was hardly worth fighting for after the Italians had capitulated and handed over their fleet. It seems to have been forgotten that the main purposes of invading Italy had been to clear the Mediterranean for Allied shipping and "to knock Italy out of the war." With the fall of Sicily and the signature of the armistice, was there any point in going on?

There was, indeed, a case for securing air bases on the Italian mainland, from which south Germany could be conveniently raided. But the value of such bases had to be weighed against the cost of securing them. If it became apparent that a long and bloody campaign would be involved, the advantages to be gained from Italian air bases could hardly justify such a price.

The occupation of Italian territory was, in more than one sense, a strategic folly. It imposed upon the Allies the responsibility for sustaining a large population whose contribution to the war effort would never be significant, while at the same time, of course, it relieved the Germans of that burden. Allied military government (A.M.G.O.T.) was an expensive and insensitive apparatus which, to put it mildly, did little to generate enthusiasm for the Allied cause. It would have been an economy for the Allies, and an additional drain on the Germans' resources, if the mainland Italians had been left entirely under their rule. And the Allies' absence might have made Italian hearts grow fonder.

One highly intelligent Allied commander, Air Marshal Tedder, quickly formed a most unfavourable view of A.M.G.O.T.'s activities. At a dinner in Palermo towards the end of 1943, he met Colonel Charles Poletti, an American of Italian descent and a former lieutenant-governor of New York State, who was serving as deputy to the

British head of A.M.G.O.T. in Italy. Lord Zuckerman, at the time Tedder's scientific adviser, describes the scene:

When Poletti walked into the . . . sitting room he was somewhat merry from drink, and had a pretty young Sicilian girl on each arm. "Meet my Botticellis," he called out as he entered. We all rose, and Tedder, no doubt remembering what I had told him about the hijacking of supplies, greeted him with the words, "I have long been wanting to meet one of the men who have taken so little time to undo what it took us so long, and cost us so much, to achieve." Poletti did not know what to say, and I certainly did not know where to look.

But whatever A.M.G.O.T. may have cost the Allies in money and goodwill, the logistical balance-sheet of involvement in Italy was even more adverse. One of Brooke's favourite arguments in support of Mediterranean strategy was that the enemy's north-south communications were, because of the Alps, only about one-seventh as efficient as his east-west communications, and it was therefore more profitable to attack him in the south than in the north-west. The countervailing inefficiency, on the Allies' part, of communications extending over land and sea for hundreds, even thousands, of miles, compared with the accessibility of north-west Europe from the Allies' great island base in Britain—this was seldom, if ever, mentioned by Brooke. But in any case, presumably the disadvantage to the Germans of their difficult north-south communications would be aggravated the more they were stretched, and eased the more they were shortened. So why should the Allies help the enemy by enabling him to operate with a shorter line of supply, while their own became proportionately longer?

It was, to be sure, most desirable that the Germans should be forced to maintain large forces in southern Europe, to hold the local populations down and to guard against Allied landings. But with the Allies controlling the whole of the south shore of the Mediterranean, and firmly established in Sicily—also, later, in Sardinia and Corsica—they would have been forced to do that in any case. A much smaller total of Allied troops than was present in the Mediterranean theatre in 1943 would have been enough to pose a constant threat of amphibious raids and backing for insurgents.

It is a fallacy to suppose that the pinning down of German troops

111

in southern Europe depended upon the Allies' maintaining a major fighting front there. By October 1943 there were, it is true, eighteen German divisions in Italy. Yet at the same time there were more divisions—twenty-one—in the Balkans, where there was no fighting front, only the threat of invasion or insurgency. In December 1943 the comparative figures were twenty-two and twenty-four, still rather more in the Balkans than in Italy.

On the other hand, it is beyond question that *two Allied armies* (comprising at first thirty divisions of greater numerical strength than the German) were pinned down in Italy from the autumn of 1943. Unlike the German forces in southern Europe, if the Allied troops had not been fighting there it would have been unnecessary for them to be present, in anything like such numbers, in the Mediterranean theatre at all. The Allies had mastery of the sea and air, so they were in no danger of having to repel amphibious raids. The indigenous peoples of North Africa were, at the time, either friendly or acquiescent, so there was no danger of any rebellions having to be quelled.

As well as pinning down a mass of soldiers who might have been used to greater effect against the Germans elsewhere, the Italian Front made immense demands on Allied shipping, which substantially offset the gain of clearing the Mediterranean and ending the necessity for so many ships to go round the Cape. On the whole, the Germans were entitled to feel that the Italian campaign, though very costly to them, was far costlier in strategic terms to the Allies.

Could this have been avoided? In retrospect, it would seem that there were two relatively good ways of tackling the Italian problem in 1943, neither of which was tried. One of them might have given the Allies control of the whole of Italy, or at any rate a large part of it, in the early months of 1943. The other would have spared them the agony and waste of a long campaign in Italy, while keeping the Germans fully stretched.

The first option depended upon invading Sicily before the Tunisian bridgehead was reduced, and upon being prepared to do a quick Darlan-type deal with any successor government to Mussolini's. The second would have involved a clear decision not to invade the Italian mainland—except for the limited purpose of cutting off enemy troops in Sicily—combined with encouragement to the Italians to rise against the Germans, wherever possible, in partisan groups. Any compromise between these two alternatives was fraught with perils which might well have been foreseen if the matter had ever been discussed in depth by the Allied leaders.

What actually happened made just about the worst of all possible worlds. Unconditional surrender was proclaimed, and the effect of the policy was to inhibit and retard negotiations with the anti-Mussolini elements in Italy, both before and after his overthrow. Though such negotiations were, in fact, inconsistent with any strict application of the policy, the advantage of being free to strike a quick bargain was completely lost.

After the fall of Mussolini, "unconditional surrender" also did the Allies no good in the eyes of ordinary Italians. Iris Origo is interesting on this point. An Englishwoman married to an Italian, she lived in Italy throughout the war and kept a diary later published as *War in Val d'Orcia.* On 4 August 1943 she wrote: "The tone of British propaganda since the fall of Fascism [ten days before] has caused much resentment, with its insistence on 'unconditional surrender' and its bland assumption that peace at any price will be welcomed by the Italian people. The Italians feel that they have succeeded, at considerable risk, in ridding themselves of Fascism, thus kindling a spark which may start similar conflagrations all over Europe—and that the Allies, who for years have been urging them to this course, have now shown that they are utterly indifferent to the liberty of Italy, except as a stepping-stone to Germany's destruction."

After the armistice—fatally delayed for six weeks after Mussolini's fall, which itself would almost certainly have occurred sooner if HUSKY had been expedited—many Italians who held no brief at all for the Germans were (according to Iris Origo) disgusted by the way that they had been betrayed by the Badoglio government, and by the fact that Badoglio and the King had run away after doing their treacherous deed—so much so as to feel morally debarred from giving any active support to the Allies. Yet in fairness to Badoglio it has to be said that he was forced to play a prolonged double game by the Allies' failure to move quickly, either in negotiation or on the ground.

The Italians may not have wanted peace at *any* price, and it was natural that they should regard the armistice as peace with dishonour. But most of them certainly did want peace, and were therefore even more distressed to find that the armistice had not brought them peace at all, but had merely turned their country into a major battle-zone. Before the war was over many of them had been killed by Allied bombs or had suffered in other ways from the experience of having their country fought over.

It must also be said again that in areas occupied by the Allies the civilian population was considerably antagonised by A.M.G.O.T., which on the whole acted as an expensive device for creating ill-will, or at any rate for forfeiting the chance to create goodwill. There was, therefore, no psychological victory to set against the strategic frustration of the Italian campaign. The hearts and minds of the people had been lost by their own rulers, but were not won by the Allied invaders.

At the end of May Churchill had told Eisenhower that he "confidently looked forward" to having Christmas dinner with him in Rome. Similar boasts have often been made, and have nearly as often been made to seem foolish in retrospect. This one has its own painful resonance in the tradition of vainglory and folly.

In fact, after four months of bitter and bloody fighting, the American Fifth Army had, by Christmas, advanced only seventy miles northward from Salerno, and was still barely half-way to Rome. It had lost forty thousand men in battle and fifty thousand through sickness. On the east coast Montgomery's Eighth Army had struggled forward an even shorter distance, also at very heavy cost.

From being over-confident Churchill became alarmed, and his alarm was shared by the Combined Chiefs of Staff. The Americans now paid the price of their failure, at Quebec, to be quite ruthless enough about the British Mediterranean strategy. Instead of imposing a veto, they had merely insisted that men, landing-craft, etc., must be transferred to Britain by November, in preparation for OVERLORD. But by November they had had to modify this decision to avert an apprehended catastrophe on the Italian Front.

OVERLORD was not displaced as the supreme commitment for 1944, and those who believed that the war could be won in the Mediterranean were in no sense satisfied by the concessions that were made. But the concessions were enough to ensure that Italy would remain the very large and distracting sideshow that it had been allowed to become.

On 20 December Eisenhower went with his aide, Captain Butcher, to the hunting-lodge of the Neapolitan Bourbons in the mountains behind Caserta (where, in their former palace, Allied headquarters had been established). It was to be his personal residence, and on this first visit it was the scene of perhaps the only shots ever fired by him on active service.

The house seemed quite attractive, until a rat was found in the general's bathroom. It was sitting on the lavatory seat, a perfect target. But Ike's marksmanship was far from perfect. As Captain Butcher records, he "put on his spectacles, growled that the light was bad . . . carefully took aim and shot—furrowing the seat under the rat. It jumped to a pipe. Always an advocate of trigger squeeze, he again took careful aim and shot. He clipped its tail. The rat jumped a foot higher, clinging to the pipe. Again Ike shot. The rat tumbled to the floor after a final shot and lay quivering."

The incident seems rich in symbolic aptness as a comment on the policy and strategy of "knocking Italy out of the war."

4   The Captive Giant

By the time of the QUADRANT conference, in August 1943, Winston Churchill had acquired the almost superhuman stature in the public imagination that he was never thereafter to lose, despite the election defeat of the Conservative Party under his leadership in 1945. His apotheosis had begun. Yet it is one of history's more malicious ironies that the beginning of it coincided with the ending of his own, and his country's, independent power.

The combination of Alamein and TORCH had saved him politically, making him more or less invulnerable as Britain's wartime leader, provided Britain herself were able to survive. But until the summer of 1943 there could still be some doubt about Britain's survival, because it was not until April–May of that year that the U-boat menace was finally countered, and it was only in July that more Allied merchant ships were being built than sunk.

At Casablanca top priority was given to winning the battle of the Atlantic, which was only natural granted that in November 1942 the tonnage of sinkings had risen, as in June, above the 800,000 mark, of which 500,000 tons had been sunk in the North Atlantic. The TORCH landings imposed a further heavy burden on Allied naval resources, especially escort ships, and the reduced rate of sinking in December and January carried little reassurance, because it was largely due to stormy weather.

In February 1943 the rate of sinkings went up again sharply, and in the first three weeks of March ships totalling 627,000 tons were sunk, two-thirds of them in convoy. According to the Admiralty, this was the period in the whole war when the Germans came nearest to disrupting communications between the New World and the Old. But salvation was near. When the crisis was at its height, Britain and Canada were given exclusive responsibility for the North Atlantic routes, while the United States assumed exclusive responsibility for the South Atlantic. At the same time, Britain was provided with the indispensable Liberator aircraft, which could operate at very long range.

These measures, combined with the improved anti-U-boat methods already devised by the British commander-in-chief Western Approaches, Admiral Sir Max Horton, did the trick with astonishing speed. During May the losses *among U-boats* more than doubled, and the German naval chief, Admiral Dönitz, master-mind of the U-boat offensive, had to make a thoroughly pessimistic report to Hitler.

At Quebec, therefore, the Allied leaders were able to note with relief that the Battle of the Atlantic was being won. This was a victory of cardinal importance for the whole Allied cause, but for Britain it was literally a vital success, in no way inferior to the air Battle of Britain in 1940, and equally deserving of the title. After 1943 the country could still have been overwhelmed by the atomic bomb, if the Germans had managed to develop and produce it in time. But in fact Britain was out of danger, and Churchill apparently destined to be not only the hero that he already was, but in due time a triumphant rather than a tragic hero. People everywhere admired—or resented—him as a potentate on the world scale, as firmly established as he was uniquely gifted.

Yet forces were at work which could only have the effect of making the ultimate victory towards which he was leading his country a Pyrrhic triumph. The domination of the world by two super-powers, the United States and the Soviet Union, foretold more than a century before by Alexis de Tocqueville, was fast becoming a reality, while the disintegration of the British Empire was already beginning, despite superficial appearances to the contrary.

Churchill sensed the underlying weakness of his position, though the aspect of which he was least aware was the loss of British imperial power, actual and impending. He never really accepted the implications of self-government within the Commonwealth, and was unwilling to contemplate the full emancipation of India or of Britain's many lesser dependencies. Yet he knew that, by the end of the war, the Soviet Union would be the greatest land power in the world, and the United States the greatest all-round power. He had no illusions of going it alone, even as a united Commonwealth and Empire.

All the same, the vision of the future that captivated him *was* illusory, and the nature of it can be observed most clearly in the summer of 1943.

It has already been mentioned that, before the QUADRANT conference, he paid a brief visit to the Roosevelts at Hyde Park. At dinner there on 14 August he raised the subject of Anglo-American partnership after the war. Mrs. Roosevelt did not much like the idea, fearing (as Harriman noted) that it "might be misunderstood by other nations and weaken the U.N. concept." But Churchill insisted that "any hope of the U.N. would be in the leadership given by the intimacy of the U.S. and Britain in working out misunderstanding [sic] with the Russians"—and the Chinese, too, if they became a nation. What Roosevelt said is not recorded, but it would have been quite in character for him to make friendly noises, for hospitality's sake, or to avoid a tedious argument.

At Quebec the President and the Prime Minister stayed at the Citadel, while their advisers were lodged at the Château Frontenac Hotel. Roosevelt was given the top floor of the Citadel, with special ramps fitted for his convenience.

Formally speaking, he and Churchill were guests of the Governor-General of Canada, Lord Athlone (an uncle of King George VI), because the Citadel—where the conference sessions also were held—was an official residence of the Governor-General. In a broader sense, they were guests of the Canadian government and people, and Churchill wrote to the King that holding the conference in Canada would, he believed, remove "a lot of fretfulness," which was noticeable in the Dominion.

Soon after he arrived, he attended meetings of the Quebec provincial cabinet and of the Federal Cabinet. He was also sworn a Canadian privy councillor. Lord Athlone gave a cocktail party in the Citadel for Canada's distinguished guests, and a dinner was also held there, at which the Canadian Prime Minister, Mackenzie King, presided.

He, for one, was probably a little fretful. Since a proposal that he should take part in the conference came to nothing, he seemed (according to Moran) rather like a man who had lent his house for a party. "The guests take hardly any notice of him, but just before leaving they remember he is their host and say pleasant things." Moran doubted that he was as enamoured of his role at QUADRANT as Churchill imagined him to be.

When the conference was over, Churchill "remained for a few days in the Citadel, pacing the ramparts for an hour each afternoon, and brooding over the glorious panorama of the St. Lawrence and all the tales of Wolfe and Quebec." *Then,* he may have reflected, the British empire was in the springtime of its greatness, whereas autumn and winter were now approaching.

On 31 August he broadcast from Quebec "to the Canadian people and the Allied world." He praised Canada's contribution to the war, which "came from no treaty or formal obligation" but "sprang in perfect freedom from sentiment and tradition and a generous resolve to serve the future of mankind." He regretted that his duties did not allow him "to travel still farther afield and tell Australians, New Zealanders and South Africans to their faces how we feel towards them for all they have done." In fact, even when he was out of office for six years after the war, he never visited those particular countries.

From Quebec he travelled, not back to Britain, but to Washington, where he stayed at the White House from 1 to 11 September. On the sixth he went to Harvard to receive an honorary degree, and to make the speech in which his Anglo-American dream found most forceful expression. The key passages are these:

To the youth of America, as to the youth of Britain, I say, "You cannot stop." There is no halting-place at this point. We have now reached a stage in the journey where there can be no pause. We must go on. It must be world anarchy or world order. Throughout all this ordeal and struggle which is characteristic of our age you will find in the British Commonwealth and Empire good comrades to whom you are united by other ties besides those of State policy and public need. To a large extent they are the ties of blood and history . . .

The great Bismarck—for there were once great men in Germany—is said to have observed towards the close of his life that the most potent factor in human society at the end of the nineteenth century was the fact that the British and American peoples spoke the same language. That was a pregnant saying. Certainly it has enabled us to wage war together with an intimacy and harmony never before achieved among allies.

This gift of a common tongue is a priceless inheritance and it may well some day become the foundation of a common citizenship. I like to think of British and Americans moving about freely over each other's wide estates with hardly a sense of being foreigners to one another . . .

There follows a plea for the dissemination of Basic English—650 English nouns and 200 verbs or other parts of speech—which might well become "a mighty fertilizing and health-giving river," bringing unity to the world as a rudimentary *lingua franca*. By the time Churchill came to write his memoirs, it was already obvious that Basic English would never come up to his expectations, so he did not include the passage referring to it in the extracts that he chose to quote from his Harvard speech.

More surprisingly, he omitted the whole of the passage about the gift of a common language and the possibility of a common Anglo-American citizenship, which is, surely, the speech's most important and striking feature. No doubt it was this passage that Robert E. Sherwood had in mind when he wrote of a statement in the speech that Churchill "would not have dared to make at any previous and less propitious moment in the war or, indeed, at any previous time since the Declaration of Independence."

Sherwood also tells us that Churchill "certainly talked to Roosevelt before suggesting even the remote possibility of 'common citizenship' and was assured by the President that the United States had advanced so far from its isolationist position that this would not outrage public opinion or provoke another Boston Tea Party." No hint that Roosevelt agreed with the idea or regarded the speech as a trial balloon: merely that he thought it would be harmless.

As a Harvard man, the President took an interest in the occasion and wanted his old university to put on a good show, with plenty of pageantry. But that seems to have been the limit of his involvement. Churchill was persuaded to wear the scarlet gown of an Oxford LL.D. (One had to be found for him at Princeton, because there was none at Harvard.) But beneath the robe appeared (according to Moran) "a pair of rather inadequate grey flannel trousers."

Despite the common language, Churchill's idea of a common citizenship between Britain and the United States was even more of a nonstarter than that of an Anglo-French union, which was mooted in 1940. Indeed, the Anglo-French idea might conceivably have worked if the French Cabinet at the time had possessed the vision and the will to stay in the war. But there was no theoretical or practical basis for the merging of Britain and America in a single polity.

Of course, what Bismarck is alleged to have said is more sensible than Oscar Wilde's familiar wisecrack about two nations divided by a common language. English is a genuine bond between the British and the Americans, but—for the purpose that Churchill was trying to advance—a demonstrably insufficient one. It was not the ties of language, history, culture, or sentiment that brought the United States to Britain's aid, before the two countries became allies *on enemy initiative*. Aid was given to Britain for the same reason that it was given to Russia, as a long-range contribution to the security of the United States.

To say this is not to impute any peculiar cold-bloodedness to the Americans or their government. It is exceedingly rare for the leaders of any country to act from motives of sentiment in matters affecting its vital interests. The British government was not moved by tender feelings for the Poles when it gave a guarantee to Poland in March 1939, or when it honoured the guarantee to the extent of declaring war on Germany in September of that year. Chamberlain acted as he did because he and his colleagues had become convinced that Hitler had to be stopped. Poland was merely the trip-wire.

There have been a few, though only a few, exceptions to the rule that self-interest determines the actions of states, as distinct from individuals (though it is also, of course, true of countless individuals). One exception was, perhaps, the action of Great Britain in August 1914. The Liberal government of the day was by no means unanimously in favour of intervention, and the realistic, to say nothing of the ideological, case for supporting France cut very little ice with Liberal M.P.s. But both Parliament and country responded emotionally to the invasion of Belgium, and it then became possible for the government to declare war.

Even more exceptional was the response of the British self-governing Dominions in 1939. Their action was, indeed, dictated more by tradition and sentiment than by self-interest, and Churchill was right to emphasise this in his broadcast from Quebec. But in the least homogeneous of the Dominions, South Africa, in which there was an anti-imperial as well as an imperialist tradition, the decision to enter the war on Britain's side was taken by a Parliamentary majority of only thirteen votes.

The Dominions were, in any case, small communities, in the habit of looking to Britain as their metropolis. Most of them were in large part ethnically British, and all of them owed allegiance to the British Crown. Though in theory quite free to decide their own destinies, in 1939 they had not yet acquired a truly independent outlook. By the end of the war things had changed markedly, and even the Australasian Dominions no longer looked to Britain as in the past, but rather to the United States—and to themselves.

The United States was very much more of an ethnic mixture than even South Africa, and its minorities included large numbers of German-Americans and Italian-Americans, as well as Americans of British stock. At the level of political ideas and prejudices, the country had always been intensely anti-imperial, anti-monarchical, and anti-British. Above all, it was a country on the up-grade, which would abandon isolationism only for the sake of world leadership.

Churchill's proposal was in one sense vague. He did not explain whether the future common citizenship would apply only to America and Britain, to America and Britain plus the self-governing Dominions, or to America and the whole British Commonwealth and Empire. But even if he meant only the first or the second, it was a fantastic proposal. There was no way that the Americans could or would have amended their Constitution to allow for such a drastic change.

As for the idea of British and Americans "moving about freely over each other's wide estates with hardly a sense of being foreigners to one another," what could be more eloquent of the spirit of make-believe in which Churchill was contemplating the postwar world? The two countries' "estates" were in no true sense comparable. America's was, essentially, her own massive heartland, inhabited by her own citizens;

Britain's was a group of more or less British, but virtually autonomous, states, combined with a much larger group of dependencies with an overwhelmingly non-British population.

In using the word "estate" to describe the British Empire, Churchill was echoing one of the political giants of his youth, Joseph Chamberlain, who said in 1895:

Great Britain, the little centre of a vaster Empire than the world has ever seen, owns great possessions in every part of the globe, and many of these possessions are still unexplored, entirely undeveloped. What would a great landlord do in a similar case with a great estate? If he had the money he would expend some of it at any rate in improving the property . . .

One of Chamberlain's ideas for "improving the property," Tariff Reform and Imperial Preference, later gave the young Churchill his pretext for leaving the Conservative Party and joining the Liberals. But that was long ago. Now he was leader of the Conservative Party, and one at least of Chamberlain's imperial concepts had evidently stuck in his mind.

But of course he knew that Britain could not maintain, or even retain, her "estate" single-handed. He wanted to bring the Americans in, and with them to create an Anglo-Saxon Co-Prosperity Sphere. That is what his notion of "moving about freely over each other's wide estates" must have been intended to suggest. It cannot have meant simply that they would be free to circulate in each other's territories, because they were more or less free to do that in any case. Taken in conjunction with the idea of a common citizenship, the implication was clearly that the Americans would become joint administrators of the British Empire, in return for the British having reciprocal rights within the United States.

The blindness of a man of genius can be no less extraordinary than his vision, and in even suggesting the possibility of a merger between the United States and the British Empire Churchill showed one of his blindest spots. Many people with no pretence to his knowledge or imagination could see what he, apparently, was unable to see—that for Americans the liquidation of the British Empire was an article of policy as well as faith. They were conditioned to regard the British Empire as an infamous institution, and moreover, at that period,

American leaders tended to believe that its successor-states would automatically feel beholden to them as the champions of emancipation.

Roosevelt was no exception, but rather the outstanding case in point. Though he was Britain's loyal ally in the war against Hitler, he was no friend at all to British interests in the world. Indeed, it is strictly true to say that even Hitler was less hostile to the British Empire as such than he was. It was, therefore, the ultimate in self-deception on Churchill's part to imagine that he could call in the New World to make the British Empire viable and respectable.

Whatever Roosevelt may have said to him before the Harvard speech was not, we may be sure, intended to give any encouragement at all to the idea of an Anglo-American condominium after the war. Roosevelt's only possible interest in American involvement in the British Empire was to assist in its demolition, and his only likely interest in common citizenship an application by the British nation, or nations, to join the American Union—which was wildly improbable on many grounds and never, of course, suggested.

He may, however, have said something about continuing military cooperation, because this was a theme in which he did have some interest, and which Churchill particularly emphasised in his speech, praising the Combined Chiefs of Staff Committee and commenting that "it would be a most foolish and improvident act on the part of our two Governments, or either of them, to break up this smooth-running and immensely powerful machinery the moment the war is over." At the end of his Washington visit, when the President had left for Hyde Park, Churchill was authorised to hold a meeting, under his chairmanship, of the Combined Chiefs in the council room of the White House, and this seemed to him a significant "event in Anglo-American history." But in fact it did not turn out to be the augury of any permanent special relationship, even in the military sphere, and after recording in his memoirs the words quoted above, he was forced to add: "Alas, unwisdom has already prevailed!"

In 1963 both Houses of Congress decided to make him an honorary citizen of the United States—a solitary swallow not heralding any summer of common citizenship. There was piquancy and pathos in the occasion. Churchill was too old to receive the honour in person, but was represented by his son, Randolph, who read a speech on his behalf. Dean Acheson had just made his famous remark that Britain had "lost an Empire" but "not yet found a role," and this had obviously stung Churchill. In his message of acceptance he said: "I reject the view that Britain and the Commonwealth should now be relegated to a tame and minor role in the world." But, some may have noted, he did not use the word "Empire."

While the Western Allies were conferring at Quebec, they were made unpleasantly conscious of their absent "friend" Joseph Stalin. Notified of the proposed deal with Badoglio, Stalin reacted sharply. "To date it has been like this," he wrote; "the U.S.A. and Britain reach agreement between themselves, while the U.S.S.R. is informed of the agreement." The situation could not be "tolerated any longer." He demanded an Allied commission to be responsible for Italy and, in due course, other defeated Axis countries.

At dinner on 24 August, Harriman observed the different degrees of indignation which this message from Stalin aroused in Roosevelt and Churchill. His account is of capital importance for understanding their respective attitudes.

The President came into the room first, after some of us had already arrived, saying: "We are both mad." He referred to the Prime Minister's, and his, annoyance over the most recent cable from Uncle Joe. His anger took the form of making him gayer than usual, both before and after dinner. The PM, however, arrived with a scowl and never really got out of his ill humor all evening—up to 3 A.M. when I left.

I asked the President if he recalled the sentence in a cable that went to Joe from the PM in which he said: "I am entirely unmoved by your statement." I said the Prime Minister had shown me this cable and asked for comments. My only comment had been [to ask] him whether this statement was entirely accurate. The President roared with laughter and, much to my embarrassment, proceeded to tell the story to the PM when he came in. Needless to say, it not only fell flat but bounced in my direction. With a scowl, he said, "Impudence.". . . The Prime Minister and President were particularly annoyed because they had attempted to keep [Stalin] fully informed. But one can't be annoyed with Stalin for being aloof and then be dismayed with him because he rudely joins the party . . . But the Prime Minister would not have any of it. After dinner, when we were alone, he said he foresaw "bloody consequences in the future," using "bloody" in the literal sense. "Stalin is an unnatural man. There will be grave troubles." He ticked off Anthony [Eden] when [he] suggested it was not so bad, saying, "There is no need for you to attempt to smooth it over in the Foreign Office manner."

Eden had come to Quebec with the official head of the Foreign Office, Sir Alexander Cadogan, whose diary for 24 August contains the comment that Stalin's message "read properly . . . really wasn't so bad." Eden himself was keen to get down to brass tacks with the Russians. He was ready to admit that neither the British nor the American government "had ever given the Russians any hint of their views," and felt that the time had come for frank discussion of political issues. Soon after his return to London he told his private secretary that Churchill was "now getting dangerously anti-Russian."

The row with Stalin was patched up. Churchill was soon "on growling terms" with him again. It was agreed that the Foreign Ministers of the three countries should meet in October to discuss political cooperation in the Mediterranean and elsewhere, and to prepare for a meeting of the Big Three before the end of the year. But Churchill had given his first clear, though private, indication of an apocalyptic view which was to be made known to the world in the Fulton speech of March 1946.

The timing was perhaps rather odd, because only a short time before Stalin had dissolved the Comintern, which was generally regarded as a friendly gesture. The substance of his message about the negotiations with Italy was not palpably unreasonable, as Cadogan appears to have felt. Italy was at war with the Soviet Union as well as with Britain and the United States. Italians had fought on the Russian Front, and above all the collapse of Italy would not have occurred but for the postponement of OVERLORD and the fact that the Russians had been left to bear the brunt of the war with Germany. On the face of it, Stalin had a right to be directly involved, and not merely informed.

Yet one can understand why Churchill began to feel seriously alarmed about Russia in August 1943, and why Stalin's tough line on the Italian negotiations was the precipitant of his alarm. It was now for the first time obvious that the war on the Eastern Front would end not in stalemate but in outright victory for the Russians. The German offensive against the Kursk salient in early July had been held, and within days the Russians had launched a big offensive themselves. On 23 August—the day before Churchill made his baleful remarks at Quebec—Kharkov fell. Liddell Hart compares the pattern of the Russian offensive in the summer of 1943 with that of Foch in 1918.

It was natural that Churchill's fear of Bolshevism should revive as his fear of Russian defeat was removed. With reason, he did not see the dissolution of the Comintern as clinching evidence that Stalin had ceased to have ideological ambitions beyond the borders of the Soviet Union. Even if it had been genuinely dissolved, it could easily be resurrected (as indeed it later was, under a different name).

But as well as being as anti-Bolshevik as ever, Churchill had the traditional British imperialist's dread of Russian expansion. Habituated to regard the Mediterranean as a British sphere of influence, he reacted instinctively against the Russian demand for direct involvement in Italy. Since it was more than likely that Communism would flourish there after the downfall of Fascism, Stalin would have a double opportunity for promoting Soviet interests. And the combination of ideology and power would serve him well in other parts of the world where Britain had interests to defend.

In his new-found, or newly rediscovered, obsession with the Bolshevik bogey, Churchill was out of step with many of his British colleagues, as Eden's comment soon after QUADRANT shows. And if his attitude was, at the time, eccentric even among his own compatriots, inevitably it could not be shared by the Americans to more than a limited extent. It was not that they were pro-Russian, still less that they were soft on Communism, but rather that they could afford to take a more relaxed view of Soviet power.

Before QUADRANT Roosevelt and his advisers had been supplied with a high-level strategic estimate of Russia's position, from which the following passage is quoted by Robert E. Sherwood in *The White House Papers of Harry L. Hopkins,* though without identifying the precise source:

Russia's post-war position in Europe will be a dominant one. With Germany crushed, there is no power in Europe to oppose her tremendous military forces. It is true that Great Britain is building up a position in the Mediterranean *vis-à-vis* Russia that she may find useful in balancing power in Europe.

However, even here she may not be able to oppose Russia unless she is otherwise supported.

The conclusions from the foregoing are obvious. Since Russia is the decisive factor in the war, she must be given every assistance and every effort must be made to obtain her friendship. Likewise, since without question she will dominate Europe on the defeat of the Axis, it is even more essential to develop and maintain the most friendly relations with Russia.

Finally, the most important factor the United States has to consider in relation to Russia is the prosecution of the war in the Pacific. With Russia as an ally in the war against Japan, the war can be terminated in less time and at less expense in life and resources than if the reverse were the case. Should the war in the Pacific have to be carried on with an unfriendly or a negative attitude on the part of Russia, the difficulties will be immeasurably increased and operations might become abortive.

We see here the basis, and the rationale, for Roosevelt's much-criticised policy towards Russia during what remained to him of life. His weakness, and Stalin's strength, was that Russia's eventual participation in the war against Japan was regarded as almost vital. This consideration would clearly take precedence over American willingness to support Britain, whose future power was in any case overrated.

In practice, Roosevelt stood quite firmly against Russian interference in the Mediterranean while the war was going on, allowing only a token and cosmetic Russian presence in Allied councils there. But at the same time he decided to make a personal bid to settle major postwar problems with Stalin, if necessary behind Churchill's back. He was convinced that he was more likely than Churchill to deal successfully with the Russian dictator.

He did not exactly see it as left talking to left—though he did regard himself as economically more "advanced" than Churchill, and was doubtless annoyed when Hopkins once told him that Churchill was "much more left" than he was. Above all, he felt that he and Stalin belonged to the modern world in a sense that Churchill did not. Both represented countries with an anti-imperialist ideology, whatever their other differences, whereas Churchill was the supreme embodiment of old-fashioned imperialism.

Roosevelt fancied himself as an exponent of foreign policy. He had many ideas, some remarkably half-baked, for re-structuring the world. As part of his campaign to establish good relations with Stalin, he appointed Harriman U.S. ambassador to Moscow, and at the beginning of September briefed him on what he (Roosevelt) hoped to achieve from the new relationship.

"He had the idea that he could explain to Stalin the world reaction he could expect from decent behavior on the part of the Russians, as opposed to the violent antagonism they would encounter if they seized certain territories . . . he hoped to persuade Stalin to grant the Baltic States the right to approve or disapprove any territorial changes through plebiscites, to be held within two or three years after re-occupation by the Russians." (On this Harriman comments that "he did not seem to realize that once the Russians occupied a territory, the plebiscite would almost certainly go their way.")

On the future of Germany, he suggested that after the war the Germans should be denied all aircraft and not even be allowed to learn to fly. He also "talked of breaking Germany up into three, four or five states." But he had "no intention of stationing large American forces in Europe after the war." He did "not want to take direct military responsibility for Europe, only supplementary." Those directly responsible should be the Russians, the British, and perhaps the French.

The inevitable result of Roosevelt's attempt at personal diplomacy was to be that Stalin would drive a wedge between him and Churchill. But the situation was further complicated by the fact that Churchill, too, hankered after a miraculous settlement to be achieved by personal diplomacy. Despite the feelings of horror and disgust that Stalin inspired in him, he was proud of his own success in dealing with the "unnatural man" in Moscow, and continued for the rest of his life to alternate between Russophobia and a rather naïve faith in summitry.

Churchill's old-fashioned imperialism was nowhere more apparent than in his attitude towards India, which remained that of the young subaltern of hussars who had done a tour of duty in India in 1896–8 and had never again visited the country. His quarrel with the Conservative leadership in the early 1930s was initially on the subject of India, because he opposed a very moderate and limited Indian constitutional reform which Stanley Baldwin, the party leader, and a majority of Tory M.P.s favoured. In his almost fanatical opposition to the measure Churchill spoke (in Baldwin's phrase) "as George III might have done had he been endowed with the tongue of Edmund Burke."

As Prime Minister he was still the same man, though in the crisis of 1942, when the Japanese were at the gates of India, he had sent Sir Stafford Cripps on a fool's errand to fix the Indian nationalists. The offer that Cripps made was inadequate and resulted, as we have seen, in the Indian National Congress's "Quit India" movement, which the authorities effectively suppressed. By 1943 the Congress leaders were in prison, and the removal of imminent danger to India from without was not accompanied by any constructive move towards a settlement within.

The Viceroy, Lord Linlithgow, had been in the job since 1936 and his term of office had been twice extended. He had shown considerable powers of administration in putting India on a war footing, and great strength of character in meeting the "Quit India" challenge. He also had human qualities which make the tone of his correspondence with Gandhi as creditable to him as it was to the Mahatma. But he lacked imagination, and was anyway tired. The choice of his successor, long overdue, was crucially important for the future of India.

In April, May, and early June Churchill tried fairly hard to persuade Eden to take the post, with the incentive that he would not be obliged, as Viceroys normally were, to accept a peerage, and so would be free to return to the House of Commons. Eden was much attracted by the offer and dithered for a long time, but at length was prevailed upon by his friends to refuse. Churchill then surprised almost everyone by appointing the commander-in-chief in India, Field-Marshal Sir Archibald Wavell, to succeed Linlithgow.

Since Eden had supported the modest Indian constitutional reform against which Churchill had fought, it might perhaps be thought that the attempt to make him Viceroy indicated a change of heart in Churchill. But it was not so. Among others whom he considered for the job was Sir Miles Lampson, ambassador (in effect, viceroy) in Egypt, whose arrogance and insensitivity in dealing with the Egyptians had already aroused the furious indignation of a young officer called Gamal Abdul Nasser. Anyone who could dream of appointing Lampson to India in 1943 had no serious interest in conciliating the nationalist leaders there.

Nor is that the only evidence. Churchill's state of mind is further revealed in Wavell's account of what was said when the Viceroyalty was offered to him. The Prime Minister "said it would probably be a war appointment only and that he would make a political appointment after the war." In other words, there was to be a moratorium on politics in India until the war was over, and the new Viceroy was merely intended to keep the Indian home front quiet.

Churchill's motive for offering Eden the post was not that he hoped for a political breakthrough in India—though in fact it is just possible that Eden might have achieved one—but rather that he wanted to get him out of the Foreign Office and out of England. In certain moods Churchill could be sentimental about Eden, describing him as a sort of political son, but more often Eden irritated him, and Eden was certainly very often irritated by Churchill. Between the two men relations were never really easy, and by 1943 both were feeling that a period of separation would be welcome.

When Churchill formed his coalition in 1940, and soon afterwards (on Neville Chamberlain's death) became leader of the Conservative Party, Eden was indispensable because his standing was so good among Conservatives, as well as among members of other parties. In 1942, when Churchill was most vulnerable, Eden alone might have been able to seize the premiership, or at least the Ministry of Defence, had he been sufficiently determined and ruthless. As it was, Churchill was able to keep him under control, fully recognizing, however, that he was the greatest potential threat.

By 1943, Churchill's position was so secure that he no longer needed Eden, while Eden could see that there was no immediate chance of becoming Prime Minister. He was tempted by the idea of having his "own show," and Churchill by the thought of having a more tractable and malleable Foreign Secretary. On quite a number of issues they tended to disagree, and on some—particularly France —Eden had the better judgment.

Friends of his were dismayed at what Churchill might do if his restraining hand was removed, and above all they were convinced that by abandoning his political base even for a few years he would forfeit his position as heir apparent. Whether or not they were right, Eden was certainly swayed by their arguments. In retrospect, one may feel that it would have been better for all if he had never been Prime

Minister, whereas his undoubted talents as a diplomat and negotiator might have enabled him, in the circumstances, to do valuable work as Viceroy.

Wavell had no diplomatic gifts, as Churchill must have known. Soldierly, scholarly, and, in a quiet way, rather vain, he was taciturn in company, preferring to express himself on paper. He also had a natural distaste for politics and a distrust of politicians. Such a man was unlikely to make much headway with the highly articulate leaders of a nation that revels in talk and argument, at a time of supreme political ferment. And it was, indeed, partly for that reason that he was appointed.

The other main reason was that Churchill wanted to "bowler-hat" him, and making him Viceroy was the politest way of doing so. A new Allied command in South-east Asia was already under discussion, and it was more or less agreed that it would go to a British officer. Wavell regarded himself as the obvious choice, but Churchill intended to appoint a younger man, hoping that Wavell would continue to hold the Indian command as a glorified intendant or quartermaster-general. Wavell, however, made it clear that he would not stay on as commander-in-chief in India if a younger man were appointed over his head to the active South-east Asia command. The result was that he was made Viceroy.

At the QUADRANT conference the choice of commander for South-east Asia was made, having first been agreed on between the President and Prime Minister at Hyde Park. The officer chosen was Mountbatten, whose work as Chief of Combined Operations had, since the end of 1942, been largely transferred from Britain to the Mediterranean. Now he was to be moved away farther still from what was to be the decisive theatre of the war.

In his broadcast from Quebec Churchill made much of the new appointment. Mountbatten, he said, was only forty-three, and

It is not often under modern conditions and in established military professions that a man gets so great a chance so early. But if an officer, having devoted his life to the military art, does not know about war at forty-three, he is not likely to learn much more about it later on. As Chief of Combined Operations Lord Louis has shown rare powers of organisation and resourcefulness. He

1 Roosevelt and Churchill at Casablanca with service advisers:
(*l. to r.*) Arnold King, Marshall, Pound, Brooke and Portal

2 Roosevelt making his 'unconditional surrender' announcement to
correspondents at Casablanca

3 The 1943 Washington conference: at the table second from *l.* Marshall, fourth and fifth from *l.* Leahy and King; third from *r.* Dill, then Portal, Brooke, Pound and Ismay

4 Roosevelt and Churchill at the 1943 Quebec conference, with Mackenzie King trying to join in

5 Teheran conference: in front (*l. to r.*) Eden, Churchill, Stalin; between Churchill and Stalin, Voroshilov; behind, lighting a cigarette, Harriman

6 Teheran conference: Roosevelt turns to shake hands with Sarah Churchill; on either side of him, Stalin and Churchill; behind (*l. to r.*) Hopkins, Molotov, Harriman and Eden

7 Mountbatten (*l.*) on a visit to Montgomery in Normandy

8 Eisenhower (*l.*) with Marshall

9 Harris (*l.*) with Eaker, commander of the US Eighth Air Force

10 Brooke arriving at 10 Downing Street

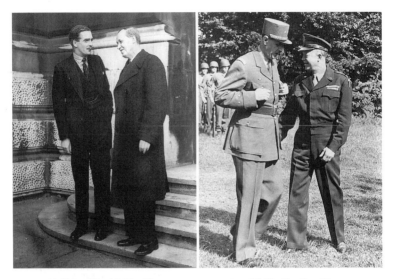

11 Eden (*l.*) with Hopkins,
outside the Foreign Office
in London

12. De Gaulle with
Eisenhower in France

13 Patton lands in Sicily

14 Alexander (*l.*) and Brooke (*r.*) in Italy

15 Admiral Ernest King

16 Churchill with Tedder in North Africa

17 Hitler with Mussolini

18 Hitler wishes Rommel good luck

is what—pedants notwithstanding—I will venture to call a "complete tri-phibian"—that is to say, a creature equally at home in three elements, earth, air and water, and also well accustomed to fire.

The point about age was unquestionably valid, since many of the greatest commanders in history have been as young as, or younger than, Mountbatten. In the Red Army, moreover, the top men tended to be younger than in the British, American, and German armies, because Stalin had liquidated most of its senior officers before the war; and this relative youthfulness of their generals is thought to have given the Russians a distinct advantage.

It was also true that Mountbatten had shown notable energy and unorthodoxy at Combined Operations, and that his experience qualified him to lead forces in all three elements. It was, therefore, surely rather unfortunate that he was sent to a theatre where the scope for large-scale operations was restricted, and where his talents as a commander, though not exactly wasted, were denied the fullest opportunity. He would, for instance, have been the right man to command in the Mediterranean, if there had been no Italian campaign but numerous raids on the southern coast of Europe to keep the enemy guessing. He would also have had much to contribute to the execution of OVERLORD.

But, above all, there is a strange and sad irony in his appointment to S.E.A.C. and Wavell's as Viceroy, because it now seems that so much more good might have resulted if the choices had been reversed. Three years later Mountbatten succeeded Wavell in the Viceroyalty, and he brought to the job all the charm, imagination, and political flair that Wavell and most other holders of it had lacked. If these qualities had been deployed in 1943, it is just possible that India might have achieved independence without the tragedy of partition. It was already very late to make amends for past errors, but perhaps not too late.

Wavell might not have been ideal in the South-east Asia command, but he would probably have been adequate; and in any case, that post mattered far less, in the perspective of history, than the Viceroyalty. But Churchill, with his reactionary views on India, was the last man to make the right choice of Viceroy, and he made his choice, explicitly, according to a negative criterion. When the situation in India called for political genius, he appointed a non-politician.

For all his waywardness and fallibility, Churchill was a giant among men. But in 1943 his own defects and the brutal realities of power were combining to make him a captive giant. As well as being the prisoner of his own prejudices and mistakes, he was also increasingly at the mercy of his allies, and of those who were supposed to be his subordinates.

Roosevelt was already showing that he did not wish to be too closely identified with Churchill, or to have his country committed to the defence of British interests, as distinct from Britain herself. Now that American power was predominant within the Western Alliance, he intended, as the repository of that power, to assert his independence and to conduct a foreign policy of his own.

Stalin's Russia was no longer struggling for survival, but advancing westwards in massive strength, evidently soon to be the greatest land power in Europe. Stalin himself knew that Churchill counted for much less than Roosevelt, in material terms, and he had reason to believe that the Western leaders would not necessarily maintain a solid front against him. Between the two material giants, who might indeed be described as the Emperors of East and West, Churchill was to find his freedom of action reduced and his importance diminished.

In the realm of strategy, he had been seduced by ideas that were not, originally, his own, but rather those of the British C.I.G.S., General Brooke. Nor was it only in military affairs that he had been captured by professional dogma. In air policy, too—as the next chapter will attempt to show—he was the victim of an *idée fixe* which a powerful group of professionals had sold to him.

It is often said that Churchill, by contrast with Lloyd George in the First World War, had his Service advisers effectively under control. In theory his position as Minister of Defence as well as Prime Minister was stronger than Lloyd George's, and he certainly sacked more generals. All the same, it seems fair to suggest that his judgment was more susceptible to Service influence than Lloyd George's was.

Even his freedom to sack, or to avoid promoting, was doubtful in at least one case—that of Montgomery, who became almost as invulnerable as Haig. Monty had been not Churchill's, but Brooke's, candidate for the command of Eighth Army. Churchill did not particularly want to appoint him and managed, at first, to have Gott preferred. But when Gott was immediately killed, Brooke was able to get his man appointed.

Thereafter, Monty's reputation, though much inflated and distorted by propaganda, became such that Churchill felt obliged to give him key roles in HUSKY and OVERLORD, for which he was by no means the officer best fitted. Had he been passed over, there might well have been an outcry.

At two periods in his career—when he was a young Cabinet minister before the First World War, and during the supreme crisis of 1940–1—Churchill's genius had its freest scope and is seen to best advantage. At other times he said, wrote, and did many marvellous things, but his performance as a whole was seriously flawed.

1943 was a bad year for him, though it seemed superlatively good at the time. His prestige had never been greater; but it far exceeded his power and somewhat exceeded his deserts.

5   Bombing On Regardless

At Casablanca the following directive was given to the British and American Bomber Commands in the United Kingdom: "Your primary object will be the progressive destruction and dislocation of the German military, industrial and economic system, and the undermining of the morale of the German people to a point where their capacity for armed resistance is fatally weakened." Within this "general concept" the "primary objectives" were to be German submarine construction yards, the German aircraft industry, transportation, oil plants, and other targets in war industry, in that order.

The directive was an attempt at compromise between two entirely irreconcilable philosophies of bombing, the first represented by Britain's Bomber Command and its commander-in-chief, Sir Arthur Harris, the second by the U.S. Eighth Air Force under Lieutenant-General Ira C. Eaker. The British doctrine, adhered to despite strong evidence that it was fallacious, was that Germany could be knocked out by general, more or less indiscriminate "area bombing" *by night,* aimed at devastating whole industrial areas rather than specific factories or other key targets. The American doctrine, as yet largely untested, was that the German war economy could be wrecked by selective precision bombing of such targets *by day.*

It was intended, on paper, that the Casablanca directive should result in a combined Anglo-American bomber offensive against Germany during 1943, and this was given the code-name POINT-BLANK. "Strategical direction" of the offensive was entrusted to the

British Chief of Air Staff, Portal, but in practice there was no combined offensive. Each of the two bomber forces interpreted the directive to suit itself and was left free to do its own thing. Each, in the eyes of history, can be seen to have done the wrong thing.

At least the Americans were trying something new, and their method had the additional merit that it was in accordance with decent standards of warfare. Moreover, we now have reason to believe that the war *might* have been won by precision bombing of vital targets, if these could have been correctly identified and bombed with the necessary accuracy until they were completely destroyed. But the American offensive was not concentrated enough and, to the extent that it was carried out beyond the range of fighter escort, proved too costly.

The British method, also very expensive to the attackers in men and machines, was neither new nor decent. It was the magnified form of a technique already tried and found wanting. Against people less tough than the Germans it might have succeeded, but German heroism should have been taken for granted. The R.A.F. bombing campaign was, on balance, a failure as well as a disgrace.

POINTBLANK came up for review at the Washington conference in May (TRIDENT), when the importance of destroying the Luftwaffe was stressed, and further lip-service paid to the need for complementary action by the two Allied bomber forces. R.A.F. Bomber Command was at the same time given a clear licence to pursue its own policy, since the plan agreed to at Washington did "not attempt to prescribe [its] major effort."

Both the Allied bomber forces sought to penetrate deep into Germany rather than to operate at relatively close range against targets on or near the enemy coast. In this at least they were alike, but it was a dubious policy, because the farther afield they went, the more vulnerable they became to enemy fighters. The Luftwaffe was thus given the chance to fight at short range against attackers who had to come, and return, a long distance. As a policy for destroying the Luftwaffe it left much to be desired.

Among British and American airmen there was a marked tendency to believe that wars could be won by bombing, even though they differed in most respects as to the method. By the end of the war, this view was less confidently held in the R.A.F., but it lingered on in the

United States until, perhaps, the experience of Vietnam produced a final disillusionment. (Ironically, in Vietnam the Americans practised area bombing.)

The U.S. Eighth Air Force had made only small-scale raids before the Casablanca conference, but in 1943 it put its philosophy to the test in a series of heavy daylight attacks on targets in various German cities. In April it raided Bremen, losing 16 bombers out of 115 employed. In an attack on Kiel in June, it lost 22 of the 66 Flying Fortresses that took part. When Hanover was attacked in July, the losses were 24 out of 92, and there was also a high, though rather less high, ratio of loss when Berlin was raided later in the same month.

But during one week in October the Eighth Air Force lost 148 bombers and crews, as they carried out missions far beyond the protective range of any fighters then in service. The most costly raid of the week was on 14 October, when out of 291 Flying Fortresses 60 were shot down and 138 damaged. Such losses were unacceptable, and it became obvious to the Americans that daylight bombing could not be continued without fighter cover all the way.

The target of the disastrous October raids was the ball-bearings factory at Schweinfurt, east of Frankfurt. This had already been attacked in August and it was certainly the right sort of target—one that might have justified the American philosophy if the first attack on it, in August, had been more concentrated than it was, and above all if it had been followed up at once.

Nobody on the German side is better qualified to judge than Albert Speer, who was in charge of German war production. In *Inside the Third Reich* he wrote of the August attack on Schweinfurt:

Ball-bearings had . . . already become a bottleneck in our efforts to increase armaments production. But in this . . . attack the other side committed a crucial mistake. Instead of concentrating on the ball-bearing plants, the sizable force of 376 Flying Fortresses divided up. 146 of the planes successfully attacked an airplane assembly plant in Regensburg, but with only minor consequences.

("Meanwhile," he added, "the British air force continued its indiscriminate attacks upon our cities.")

The August raid cut production at Schweinfurt by 38 per cent, and further attacks at the time might well have put the place totally out of action. This, according to Speer, would have been catastrophic for Germany, because ball-bearings were so vital that he could not afford the three or four months that would have been needed to relocate the industry. He had no choice but to "patch up" the facilities at Schweinfurt, and the Eighth Air Force gave him two months in which to do so.

The raids in October cut production by 67 per cent, but by then the German defences were so well organised that the cost to the Americans reached, as we have seen, a deterrent level. "The countryside was strewn with downed American bombers." Even so, Speer was surprised to be let off again. The Germans were able to meet the crisis partly by substituting slide bearings for ball-bearings, but (in Speer's words) "what really saved us was the fact that from this time on the enemy to our astonishment once again ceased his attacks on the ball-bearing industry."

It would seem that the American philosophy was basically sound, but flawed in execution. If Intelligence had made sure that the right targets were attacked—with the right degree of persistence—the policy of precision bombing by day might have done the trick. But perhaps it would never have been possible, with so many targets to choose from, to be sure of destroying the ones that were, in fact, vital.

All the same, the Americans came tantalisingly near to success at Schweinfurt, and they might have finished the place off if they had returned to the attack. This they might well have done if their bombers had been able to fly the whole distance there and back with fighter protection, instead of losing it about half-way out.

British air chiefs, however—in particular Portal—felt that their scepticism of daylight bombing was wholly vindicated, and were no less sceptical of the chances of developing a long-range fighter which would be capable of dealing with German fighters operating over their own homeland. In Portal's view, even long-range fighters whose auxiliary fuel tanks could be jettisoned would never be a match for good short-range fighters sent up to meet them. For this reason R.A.F. Fighter Command was still equipped very largely with the sort of interceptors that had won the Battle of Britain, while the very machine that the situation required was used only in low-level operations by the Army Co-operation Command.

This aircraft—the P–51 Mustang—was originally manufactured by North American Aviation, Inc., to a design approved by the R.A.F. The prototype was built in mid-1940 (it took only 127 days to build) and an order was immediately placed. But in its original form the Mustang proved to be insufficiently powered, and to lose speed as it gained height. Its performance was then revolutionised by the insertion of a Rolls-Royce Merlin engine, and the new improved version was tested in October 1942. In America a similar model was soon developed, with a Packard-Merlin engine.

But it was not until after the trauma of October 1943 that the Americans decided to mass-produce Mustangs. In retrospect, it seems very odd that they did not take the decision sooner, in view of the appallingly heavy losses that their bombers were suffering. The R.A.F. chiefs' lack of enthusiasm for the aircraft which they had bought three years before, and since transformed, is less to be wondered at, because they still had no faith in the utility of long-range fighters of any kind, however impressive their performance in tests.

The new Mustang was certainly one of the outstanding technical achievements of the war. Instead of losing speed at higher altitudes, it could reach 455 m.p.h. at 30,000 feet, compared with 375 m.p.h. at 5,000 feet. It was at least as manoeuvrable as the best fighter in the Luftwaffe, and could escort bombers up to 600 miles from their bases. If the Americans had acted swiftly enough in supplying Mustangs to the Eighth Air Force, their precision bombing programme in 1943 might have succeeded.

It would also have had a good chance of success if R.A.F. Bomber Command had followed the Americans' daylight raids on Schweinfurt with night attacks on the same area—if (in other words) the Combined Bomber Offensive had been anything more than a phrase. But Harris was utterly opposed to the doctrine of concentration upon supposedly vital targets. To him they were merely "panaceas," and those who believed in them "panacea-mongers."

Of course he was a panacea-monger himself, but his panacea was area bombing. Many British airmen shared his view, and he differed from them only in the fanatical certainty of his belief and the exceptional force of his personality. To understand how and why the doctrine of area bombing caught on in the R.A.F., it is necessary to look back.

Between the two world wars, when the R.A.F. was evolving as a separate service, the idea that wars could be won by strategic bombing helped to justify its independence, and a leading exponent of the idea was the man who came to be regarded as the "father" of the R.A.F., Lord Trenchard. As a result, bombers were given a marked preference over fighters in the equipment of the R.A.F., and it was only in the last year before the outbreak of the Second World War that the ratio of fighters to bombers was increased from 1 to 2 to about 3 to 5—an increase strongly opposed by Trenchard but, as it turned out, providential for the country.

Despite the bomber-orientated thinking of the R.A.F., Britain was in no position to put theory into practice when the war broke out. Neither the types of bomber in service with the R.A.F. nor the training of their crews made any sustained strategic air attack upon Germany possible. During the "phoney war" period, moreover, the British government was reluctant to provoke retaliation by the German bomber force, which was known to be twice as strong as the British. Apart from a few daylight attacks, mainly on naval targets, most of Bomber Command's activity at the time occurred at night and took the form of dropping propaganda leaflets.

This was important for the future in one way only. Since the few daylight raids were extremely costly, whereas the nocturnal sorties over Germany were accomplished without loss between November 1939 and March 1940, it became accepted in the R.A.F. that the axiom popularised by Baldwin in the mid-1930s—"the bomber will always get through"—was true by night, though not by day. Hence the R.A.F.'s commitment, three years later, to night bombing, while the American air leaders were committed to daylight bombing, for the sake of precision.

It did not, however, seem to follow that bombing at night had to be area bombing, and in 1940–1 the R.A.F. directed the greater part of its effort against specific targets, though there was already a policy of bombing cities on unclear nights. At first Bomber Command was grossly over-optimistic about the effects of its supposedly precise attacks, but, as photographic reconnaissance improved, it became evident that the standard of accuracy was, in fact, so low as to be hardly worth the name. A report in August 1941 showed that, in raids on the Ruhr, only one in ten of the bombers found its way to within five miles of the assigned target.

When excessive hopes of precision bombing by night were thus disappointed, the tendency in the R.A.F. was to swing towards a faith in area bombing that was even more excessive. There was, too, another reason for the change. German attacks on London, Coventry, and other British cities created, inevitably, a demand for retaliation. Whether this was a truly popular demand, as distinct from one made by politicians and the press in the name of the people, will always be a matter of conjecture. (According to Tom Harrisson's system for testing public opinion, "Mass Observation," the demand for retaliation was never really strong, but strongest in areas *not* affected by bombing.)

In fact, the German attacks on cities represented a major, not to say decisive, error on their part. Their policy for bombers had been to use them almost exclusively in support of military operations, and in the summer of 1940 they came near to establishing air supremacy over Britain—which was the essential prerequisite of invasion—by knocking out R.A.F. airfields. When they allowed themselves to be diverted into attacking London, they forfeited what may well have been their best chance of victory.

In any case, the effect of the city raids was minimal, both on British war production and on civilian morale. If Britain's war leaders had been guided by the lessons of the Blitz, they would have dismissed area bombing from their thoughts, at any rate as a means of winning the war. The Germans' experience over Britain pointed clearly to the need to use air power for specific tasks related to actual or impending military operations, the first and paramount task being the destruction of enemy air power.

At moments Churchill perceived this truth with dazzling lucidity, and drew the right lessons from German area bombing in 1940 and British area bombing in 1941. In September of the latter year he wrote to the Chief of Air Staff, Portal: "It is very disputable whether bombing by itself will be a decisive factor in the present war. On the contrary, all that we have learnt since the war began shows that its effects, both physical and moral, are greatly exaggerated . . . The most we can say is that it will be a heavy and I trust a seriously increasing annoyance."

When Portal replied sharply, reminding Churchill that he had agreed to the policy of treating bombing as the weapon on which Britain "must principally depend for the destruction of economic life and morale," Churchill wrote again in terms so prophetic that he must be quoted, this time, at some length:

I deprecate . . . placing unbounded confidence in this form of attack . . . It is the most potent method of impairing the enemy's morale at the present time. If the United States enters the war, it would have to be supplemented in 1943 by armoured forces in many of the conquered countries which were ripe for revolt . . . Even if all the towns of Germany were rendered uninhabitable, it does not follow that the military control would be weakened or even that war industry could not be carried on . . . It may well be that German morale will crack and that our bombing will play a very important part in bringing the result about. But all things are always on the move simultaneously, and it is quite possible that the Nazi war-making power in 1943 will be so widely spread throughout Europe as to be to a large extent independent of the buildings in the actual homeland.

A different picture would be presented if the enemy's Air Force were so far reduced as to enable heavy accurate daylight bombing of factories to take place. This however cannot be done outside the radius of fighter protection . . .

Unfortunately, Churchill did not stick to this line. Both before and after he not only acquiesced in, but at times urgently pressed for, heavy indiscriminate bombing of enemy towns. Even in the passage quoted, the ambiguity of his attitude may be seen, for instance in the words: "It may well be that German morale will crack and that bombing will play a very important part . . ." The R.A.F. exponents of area bombing observed his ambiguity and took full advantage of it.

Churchill's enslavement to the policy, despite occasional efforts to escape, resulted partly from his desire to satisfy the Russians with some form of offensive action, partly from the belief that it would be good for British morale, and partly from sheer wishful thinking. The idea of winning the war without large-scale amphibious and land operations was naturally tempting to him, especially when his faith in British military stamina was shaken by Singapore and Tobruk. In 1942, moreover, he was politically vulnerable, and therefore in a mood to clutch at anything that seemed to offer the hope of a magical denouement.

For all the reasons outlined, terror bombing became the explicit prime activity of the R.A.F. in 1942, and so remained until early 1944. A directive sent to Bomber Command in February 1942 stated that bombing should be focussed in future "on the morale of the enemy civil population and, in particular, of the industrial workers." At about the same time Arthur Harris was appointed commander-in-chief, Bomber Command.

At the end of May Harris launched, against Cologne, the first of his "thousand-bomber" raids, which laid six hundred acres of the city waste, at the cost of forty bombers. A simiiar attack on Essen two days later did far less damage, because the night was cloudy, and at the end of June Bremen was attacked with disappointing results and a 5 per cent ratio of loss among the attackers. That was the end of "thousand-bomber" raids until a later stage in the war. But it was by no means the end of area bombing.

During 1942 German war production increased by about 50 per cent, and civilian morale was unshaken.

Returning now to the Casablanca bombing directive, we find that Harris not only interpreted it in his own way but subtly (and no doubt unconsciously) distorted it. In a letter to the Air Ministry dated 6 March 1943, he quoted the key passage as "the progressive destruction and dislocation of the German military, industrial and economic system *aimed at* undermining the morale of the German people to a point where their capacity for armed resistance is fatally weakened." In fact, the directive had referred to "the progressive destruction and dislocation of the German military, industrial and economic system, *and* the undermining of the morale of the German people," etc. (J.G.'s italics).

Instead of the compromise that the directive sought to achieve between two quite different and irreconcilable doctrines, Harris was thus presenting an uncompromising statement of his own doctrine. The terror campaign was made out to be not separate from, but the true purpose of, the assault on German war production and the

German economy. This crucial change of wording, and of meaning, went uncorrected. In the tactful language of the official history, it does "not seem to have engaged the attention of the Air Staff."

Perhaps the Air Staff, or at any rate its chief, deliberately turned a blind eye to the misquotation. Portal has been credited with a less blinkered outlook than Harris, but in reality the difference between them was more one of function than of conviction. As professional head of the whole R.A.F., and as a member of the British and Combined Chiefs of Staff Committees, Portal had to show some regard for the roles of other services, and of activities other than bombing within the R.A.F. Though on paper, and in discussion with outsiders, he was usually careful to hedge the position, at heart he believed, like Harris, that area bombing could win the war.

He was Trenchard's blue-eyed boy. Before he became Chief of Staff he was, himself, Britain's bomber chief. It was he who selected Harris for Bomber Command, and who kept him there long after many even within the R.A.F. had lost faith in his "panacea." Certainly Harris had direct access to Churchill, which was facilitated by the proximity to Chequers of his headquarters at High Wycombe. But if Portal had disapproved of Harris's meetings with the Prime Minister behind his back, he would have lost no time in protesting, and—such was his influence with Churchill—the meetings would have stopped. In fact, surely, he must have welcomed them as a reinforcement to his own influence on the bombing issue.

Apart from being *ex officio* more obviously confined to bombing than Portal was, Harris had less tact and less ability to seem accommodating. He also had a sarcastic wit which not everybody appreciated, and which was particularly uncongenial to Americans. (In 1941, as head of the R.A.F. delegation in Washington, he had to be withdrawn, on the British ambassador's advice.) But although he lacked Portal's quasi-political gifts he was, in all essentials, Portal's man, and it is not fair that he should bear the whole, or even the main, responsibility for a policy of which he was the dedicated executant, rather than the author.

The R.A.F.'s bombing campaign against German cities reached a terrible crescendo in 1943. With better machines, notably Lancasters and Mosquitoes, and with superior aids to navigation and bomb-aiming, including the new Pathfinder force, the attack was far more effective than in 1942. So also, however, was the defence, and by the end of the year it was apparent that unescorted bombing by night was scarcely more tolerable, to the attackers, than unescorted daylight bombing.

The principal phases of the 1943 campaign were the so-called Battle of the Ruhr between March and July, the Battle of Hamburg between July and November, and the Battle of Berlin, which began in November and extended well into 1944. In addition, there were numerous attacks upon other places, including the famous precision raid on the Möhne and Eder dams. (This atypical operation, carried out by a specially trained squadron, was later used by Harris as an argument against the doctrine of vital targets, because despite its success it failed to win the war. But, in fact, the dams were not vital.)

Immense damage was done to most of the places attacked, but the effect upon the German war economy was relatively limited. Above all, the true objective of the campaign was not attained, since the morale of the German people stood up to the ordeal. In Hamburg, for instance, which was perhaps the hardest hit of all German cities, fifty thousand people were killed and a quarter of a million houses destroyed. At first, nearly a million people left the city, but most of them soon returned and got back to work. In the event, only about 1.8 months' production was lost.

Towards the end of the year, the impact of the campaign was diminishing, while the losses to Bomber Command were growing ominously. Over a thousand bombers had been lost, and about 1,600 damaged. The ratio of loss had risen from 4.7 per cent during the Battle of the Ruhr to 5.2 per cent during the Battle of Berlin. But it was not until the Nuremberg raid in March 1944, when 94 bombers were shot down out of 795 employed, that the case for a change of policy became unanswerable.

There had already been weighty demands for it in the course of 1943. Opinion in the higher echelons of the R.A.F. was by no means unanimously favourable to the Portal-Harris policy. During the summer Air Commodore S. O. Bufton, Director of Bombing Operations, did his best to secure a night raid by the R.A.F. to follow the first daylight raid by the U.S. Eighth Air Force on Schweinfurt. "If both operations are successful," he wrote, "German resistance may be broken and the war ended sooner than could be possible in any other way." But the commander-in-chief ignored the director's views.

After the Eighth Air Force's extremely costly raid on Schweinfurt in mid-October, the Ministry of Economic Warfare strongly advised that the R.A.F. carry out a night attack on the place. Bufton was quick to underline this advice. A successful attack "would have an immediate and far-reaching effect upon Germany's war effort and, incidentally, upon her morale, as work in all kinds of factories would be held up through lack of ball-bearings." Though Bomber Command had firmly set its face against "panaceas," if one existed it was the Axis ball-bearing industry.

This strong pressure was reinforced by the Deputy Chief of Air Staff, Air Marshal Sir Norman Bottomley, who eventually persuaded Portal himself to give Harris a direct order on behalf of the Allied air staffs. Even so, Harris managed to avoid bombing Schweinfurt until the end of February 1944.

Bottomley was the most consistent critic of the Harris policy among senior R.A.F. officers. In September 1943 he told Portal that, unless means could be found of stopping the increase of German night fighters or combating their effectiveness, it might be impossible to maintain the night offensive against Germany. He suggested, therefore, that priority should be given to the selective task of disrupting German fighter production.

But Harris was convinced that attacking Berlin should be the top priority and that, if the Americans would join in the attack, the Allies could "wreck Berlin from end to end" and, at a cost of 400–500 aircraft, win the war outright.

The fact that Harris was not brought to heel until well into 1944, despite such powerful and reasoned criticism of his policy, shows that Portal fundamentally shared his infatuation, though not his absolute candour. It is inconceivable, otherwise, that a man who was charged at Casablanca with the "strategical direction" of the Combined Bomber Offensive would not have insisted, in August and again in October, that Harris act jointly with the Americans in the attempt to destroy Schweinfurt.

Portal's state of mind may be judged from comments that he made in early December 1943. While admitting that the "progressive destruction of the German fighter force" was the "essence" of the first stage of POINTBLANK, he also said that he had "no shadow of doubt" that German morale was "at an extremely low ebb," and he thought that Germany might be "at least half-way along the road of industrial devastation towards the point where Germany [would] become unable to continue the war." To this extent, the official history remarks, he "lent his high authority to both the claims and the expectations [of] Sir Arthur Harris."

Even in 1944 and 1945, the Harris policy was never totally and permanently scrapped. Though in the two months before D-Day Bomber Command's effort was diverted, with the greatest difficulty, to attacking road and rail communications leading to the French coast, towards the end of 1944 Harris was once again showing his reluctance to cooperate in a common policy with the Americans, aimed at a specific type of target. In late September, oil was designated the top priority for Allied bombing, but Harris was slow to treat it as such, and for at least a month General Carl A. Spaatz—now commander of the U.S. Air Forces in Europe—was carrying out the "Allied" policy more or less single-handed.

During the whole of October, Harris concentrated upon area bombing, sparing only one-third of Bomber Command's effort for specific targets such as oil and communications. Portal's biographer seems to regard it as no serious reflection upon his subject that the first month after the oil directive was issued "witnessed a relatively light scale of effort by Bomber Command against oil." At the beginning of November, he tells us, "Portal's pressure began" and before long he was "reasonably content" that the policy was being carried out. But surely it was rather remiss of him to allow a whole month to pass before showing concern at the disregard of official orders, and even then to address Harris in a tone more argumentative than peremptory.

In the last months of the war, area bombing was resumed with a vengeance, and the Americans joined in the ghastly business. The Luftwaffe was so weakened that long-range penetration of German air-space could be achieved with relative impunity, and it was thought helpful to the Russians, and therefore desirable, to bomb the centres of cities crowded with refugees from the East. In late January Churchill asked the British Air Minister "whether Berlin, and no doubt other large cities in East Germany, should not now be considered especially attractive targets."

A resounding answer was given to him on 14 February, when the British and American bomber forces combined to devastate the city of Dresden and to kill, in the process, at least sixty thousand people. By the end of March, Churchill's conscience was troubled, and he was also, perhaps, feeling some apprehension about the verdict of history on Allied terror bombing. He then wrote to Portal:

It seems to me that the moment has come when the question of the bombing of German cities simply for the sake of increasing the terror, though under other pretexts, should be reviewed . . . The destruction of Dresden remains a serious query against the conduct of Allied bombing . . . I feel the need for more precise concentration upon military objectives, such as oil and communications behind the immediate battle zone, rather than on mere acts of terror and wanton destruction, however impressive.

Portal was furious and persuaded Churchill to withdraw the minute as originally phrased. Two days later it was sent in revised form, with the query about Dresden removed and no mention of terror—only of the inexpediency of area bombing "from the point of view of our own interests," since there would be "a great shortage of accommodation for ourselves and our Allies" if Germany, when conquered, were to be "an entirely ruined land."

Churchill was thus forced to accept the responsibility, which was, indeed, justly his—though shared by Roosevelt, whose remote control of operations is no excuse for his failure to prohibit such barbarism.

Was area bombing a war crime for which the victors, being victors, were not punished? Some would argue that the phrase "war crime" is a tautology, since war itself is such a gigantic crime that everything that happens in it is, of necessity, criminal. According to this view, any attempt to draw a line between what is and what is not acceptable conduct in war merely distracts attention from the true moral issue.

That is the pacifist view. Most pacifists would, however, readily agree that even in the comprehensively odious state of war some actions are more odious than others. For instance, it would be hard to maintain that shooting a prisoner in cold blood was no worse than shooting an armed enemy in the heat of battle.

Another argument is that the Second World War was total war, in which the old distinction between civilians and combatants ceased to apply. At best this is no more than a half-truth. Certainly the distinction was much less clear-cut than in former wars, but it would be absurd to suggest that it ceased to exist. Women and small children, for instance, were not trained to kill, and it would seem, therefore, that they should not have been exposed to deliberate murderous attack from the skies.

But the Germans started it—that is a familiar excuse. After Rotterdam and Coventry, why not Hamburg and all the other places, including even Dresden? To this, there are two rather obvious answers. First, Bomber Command's onslaught upon German cities was on a vastly larger scale than the German Blitz; the difference in degree was so great as to be almost a difference in kind. But second, there is the old maxim that two wrongs do not make one right, which presumably is even more applicable when one wrong is out of proportion to the other.

When the war began, the British Prime Minister at the time, Neville Chamberlain, said in the House of Commons: "Whatever be the lengths to which others may go, His Majesty's Government will never resort to the deliberate attack on women and children and other civilians for purposes of mere terrorism." And the British Chiefs of Staff also pledged themselves to refrain "from attack on civil population as such for the purpose of demoralisation." In the event, so far as bombing was concerned, Britain far exceeded the worst excesses of the Germans.

One further quasi-moralistic argument has to be considered—that it was salutary for the German people as a whole to be "taught a lesson," since it was their love and worship of war that had caused all the trouble. But even if we forget Burke's powerful statement, "I do not know the method of drawing up an indictment against an whole people," it should not be forgotten that in 1939 there was very little popular enthusiasm for war in Germany. The lesson of 1914–18 had not been altogether lost on the Germans.

Moreover, it is only fair to recall that, despite mass unemployment and the sense of national grievance that Hitler was able to exploit, his compatriots never gave him more than 37 per cent of the vote in a free election. As Alan Bullock has written: "Hitler came to office in 1933 as the result, not of any irresistible revolutionary or national movement sweeping him into power, nor even of a popular victory at the polls, but as part of a shoddy political deal." It cannot be said that the German people, as distinct from their rotten politicians, got the leader they deserved when Hitler came to power.

Once he was in office, he swiftly turned Germany into a totalitarian police state, and thereafter the Germans were no more free to decide their own destiny than any of the people they conquered. If their condition was preferable, it was only to the extent that an indigenous tyranny may be easier to bear than an alien one, and that even slaves derive some advantage from being on the winning side.

Of course the Germans' patriotic pride was aroused by their triumphs in 1940, and being the people they were it was also natural that their loyalty and discipline should not crack when the tide turned against them. But they cannot in justice be blamed for the war itself. Indeed, they were less to blame than the citizens of free countries, and much less to blame than the *leaders* of those countries, who failed to use their power to stop Hitler.

Churchill was right to feel uneasy about the moral aspect of area bombing. As a calculated policy for terrifying civilians of all ages into submission, it was a grave affront to those minimal standards of civilisation which a civilised country should respect, even when engaged in a life-and-death struggle. If it had been the only conceivable way to save the world, including Germany, from Hitler, its brutality might have been justified on grounds of dire necessity. In the absence of such justification, it was simply heinous.

As a rule Churchill was a humane and deeply sentimental man who could be moved to tears by the sufferings of ordinary people, and who even, during his last premiership, was so upset by the sight of a rabbit afflicted with myxomatosis that he called at once for action by the Minister of Agriculture. But there was another and contradictory side to his character—a capacity for ruthlessness amounting to heartlessness—which was caught by Graham Sutherland in the portrait of him commissioned by Parliament on the occasion of his eightieth birthday.

It was probably this that made him hate the portrait so much that it was destroyed to please him. If he had disliked it for no other reason than that it made him look rather senile (one reason that was put around), it is hard to believe that he would have shown such ingratitude for the work of a major artist, presented to him by Parliament.

The cruelty of time is nothing to be ashamed of, but the consciousness of a streak of callousness in himself is enough to make any decent man ashamed.

That there *was* a streak of it in Churchill can hardly be doubted, though it conflicted with the prevalent tendency of his mind and nature. In November 1942, for instance, he said that the Italians should be bombed relentlessly. It might make them hate the British, but on the other hand, "the demoralisation and panic produced by intensive heavy air bombardment [would outweigh] any increase in anti-British feeling." There was "everything to be said for keeping up and increasing our heavy indiscriminate raids on Italian cities." Such words ill became a champion of civilisation.

The motive for bombing German civilians was not only that their morale might be broken (though this was inherently less likely than that the Italians' would be) but also, and perhaps more especially, that after Singapore and Tobruk Churchill felt unable to rely wholeheartedly upon the morale of British troops. The astonishing prowess of the German Army had so impressed itself upon his mind that he could not help rather dreading the prospect of a fight to the finish on land. Instead, he was tempted into the ignoble policy of trying to defeat the German Army indirectly by destroying German homes and slaughtering German families.

But he did not, as we have seen, adhere to it consistently, any more than he was consistent in shrinking from a decisive trial of strength between the British and German Armies. His attitude changed with his mood, and with the fortunes of war. Unfortunately, his emotional ambiguity and lack of definite principle on the bombing issue—as on Mediterranean strategy—played into the hands of those who knew all too well what they wanted.

The outstanding public critic of the area bombing policy was Bishop George Bell of Chichester. A typical statement of his view appeared in the Chichester diocesan gazette in September 1943:

When a Minister of the Government speaks in exulting terms of a ruthless and destructive bombing of the German people; or quarters, supposed to be authoritative, contemplate the subjection of fifty German cities to the same terror as Hamburg (or Coventry) has suffered . . . then we have a real cause to grieve for a lowering of moral tone, and also to fear greatly for the future

. . . To bomb cities as cities, deliberately to attack civilians, quite irrespective of whether or not they are actively contributing to the war effort, is a wrong deed, whether done by the Nazis or by ourselves.

But the government denied that the R.A.F. was indulging in purely terror raids, and Bell received very limited support, even from his fellow-clergymen. Some, indeed, had no sympathy at all for his views. When William Temple, the much-admired and socialistic Archbishop of Canterbury, was approached, this was his reply: "I am not at all disposed to be the mouthpiece of the concern which I know exists, because I do not share it." Bell, needless to say, never became an archbishop, though earlier in his career he had seemed destined for the highest places in the Church of England.

If the bombing policy was morally wrong, no moral stigma attaches to the air crews of Bomber Command, who did their distasteful duty at great personal risk and in spite of mounting losses. They had to experience quite as much fear as they inflicted, and their exceptional courage was worthy of more honourable employment.

Was the policy on balance a mistake, which some would regard as worse than a crime? Clearly it did not achieve what it set out to achieve. Though the weight of bombs dropped on Germany by Bomber Command in 1943 was five times that dropped in 1942, German armaments production increased again—as in the previous year—by 50 per cent. And there was no sign of the anticipated psychological collapse on the German home front.

All the same, such a tremendous onslaught could hardly fail to have some important effects, even if they were not the ones predicted, and the policy may, as it were, accidentally, have helped more than it hindered the Allied cause. To decide whether or not it did so, we must try to look at all the implications and consequences.

There can be no doubt that Bomber Command's effort diverted an enormous amount of German manpower and matériel which might otherwise have been used on the Eastern and Western Fronts. Since Speer was quoted earlier as a witness to the war-winning chance that was missed at Schweinfurt, it is only fair to quote him again on the subject of the general bombing offensive. In *Spandau: the Secret Diaries* he wrote:

The real importance of the air war consisted in the fact that it opened a second front long before the invasion of Europe. That front was the skies over Germany. The unpredictability of the attacks made the front gigantic; every square metre of the territory we controlled was a kind of front line. Defence against air attacks required the production of thousands of anti-aircraft guns, the stockpiling of tremendous quantities of ammunition all over the country, and holding in readiness hundreds of thousands of soldiers, who in addition had to stay in position by their guns, often totally inactive, for months at a time . . . no one has yet seen that this was the greatest lost battle on the German side. The losses from the retreats in Russia or from the surrender of Stalingrad were considerably less. Moreover the nearly 20,000 anti-aircraft guns stationed in the homeland could almost have doubled the anti-tank defences on the Eastern Front.

As a gesture to his former adversary, Speer inscribed some of those sentences in the copies of his two books that he sent to Harris.

Beyond question the diversion of resources described by Speer was extremely hurtful to Germany, and it is worth noting, as well, that many of the twenty thousand anti-aircraft guns deployed for the defence of the Reich were of the famous 88-mm. type, which could have been used as effectively in tanks or for anti-tank purposes. Another result beneficial to the Allies, and above all to Britain, was that production for the Luftwaffe had to be largely of fighters to meet the attack, so that Germany's own bombing capability ceased to be of much account—until the V-weapons came into play.

So much for the favourable (to the Allies) side of the balance-sheet. What of the other side? The first point to be stressed is that the alternative to a policy of area bombing was not one of no bombing. Granted that large-scale raids on Germany and German-held territory were desirable, and leaving aside moral considerations, which were better value—indiscriminate area raids or selective precision raids? That is a question that has to be answered.

All the evidence suggests that the war which was manifestly not won by area bombing *might* have been won by a combined and sustained policy of selective bombing. The Americans' basic approach was right, though in 1943 they prejudiced their case by attacking the right sort of targets in the wrong way—by daylight and without fighter protection.

In 1944–5 the Americans were able to prove their point through the overwhelming success of their offensive against oil targets, despite non-cooperation for a time by Harris. In May 1944 the Germans were producing 156,000 tons of aviation gasoline, but in that month the Allied air forces dropped only 5,100 tons of bombs on German and Roumanian oil installations (understandably, in the month before D-Day).

When the oil offensive began, the results were immediately most telling. In August, for instance, when 26,300 tons of bombs were dropped, German gasoline production dropped to 17,000 tons. By January 1945 it had fallen to 11,000 tons, and by March it had come to a full stop. The pattern was similar in the output of fuel for road vehicles. This alone would have been enough to bring Germany down, even if the German Army had still, in other respects, been capable of prolonged resistance.

Daylight raids deep into Germany became practicable, without undue loss, as soon as the Mustangs came into service, and, if there had been less delay in mass-producing the improved model of that marvellous aircraft, the decisive attack on German oil targets might have been launched much sooner. But even Bomber Command, operating by night, might have damaged the German economy more grievously by going for oil targets than it did by the indiscriminate blasting of cities.

Despite the remarkable accuracy shown by his own "dambusters" Harris remained sceptical of precision bombing at night, until the effectiveness of it was finally demonstrated in the attacks on enemy communications before D-Day. If, in 1943, he had devoted the effort of his command mainly to selective bombing of vital targets, he would almost certainly have contributed far more to Allied victory. It is even possible that he might have incurred fewer losses among his own aircraft and air crews, though for that he really had to be converted —as he eventually was—to the necessity for night-fighter escorts.

There is no reason to suppose that the preparations which the Germans would have had to make against selective bombing would have been any less elaborate and costly than those, described by Speer, which they had to make against area bombing. A campaign directed against a variety of key targets, or types of target, would have been just as much a "second front" in the sky over Germany, while the danger of actually losing the war if the targets were not properly defended would have forced the Germans to make the same dispositions of anti-aircraft guns and personnel, as well as of fighter aircraft.

In the battles of the Ruhr, Hamburg, and Berlin, Bomber Command gave the Germans a chance to concentrate their defence. If the strategy had been more subtle and elastic, with less of what has later come to be known by the unpleasant word "overkill," the defence would have been kept guessing and its task would have been made far harder.

Moreover, if British and American bombers, whether on daylight or nocturnal missions, had been provided with long-distance fighter escort in 1943—as they well might have been—heavy losses would have been inflicted on the German interceptors. As it was, the Luftwaffe, though certainly forced on to the defensive, and over-equipped with fighters at the expense of bombers, was nevertheless able to score within its own air-space a victory not unlike the Battle of Britain (though of course less enduring).

In 1941 and 1942 an attempt had been made to draw the Luftwaffe into battle by attacks on coastal areas, with fighter escort. The idea was sound, but the range of British fighters was then so short that the results were inevitably disappointing. In 1943 the means were available, if only they had been developed with sufficient swiftness, to fight and defeat the German air force over the Continent. Area bombing, without fighter escort, was doubly wasteful, since it sacrificed men and machines to the German fighters without destroying the installations on the ground which enabled them to fly.

In one sense, area bombing was actually of benefit to the German war economy. In the cities affected there was rigid enforcement of the decrees shutting down inessential works and business premises, with the result that much additional manpower was released. The acute emergency acted as a stimulus not only to Speer's magnificent organising talents but to the efficiency and powers of improvisation of many lesser people. (It is notorious, too, that area bombing was of substantial benefit to the Germans' postwar economy, in that it destroyed many obsolete plants and so cleared the way for technological advance.)

While area bombing did not prevent German armaments production from increasing dramatically, it had—to say the least—a distorting effect upon British armaments production, one-third of which was pre-empted for the output of bombers. Of course, selective bombing would also have made a large claim upon the country's productive resources, but probably less large, because rather fewer bombers would have been needed for precision attacks, and fewer might have been lost if there had been more variety in the pattern of attack.

Finally, there is a political argument against area bombing which is akin to the moral argument, though the two should not be confused. Area bombing, like unconditional surrender, was a gift to Nazi propaganda. It made the Western Allies seem scarcely less brutal and implacable than the Russians, and so made nearly all Germans feel resigned to a desperate, forlorn-hope struggle against all their enemies. Indeed, it was in one way even worse than that, because while the barbarous Russians were killing chiefly German soldiers, the civilised British were killing chiefly German civilians, including women and children by the tens of thousands.

Churchill once said to Portal that in war it was not necessary to be nice, only to be right. Area bombing had the double defect of being thoroughly nasty—and wrong.

6 Fallacies about France

In September 1939 Britain and France went to war together against Hitler, as in August 1914 they had gone to war together against the Kaiser. But whereas in the first war their alliance held firm from start to finish, in the second it was broken within a year by the German *Blitzkrieg*, and by the separate French armistice that followed.

At the best of times they were uneasy allies, because for centuries there was a tradition of rivalry between them which was only ended when, at the beginning of the present century, realistic politicians on both sides saw that they had more common than conflicting interests. But the so-called Entente Cordiale was more an intellectual understanding than a union of hearts. Even the shared ordeal of 1914–18 did not create a truly cordial relationship, and between the wars there were periods of tension, even of estrangement, though the alliance remained formally in being.

After the French armistice in 1940, both countries felt let down. The British were indignant that their ally had sued for terms without their permission, rejecting the option of carrying on the war from French territory overseas. To the French it seemed that, after making far larger sacrifices than the British in the First World War, and having then maintained their large conscript Army while the British reverted to a small volunteer army, at the outbreak of war in 1939 they again had to face Germany with grossly inadequate British support. And since, in the crisis of the battle of France, the British were not prepared to commit their reserves of fighter aircraft, it was equally natural that they (the French) should put their own national interest first.

So far as it went, there was more justice in the French than in the British case, but the crucial flaw was that coming to terms with Hitler was not, in fact, in France's best interest. Though the shadow of independence was gained for part of metropolitan France, even that dubious advantage proved only temporary. In other respects, the armistice meant disaster as well as disgrace for the country.

No Frenchman saw this more clearly than a young general officer recently turned politician, who set himself there and then the task of righting the wrong that had been done to his beloved France. Charles de Gaulle was still under fifty when he came to England in June 1940. Though at first utterly dependent upon his hosts, and spurned if not condemned by most of his compatriots, he gradually established his bold claim to be the authentic representative of a France that had, as he put it, lost a battle but not the war.

His first power-base was in French West and Equatorial Africa, where several colonies rallied to him in August 1940, and it was from Brazzaville that he issued, two months later, a manifesto denouncing the Vichy regime as unconstitutional and promising to account for his actions to the French people, as soon as they were again free to elect an assembly. Early in 1941 he proclaimed a state of Free France, but this was not recognised as such by the British government, with which, indeed, he had sporadic disagreements and disputes throughout that year, notably over the Levant.

Nevertheless, Britain continued to support his movement, which was valuable for the sea and land forces that it controlled—small as yet, though by no means negligible—and still more, perhaps, for the Intelligence network that it built up inside France. De Gaulle himself was well regarded by the British public, though seriously misunderstood and underrated by most people in high places.

It was said at the time, and is often said even now, that he was an obscure man who became important only because Britain gave him the chance to shine. This was by no means true. Though relatively junior in rank, he was already, in June 1940, a man of considerable achievement and evidently of striking originality. His experience of the terrible struggle at Verdun in the First World War had not made him "Maginot-minded" (as it did Maginot himself and a whole generation of French officers), but on the contrary had convinced him of the necessity for mobile warfare.

His books on military theory and practice during the interwar years cut little ice with the French general staff—they helped, indeed, to get him struck off the list for promotion—and foreigners ignored them. (It is a myth that they influenced the German exponents of mechanisation.) But they made one very significant convert among leading French politicians—Paul Reynaud. When Reynaud became France's Prime Minister in March 1940, he would have liked to give de Gaulle political office at once, but was prevented by the outgoing Prime Minister, Edouard Daladier, who said he would leave the Cabinet if de Gaulle was appointed.

As a result, he had the chance to put his theories into practice on the battle-field when the Germans attacked in the West, and he did so with outstanding, though necessarily limited, success. He was promoted temporary brigadier in command of a division, and so became the youngest general in the French Army. Then Reynaud, conscious of being surrounded by defeatists—who included the aged and revered Marshal Pétain—decided that he must have de Gaulle in the government. On 5 June the young general became Under-secretary for National Defence. In effect, this meant that he was deputy to Reynaud in his capacity as war leader.

At the time of his flight to England he was, therefore, "obscure" only to the blind and ignorant. If the circumstances of France and Britain had been reversed, it was as if Liddell Hart, no longer captain but promoted general in recognition of very recent success in battle, had been appointed deputy to Churchill as Minister of Defence; and then, with Churchill's spirit broken and the British state in the process of being subverted, had flown abroad to carry on the fight as his country's self-appointed champion.

Apart from de Gaulle's impressive record, it should soon have been apparent to any moderately perceptive Englishman who came into contact with him that he had political genius allied to formidable will-power and eloquence. The eloquence was, it is true, largely lost on those who could not understand French, but there was no excuse for failing to observe his other great qualities. Unfortunately, the British establishment, with only a few exceptions, treated him as a rather absurd megalomaniac, troublesome, touchy, and only worth supporting *faute de mieux*.

Churchill's attitude toward de Gaulle was complex, though after America's entry into the war it hardened into a hostility which was at times almost pathological. He always prided himself upon being a friend of France. Yet his acquaintance with the real France, whether in human or cultural terms, was very slight. Indeed, his knowledge of the country did not extend far beyond restaurants in Paris and villas on the Côte d'Azur.

De Gaulle represented a French intellectual tradition and French virtues that were alien to Churchill. His disciplined mind, part-Jesuitical, part-Jacobinical, had little in common with Churchill's expansively Whiggish thought-processes, and his reserved private character and cherished bourgeois domesticity did not harmonise too well with Churchill's gregarious habits and eccentric hours.

Yet it would not be true to say that the two men failed altogether to appreciate one another. De Gaulle wrote later of Churchill as "the great artist of a great historical drama," and Churchill claims to have described de Gaulle, even before the fall of France, as the man of destiny. He was also grateful for de Gaulle's "magnificent" demeanour when the French fleet at Oran was attacked without prior consultation with him, and after their joint failure at Dakar Churchill told the House of Commons that his confidence in de Gaulle was greater than ever.

In the course of 1941, however, things turned very sour between them. Churchill wanted a French leader whom he could both get on with and patronise, but he found that neither was possible with de Gaulle. Lesser men took their cue from the Prime Minister, with the result that the Free French movement was supported in an increasingly equivocal manner. Though France was by far the most important of the countries overrun by Hitler, and de Gaulle by far the most distinguished individual among the patriotic leaders in exile, the British official attitude towards him and his movement was at best cool, at worst churlish.

This state of affairs was much aggravated when the United States became a belligerent. Since the armistice the American government had shown, on the whole, more respect for Pétain than the British government had shown for de Gaulle. The Vichy regime, which had sentenced de Gaulle to death *in absentia*, was not only recognised but courted by the United States, and the American ambassador to Vichy was Roosevelt's friend Admiral Leahy.

Shortly after Pearl Harbor, moreover, there was a huge row between de Gaulle and the Americans over the tiny French islands of Saint Pierre and Miquelon, near Newfoundland. On Christmas Eve, 1941, these were occupied by the Gaullists, who were welcomed by the local population with wild enthusiasm, and whose bloodless coup was soon endorsed in a plebiscite. But the U.S. government, and in particular the Secretary of State, Cordell Hull, chose to treat the incident as a defiance of the Monroe Doctrine. Hull even issued a statement in which he referred to the Gaullists as "so-called Free French."

Roosevelt's initial reaction was calmer, but as time went on he became scarcely less prejudiced against de Gaulle. It is tempting to look for a partial explanation in his Dutch and French Huguenot ancestry, but that may be too far-fetched. What cannot be doubted is that his ignorance of France was profound, yet no impediment to the holding of obstinate views on the subject. And one of his views, of course, was that the French empire should be allowed, even encouraged, to disintegrate.

When dealing with Britain, his anti-imperialism had to be slightly muted and masked, because the British were making a rather large contribution to the war. But the French seemed a defeated and divided people whose national interests he could override with much less compunction. Pétain had neither the means nor the inclination to assert France's position as a power in the world. He was an inward-looking quietist. But Roosevelt could see that, in de Gaulle, he had to reckon with a very different sort of Frenchman.

Roosevelt's cavalier attitude toward France was not confined to her territories overseas. Even her metropolitan territory would not have been immune if he had had his way. Discussing the future of Europe with Anthony Eden in March 1943, he proposed that a new state be set up called Wallonia, which "would include the Walloon parts of Belgium with Luxembourg, Alsace-Lorraine and part of northern France." Eden poured cold water on the idea and the President did not revert to it, at any rate with him.

In fairness to Roosevelt, it must be said that he wanted the inhabitants of France—or what remained of the country after he had lopped limbs off it—to be genuinely free to determine their own future, and he suspected de Gaulle, quite mistakenly, of having Bonapartist tendencies. Either he had not read the Brazzaville manifesto or he did not believe that the General was sincere in promising to submit himself to the people's representatives, freely elected. In fact, de Gaulle, as a disciple of the passionately anti-Bonapartist Chateaubriand, was the last man to aim at establishing a military dictatorship, and it fell to him, later, to save his country from just such a fate.

It was not until Casablanca that Roosevelt and de Gaulle actually met. The President had meanwhile become disillusioned with Vichy, but without relenting towards the Fighting French (as the Free French were re-named in July 1942). Instead, he and his agents had turned to the lightweight Giraud. Unfortunately, meeting de Gaulle produced no change of heart in Roosevelt. Though he expressed admiration for the "spiritual" look in the General's eyes, he was soon making snide and facetious remarks about him.

Up to a point Churchill defended the Fighting French against the Americans, but more often he tried to coerce de Gaulle in order to placate Roosevelt. Since his own feelings towards the General were mixed, he was disinclined to risk his vital relations with the President for de Gaulle's sake. At times he would seem even more anti-Gaullist than the Americans, yet at other times his awareness of the General's heroic stature would get the better of him. Moran, for instance, records this exchange at Casablanca:

When at last [Churchill and de Gaulle] emerged from the little sitting-room in our villa, the P.M. stood in the hall watching the Frenchman stalk down the garden path with his head in the air. Winston turned to us with a whimsical smile:

"His country has given up fighting, he himself is a refugee, and if we turn him down he's finished. Well, just look at him! . . . He might be Stalin, with 200 divisions behind his words. I was pretty rough with him. I made it quite plain that if he could not be more helpful we were done with him."

"How," I asked, "did he like that?"

"Oh," the P.M. replied, "he hardly seemed interested. My advances and my threats met with no response."

Harry Hopkins told me of the President's quip that de Gaulle claimed to be the lineal descendant of Joan of Arc. I repeated this to the P.M. He was not amused. It did not seem at all absurd to him.

"France without an Army is not France. De Gaulle is the spirit of that Army. Perhaps," he said sadly, "the last survivor of a warrior race."

It was wrong to imply that France had lost its martial spirit and that de Gaulle was no more than a soldier. The words quoted reveal blindness as well as insight. But they also show that Churchill could feel uncomfortable about acting as Roosevelt's henchman against de Gaulle.

Perhaps it was a further complication in the Prime Minister's attitude that he had a sneaking feeling that he ought, himself, to be standing up to Roosevelt rather more than he was. Though he did not have Stalin's two hundred divisions, he had vastly more than de Gaulle. Yet he had allowed the Americans to present TORCH as an American expedition, in which the very large British presence had to be played down for the sake of appearances. De Gaulle, he may have reflected, would never have made such a sacrifice of his country's dignity, even as a means of securing acceptance of his strategic ideas.

To Churchill—until the shock of 1940—the Entente between Britain and France had been a familiar, established concept, whereas his own dream of an Anglo-American condominium was new and speculative. For all that the dream meant to him, even he must have had occasional doubts. French and English might have quarrelled for centuries, and did not speak the same language; yet they belonged to the same continent and were separated by thirty rather than three thousand miles. Their countries were of comparable size, and they had many common interests. Were they not, perhaps, more natural allies than Britain and the United States?

De Gaulle himself was definitely thinking along these lines during the war. Entertained at dinner in London by a small group of politicians and Foreign Office officials on 4 July 1942, he was asked what he thought were the prospects for Anglo-French friendship in the postwar world. At present, he replied, French sympathy was divided equally between Britain, America, and Russia, but in his view Britain would eventually become once again the favourite ally, because "the Americans would become too wearisome and the Russians too alarming" (*"car les Américains deviendront trop fatiguants et les Russes trop inquiétants"*).

After the Liberation, in November 1944, he outlined to Churchill his reasons for believing in a revived Entente as the basis of a sound foreign policy for Britain and France. Both countries, he said, would emerge from the war diminished in power. France could never hope to regain her former position, and even Britain, though covered with glory, would suffer from the centrifugal forces in the Commonwealth and from the ascendancy of Russia and the United States. Acting together, however, the two countries could still have a decisive influence.

Churchill replied that he did not wish France and Britain to be separated, but that he set more store on using his own influence with the super-powers than on attempting to act independently of them. In particular, he mentioned his close personal relations with Roosevelt. In one sense the whole question was a little academic, granted that Roosevelt would soon be dead, Churchill out of power for six years, and de Gaulle out of power for twelve years. But the principles involved were of the utmost importance, and in retrospect the discussion seems rather fateful.

If Churchill could still talk about close personal relations with Roosevelt in the autumn of 1944, it is hardly surprising that he still had a lot of faith in the special relationship—despite misgivings—in 1943. This was, consequently, a year in which his ambiguity on the subject of France and de Gaulle became increasingly apparent.

In May 1943 de Gaulle left England and went to Algiers, where it was soon demonstrated that Giraud was no match for him. The Vichy men who still lingered in positions of authority were removed, and by the end of July de Gaulle was sole chairman of the French Committee of National Liberation, as well as of the Committee for National Defence, while Giraud occupied the largely ornamental post of commander-in-chief.

These developments were viewed with extreme distaste by the American government. Every effort was made to stop de Gaulle from going to Algiers, and to impede his progress once he was there. Shortly before leaving for Algiers, Churchill, who was in Washington attending the TRIDENT conference, telephoned Eden in London requesting that the British Cabinet break with de Gaulle. It seemed to Eden's private secretary that Churchill had come to feel about the General almost as Cordell Hull did. "The American atmosphere goes to his head."

In mid-July Eden wrote a paper on American policy towards France, in which he said that the U.S. government "did not wish to see a strong central administration for the French Empire built up in Algiers" but would prefer "to deal separately with each part." This had some effect upon Churchill, but the tug-of-war in him was violent and painful.

On French affairs, Eden had got the P.M. to agree that as a long-term policy he could not accept the American ideas of keeping France in leading-strings and demoting her to a second-class Power . . . The P.M. said he would be prepared eventually to have a showdown with the President on this. But on the question of immediate recognition, he was adamant and said menacingly, "I will fight you to the death . . ."

A day or two later he burst out against de Gaulle in the presence of the American ambassador, saying, "I entirely share your President's views about him."

Stalin, meanwhile, was impatient to recognise the French National Committee, but delayed doing so until the "Anglo-Saxons" had decided in what terms, if at all, to recognise it. Eventually, at the end of August, recognition was accorded with varying degrees of warmth. The Russians acknowledged that the committee represented "the State interests of the French Republic," whereas the Americans merely recognised it "as administering French territories overseas." The British formula was nearer to the Russian than to the American, but Stalin was allowed to seem friendlier to de Gaulle than the people who were supposed to be his backers.

In the last stages of the argument with Roosevelt over recognition, Churchill more or less took Eden's line. But there is no evidence that he ever tried, in any of his personal encounters with Roosevelt, to change the President's mind about the General—probably because his own opinions and emotions were so confused.

The "Anglo-Saxons'" shabby treatment of de Gaulle was symptomatic of an even more tragic error in their war policy—their failure to note the multiplying signs of French revival and, therefore, to realise that France was the key to victory. Instead of bothering so much about "knocking Italy out of the war," they ought, surely, to have been devoting their thoughts to bringing France back into it.

Against the background of French history since 1914, and in view of the wholly unprecedented character of the *Blitzkrieg,* it is not to be wondered that France went through a period of moral prostration, in which the ideology of Vichy made a strong appeal. Apart from the trauma of sudden military defeat, between six and ten million French people, and about two million Belgians, fled to the southern part of the country, creating a social problem of nightmarish proportions.

Whatever response there may have been to de Gaulle's first broadcasts from London, loyalty to Vichy was boosted by the British attack on the French Fleet at Oran, on 3 July. This incident stimulated traditional Anglophobia in France, just as it gratified traditional Francophobia in England. (When Churchill spoke about it in the House of Commons, he was for the first time warmly cheered by Conservative M.P.s, who had previously shown some reserve towards the man who had supplanted their leader, Neville Chamberlain, as Prime Minister.)

But, in spite of Oran, the spirit of opposition soon began to grow in both Occupied and Unoccupied France, and de Gaulle was the principal focus for anti-German and anti-Vichy feeling. His name was convenient. Fishermen or pseudo-fishermen carrying two rods *(deux gaules)* could feel that they were making a political gesture, and—as H. R. Kedward says—" *'Vive de Gaulle'* written on walls or across Vichy and German posters, with the symbol of the cross of Lorraine, became the popular iconography of Resistance."

Laval's return to power in April 1942 turned many waverers against Vichy, and his labour schemes, which were designed, in effect, to put French workers at Germany's disposal, aroused bitter opposition. Under the so-called *Relève,* volunteers were encouraged to opt for work in Germany as a means of obtaining the release of French prisoners-of-war. But only one prisoner was returned for every three skilled workers who went to Germany. At first, labour was conscripted only for work judged by the government "beneficial to the over-all interest of the nation" inside France, but in February 1943 it was extended to the *Relève* as well. This drove many workers underground.

The Resistance began as a very fragmentary affair, but it gradually acquired coherence, largely through the courage and organising ability of Jean Moulin. More or less a contemporary of de Gaulle, he had been the youngest prefect in France when the war broke out. Towards the end of 1941 he made his way to London and concerted, with the General, a plan for unifying the various Resistance groups. He was then parachuted back into France and by March 1943 had set up a Conseil National de la Résistance, which was pledged to get rid of the Germans and the Vichy regime, and to work under de Gaulle's leadership.

Sadly, Moulin was captured soon afterwards and died in German hands, without giving anything away under torture. But his brief career is eloquent of the French renascence. No less so is the letter of another, and much younger, French Resistance hero, Olivier Giran, who was only twenty-one when he was executed by the Germans in April 1943. This is what he wrote to his parents just before his execution (as quoted by R. V. Jones):

Among men I did what I thought was my duty—but I did it with joy in my heart. It was war, and I fell, as others did, and as many more must do . . . I saw them on the Marne, buried in long rows. Now it is my turn—that is all . . . Yes, France will live. Men are cowards, traitors, rotters. But France is pure, clean, vital.

I am happy. I am not dying for any faction or man, I am dying for my own idea of serving her, my country . . .

Meanwhile, Frenchmen had also been showing great valour outside France. In June 1942 the 1st Free French Brigade held Rommel's forces at bay for ten days at Bir Hacheim, and could not be shifted until Rommel had taken personal command of the battle. Nowhere in Africa, he said, was he given a stiffer fight. This was not the behaviour of a nation which had lost its martial spirit.

After TORCH there were about 300,000 French troops in North Africa, but few were immediately available to go into action, because their equipment and transport were out of date and they lacked technical support. The Americans were keen to give them the wherewithal to fight, trusting that they would remain under Giraud's—that is to say their own—control. Brooke, on the other hand, was against giving them a combatant role. He favoured using them only for static duties, thereby releasing British and American troops for operations against the enemy.

In the event, a French corps took part in the battle for Tunisia, and by the end of 1943 there were three French divisions fighting on the Italian Front. De Gaulle insisted, when his authority was established at Algiers, that French forces should not be treated as pawns on the Anglo-Saxons' chessboard, and above all that they should take part in the liberation of France, both from the north and from the south. But he was never seriously consulted about Allied strategy, which is hard to believe given his credentials as a military thinker.

The Allied governments had plenty of evidence to go on concerning the state of opinion in France, but they do not seem to have given enough attention to what they heard. Jacques Kayser, for instance, formerly *chef de cabinet* to Daladier, who left France in July 1943 and made his way to London via Spain, Portugal, and North Africa, said that

From the French internal point of view invasion couldn't begin too soon. The French expected it almost hourly. The longer it was postponed, the less French powers of resistance would become from sheer physical weakening by starvation and the gradual rounding-up of all able-bodied men for work in Germany.

At about the same time a leading French resister, Albert Kohan, soon to be dropped back into France, told senior men in the Foreign Office

of the absolute necessity of recognising the [National Liberation] Committee as a Provisional Government which would take over as French territory [was] freed. All France, or rather 95% of France, was resistant and looked to the Committee as its authority . . . There was no danger of de G. becoming dictator. The French people would have no dictators.

The Americans were blind and deaf to reports showing how over-whelmingly the French people supported de Gaulle's movement, and the British high command was scarcely less anti-Gaullist. M. R. D. Foot, in his account of the work of the British Special Operations Executive (S.O.E.) in France, quotes a comment by the head of the

Intelligence service to the executive director of S.O.E. that "Giraud would be more popular than de Gaulle, and that de Gaulle had not a great following but only a symbolic value." S.O.E. knew better, but the views of the high command naturally carried great weight.

Worse still, the Allies were unmoved by evidence of what delaying the invasion of France would mean to the French. Brooke's Mediterranean strategy implied a callous indifference to the needs of Britain's original ally. Many brave Frenchmen who were expecting the invasion in 1943 were not alive to assist it, or to rejoice at the liberation of their country, the following year. Many more suffered intensely from the effects of another year's occupation, or from being deported as slave-labour to Germany.

French sacrifices in the Second World War are still insufficiently appreciated, as they were at the time. Most "Anglo-Saxons" have tended to assume that the French Army hardly fought at all in 1940, and that, after the armistice, France was for all practical purposes out of the war, apart from the creditable, but relatively small-scale, contribution of French contingents serving with the Allied armies.

A glance at the casualty figures should help to set the record straight. The rough total of French military dead in the Second World War was 211,000, which compares with 293,000 for the United States and 354,000 for the British Commonwealth and Empire. The totals of military wounded were France, 400,000; United States, 590,000; British Commonwealth, 890,000. These figures show that even in the military sphere the sacrifice of French life was not much less than that of American life, and the number of Frenchmen wounded not very far below that of Americans. Moreover, the totals of French military killed and wounded were more than twice the totals for Italy, which were, respectively, 78,000 and 120,000.

Among civilians France's losses were the worst of the Western Allies—400,000 dead, compared with 70,000 British and perhaps 1,000 American. (The Italian figure—80,000—is also less than the French.) But the scale of French sacrifice on the home front cannot be measured in purely statistical terms. Indeed, it cannot be measured at all. The only certainty is that it would have been far less if France could have been liberated a year earlier.

Considerations of honour, as well as humanity, should have influenced the British to expedite the invasion. These could not apply in the same degree to the Americans, however, who had not entered both world wars as allies of the French, and who were in less close touch with the French underground. All the same, it is very hard to understand why they did not emphasise the positive and practical advantages of bringing metropolitan France back into the war, during all their arguments with the British about cross-Channel as opposed to Mediterranean strategy.

The Americans argued that the Allies should deliver a direct blow at the heart of enemy power, with a fairly short sea crossing and massive air cover. The case was strong, but it could have been made so much stronger if they had, as well, stressed the value of landing in a country whose people were allies in spirit, if not in strict protocol, and fervently anxious to regain their liberty and redeem their national honour. Every step by the Allies on French soil would not only be so much territory denied to the Germans but, more positively, would provide the chance of new recruits for the Allied cause. France was a country of forty million inhabitants: to liberate it would be to bring about a decisive shift in the balance of manpower as between Germany and the Western Allies. Whereas occupying Italy—quite apart from the physical and military difficulties—meant taking on a heavy burden of administration with virtually no compensating advantage, advancing into France would bring the Allies a rich dividend of new combatant power.

Stalin hinted at this vital point during one of his meetings with Churchill in August 1942. In an attempt to explain to Stalin the difficulties of cross-Channel invasion, Churchill (it will be recalled) asked him rhetorically why Hitler did not invade Britain in 1940, when the country was defended by only twenty thousand trained troops, two hundred guns and fifty tanks. And Stalin replied that this was no analogy, because "the landing of Hitler in England would have been resisted by the people whereas in the case of a British landing in France the people would be on the side of the British." Regrettably, this line of argument was used, if at all, with insufficient force by Marshall and other American proponents of cross-Channel action.

They also seem to have been too little aware of what the French Resistance was already doing, and of what, with greater help and encouragement, it might have been able to do. In Jean Moulin's original report, dated October 1941, he said:

171

Tens and even hundreds of thousands of Frenchmen, mainly in occupied France, yearn to join the FFL [Forces Françaises Libres] in order to continue the fight at England's side. Those who were lucky enough to do so after the Armistice represent only a small minority. The others have had to abandon the idea in face of the impossibility of finding the necessary help. This ardent mass of Frenchmen, which has remained under the yoke, is champing the bit and is only awaiting the opportunity to shake off this yoke. It would be mad and criminal not to make use of these soldiers, who are prepared to make the greatest sacrifices, in the event of any widescale operations by the Allies on the Continent; scattered and anarchical as they are today [this was before Moulin himself pulled them together], these troops can tomorrow constitute an organized army of "parachutists" *on the spot*, knowing the country, having singled out their opponents and decided on their objectives.

That he was not exaggerating the potential of the Resistance was shown three years later when the Allies invaded France. The Germans had to devote eight divisions to holding down their rear areas while OVERLORD was in progress, and even so one SS armoured division took twenty-three days to fight its way from Strasbourg to the formal battle-front at Caen, mainly on account of informal activity by resisters. In southern France, the Allied commander-in-chief in the Mediterranean, General Maitland Wilson, estimated that the French Resistance numbered 150,000 and reduced the efficiency of the local Wehrmacht by 60 per cent.

During the years of occupation, countless acts of sabotage were committed—ranging from major value to nuisance-value, but all unquestionably valuable to the Allies—and marvellous Intelligence work was done. But even more would have been accomplished if there had been more cooperation from the high command, and particularly from the air staff. In August 1943 Portal said that it would be hard to allow the S.O.E. more than twenty-two aircraft in Western Europe as a rule, even though it was explained to him that this number was inadequate even for existing tasks.

Churchill was appealed to, and he made a general statement about the importance of stimulating resistance. Even so, M. R. D. Foot tells us, "Harris fended off for several months more any extensive participation by his squadrons in SOE's work." (It is interesting, by the way, to compare, or rather contrast, the material cost of sabotage carried out by resisters with that of Harris-type devastation. All the principal acts of industrial sabotage in France together used only about three thousand pounds of explosive, which was less than the load of a single R.A.F. Mosquito light bomber.)

France was the biggest neglected asset of the Second World War. It was a reservoir of power on which the "Anglo-Saxons" drew too little and too late.

Instead of the cross-Channel invasion that Frenchmen and others were praying for in 1943, there was, in September of that year, a large invasion exercise in the Channel, code-named STARKEY. This was organised by General Frederick Morgan, the Chief of Staff to the Supreme Allied Commander (designate), whose post had been established at Casablanca as a gesture to cross—Channel strategy.

COSSAC—as Morgan was acronymously called—intended the operation "to afford relief to our Eastern and Southern fronts by pinning down potential reserves in Western Europe," to enable the R.A.F. possibly to "pick up a nice bag of Luftwaffe," to "induce the enemy to show at any rate part of his hand," and to "convince him that he was about to be assaulted from our north-western side."

In the event, only the last of these objectives was attained, in the sense that STARKEY may have contributed to the following year's highly successful deception plan, whereby the enemy was made to believe that the main invasion would be in the Pas de Calais rather than in Normandy. But whether STARKEY, in fact, helped to deceive the Germans and, if so, to what extent, is doubtful.

It is most unlikely that the exercise pinned any troops in the northwest who would not have been there in any case, and it definitely failed to draw the Luftwaffe or tempt the enemy to show his hand. As Morgan himself has written:

The sky reverberated with the roar of great formations of American and British fighters racing for the battle that they failed to find. [These were the short-range fighters which had nothing much else to do, because they were useless as escorts to long-distance bombers.] We were told that a German coast artillery subaltern on the far shore had been overheard calling his captain on the radio to ask if anybody knew what all this fuss was about. Were our faces red?

But STARKEY was encouraging to Morgan in at least one respect. The troops who had been mobilised ostensibly in preparation to invade (their part of the exercise was called HARLEQUIN) seemed bitterly disappointed when they were told that it was not, after all, the real thing. "Once one had seen the expression on those men's faces there could no longer be any vestige of doubt as to the spirit that animated the British Army in England." The fact that he mentions that vestige of doubt is clear corroboration that people in high places had been uncertain about the British Army's morale.

Their uncertainty derived, as we have seen, above all from the shameful catastrophes of Singapore and Tobruk. But these were unreliable guides to the state of military morale nearer home. In the Western Desert, and still more in the Far East, British soldiers did not feel sure of what they were being asked to fight and die for. If it was simply a question of defending their country, or of taking action manifestly designed to bring the war to an end, their morale was as good as anybody's. But in remote outposts their sense of purpose was much less sure.

Why was it not the same with the American soldiers in the Bataan peninsula or on Guadalcanal? The reason is obvious. The Americans were at the beginning of the imperial phase of their history, whereas the British were nearing the end of theirs.

Morgan spares a thought for "the great underground army deployed behind and among the Germans that was awaiting with growing impatience our actual arrival amongst them so that they might rise up to help us." It was impossible, he says, "to tell them beforehand that what we were doing would not culminate in that which they so keenly anticipated and desired." All that could be done was "to drum into these sorely-tried people the absolutely vital necessity, come hell or high water, of waiting for the word from London."

The word from London never came—in 1943—and the disappointment of the people in France was more profound than that of the British soldiers. The few who were familiar with Barrie's *Peter Pan*, had they known the code-name of the exercise, would have thought of it as "miserable STARKEY" rather than "happy STARKEY."

7 The World-Sharers

The year 1943 ended with three summit conferences—at Cairo, Teheran, and Cairo again. Of these Teheran was the most important as well as the most dramatic, because it was the first at which Roosevelt and Churchill were joined by Stalin.

The conference was code-named EUREKA (Greek: I have found), after Archimedes' joyful exclamation when he discovered how to determine the proportion of base metal in Hiero's crown. At Teheran, Roosevelt had a similar joy in the discovery that Stalin was "get-at-able"—and Stalin, for his part, in finding that Roosevelt could easily be got at.

Until a late stage there were doubts that the conference would ever take place. Teheran was as far outside Russia as Stalin would consent to go, but Roosevelt was reluctant to travel such a distance from Washington, more especially when Congress was in session and he had to sign or veto bills within ten days of their passage. (Air transport alone made it possible for this Constitutional requirement to be met, but with the President in Teheran there would have to be a very quick turn-round of couriers, and no mishaps.)

When, as agreed at Quebec, the Foreign Ministers met in Moscow towards the end of October, among other things to complete arrangements for the summit meeting, Stalin tried to wriggle out of attending it himself, suggesting that Molotov go as his representative. But Eden and Cordell Hull were adamant that the other two heads of government would not travel to Teheran for any other purpose than to meet Stalin. So at length the rendezvous was fixed.

On 12 November Churchill sailed from Plymouth on H.M.S. *Renown,* and the following day Roosevelt sailed from Hampton Roads, Virginia, on U.S.S. *Iowa.* Both men were bound for Cairo, where a preliminary conference was to be held. Churchill had intended that this should be a bilateral affair, involving only the President and himself and the Combined Chiefs of Staff. But Roosevelt had other views.

He did not want to arouse Russian suspicions by any appearance of an Anglo-American gang-up before Teheran. And it would seem that he also rather wanted to put Churchill in his place. Though Egypt was a British zone of occupation, as Morocco at the beginning of the year was American, Roosevelt went out of his way to show that he, and not Churchill, was the master of ceremonies in Cairo. Without consulting the British Prime Minister, he invited Generalissimo Chiang Kai-shek and Molotov to attend the conference there.

The two invitations proved to be mutually exclusive, because the Russians could not overtly discuss the war against Japan, in which they were not yet engaged. But Chiang Kai-Shek came, and so did the inevitable Madame Chiang, as well as Mountbatten and other senior Allied officers from South-east Asia. As a result, the conference was almost monopolised by discussions relating to a theatre in which Churchill had very little interest.

This suited the Americans, who did not wish to give him any opportunity for lengthy debate on European strategy. Churchill's commitment to OVERLORD in the spring of 1944 was, they believed, uncertain, despite his protestations to the contrary, and it was obvious that he hankered after more "sideshows" in the Mediterranean. Indeed, he had specifically told Roosevelt that he thought the decisions taken at Quebec should not "be interpreted rigidly and without review in the swiftly changing situations of war."

It was a bad moment for Churchill to try to kindle enthusiasm for Mediterranean projects. His optimism about the campaign in Italy had turned out to be vain. On his own admission Rome, whose early capture he had prophesied, would not now be taken in 1943. Moreover, the Germans had evicted British garrisons from three islands in the Dodecanese which had been occupied when the Italians surrendered. The cost in men and ships had been surprisingly heavy, and the cost in prestige very serious, too.

In particular, Britain's failure in the Dodecanese was hardly likely to encourage the Turks to abandon their policy of neutrality, and Churchill's persistent belief that they could be brought into the war was made to seem more illusory than ever. But above all Roosevelt and his advisers were determined that the absolute priority of OVER-LORD should be maintained, not only for its own sake, but also because they felt the need to satisfy the Russians, whose active participation in the war against Japan they regarded as vital.

If the Americans were justly irritated by British Mediterranean obsessions, the British had an equally just grievance about the American infatuation with China. To them it seemed that the Chinese war effort did not amount to much, and they were not at all impressed by the Chiang Kai-Shek regime. When Roosevelt gave the Generalissimo a pledge that the Allies would launch an amphibious operation across the Bay of Bengal, he did so against Churchill's strong protests.

In retrospect, Robert E. Sherwood appears to admit by implication that the British view of China at the time was correct. "There is no doubt that Roosevelt and the U.S. Chiefs considered the maintenance of the Chinese front to be essential, and there is also no doubt that the Japanese were finally defeated by the attacks from the Pacific, with no decisive battle being fought anywhere on the mainland of Asia. The huge Japanese forces on the mainland were left stranded and largely unengaged, just as were those in the garrisons of Rabaul and Truk."

Japan, unlike Germany, was a country that *could* be defeated by a combination of sea and air power. But the Americans remained convinced that, unless Chiang could be helped to defeat the Japanese on the mainland, the war might go on for ever. And Chiang, in turn, insisted that Burma was the key to victory in Asia.

While in Cairo, Roosevelt entertained Churchill at a Thanksgiving Day dinner at the American ambassador's residence, where he was staying. It was quite a large party, including his son Elliott, son-in-law John Boettiger, Churchill's daughter Sarah, Hopkins's son Robert, and others. Proposing Churchill's health, Roosevelt described the origins of the festival and claimed that it was being spread by American soldiers all over the world. It was a special pleasure to him to be spending it in the company of his great friend the Prime Minister.

At this point Churchill rose to reply, but had to sit down again because the President had not quite finished. With considerable unction and hypocrisy, Roosevelt ended by saying that Thanksgiving was traditionally a family festival and that Britain and America formed one family, now more united than ever. Churchill then got up again and said his piece.

There is no mention, in Churchill's memoirs, of Roosevelt's reference to the Anglo-American family and its unprecedented unity. The speeches at the dinner are recalled only in general terms, as being "of warm and intimate friendship." But Roosevelt's skill in carving turkeys is described in some detail.

Two days later, on 27 November, the American and British parties flew on to Teheran. Persia (or Iran, as it was beginning to be called) was, like Egypt, nominally independent, but in fact under foreign control. The twenty-two-year-old Shah had been brought to the throne in 1941, when his pro-German father was forced to abdicate. The country was then occupied by British and Russian troops, and later American troops came in as well.

The Shah's position during the conference was even more humiliating than Mackenzie King's at Quebec, but at the end he obtained the bonus of a declaration, signed by the three leaders, in which they committed themselves to respect his country's territorial integrity and to help it economically. (Having been educated in Switzerland, he spoke French more fluently than English; but he was well disposed towards Britain, and keen to attract American interest and support. In this he was later more successful than was good for him—or the Americans.)

Churchill stayed at the British legation and Stalin at the Russian embassy, which were close together. But the American legation, where Roosevelt was at first accommodated—having declined the Shah's offer of a palace—was about a mile away. Stalin then suggested that Roosevelt move to the Russian embassy, for the sake of security, and after some hesitation Roosevelt agreed.

The symbolism of this move was ominous to the British, though in keeping with the President's diplomatic aim at the conference. For Stalin it was an early triumph, not least in that it put Roosevelt under twenty-four-hour surveillance by the N.K.V.D.

Teheran was pre-eminently a political conference. For the British and American staffs it was largely a waste of time, because there was very little exchange of information or free discussion with their Russian opposite numbers. Indeed the only "opposite number" was Marshal K. E. Voroshilov. At the professional level the alliance between the Soviet Union and its Western partners might not have existed, for all the practical effect the Russians allowed it to have.

But at the political level the meetings were of boundless importance, particularly those at which Roosevelt and Stalin talked behind Churchill's back. The first of these was at 3 P.M. on 28 November, after Roosevelt had refused to see Churchill in the morning or for a *tête-à-tête* lunch.

The conversation lasted three-quarters of an hour, though much of the time was taken up by translation. Roosevelt said that Britain and the United States would, at the end of the war, have more merchant ships than they could possibly need, and that some of them should be made available to the Soviet Union. There is no evidence that Churchill had authorised this generous offer, so far as Britain was concerned, but Stalin welcomed it and said that the Western powers would get raw materials in exchange.

The topic of France was raised—by Stalin—and it is easy to explain both why he raised it and the line that he chose to take. In Cairo Roosevelt had seen Andrei Vishinsky (the Soviet representative on the Allied Advisory Council for the Mediterranean) and had talked to him at length of his lack of confidence in de Gaulle. Vishinsky—according to Harriman, who was present—was "obviously much impressed with the President's frankness but somewhat surprised that [he] felt so seriously about de Gaulle." No doubt he reported Roosevelt's outpouring to Stalin, who therefore opened his remarks about France with the statement that Pétain rather than de Gaulle represented "the real physical France." The two men agreed that the French nation would have to be punished for its collaboration with Germany.

Stalin must have been amused to hear Roosevelt say that no Frenchman who had taken part in the Vichy regime should be allowed to hold public office after the war, since he must have remembered, even if Roosevelt preferred to forget, that for a long time the Vichy regime had been warmly recognised by the United States. But he played for all he was worth on Roosevelt's prejudice, adding that the Allies should not shed blood to restore Indo-China to French colonial rule. With this the President "agreed 100 per cent." After a century of French rule, he said, the people of Indo-China were worse off than ever before.

Mention of Indo-China led naturally to the subject of India, which Roosevelt advised Stalin not to raise with Churchill, while commenting gratuitously that reform there should start "from the bottom, somewhat on the Soviet line." Stalin replied that that would mean revolution, but also observed that India was a complicated society with different levels of culture and an absence of relationship between castes. Harriman was struck by his well-informed and sophisticated view of India, contrasting it with Roosevelt's ignorance and over-simplification.

At their second private meeting, on the following day, the two leaders mainly discussed Roosevelt's ideas for a future world organisation, in which "four policemen"—Russia, America, Britain, and China—would "deal immediately with any threat to the peace or sudden emergency." Stalin's reaction to this proposal was that it would not be favourably received by the small nations of Europe, that he did not believe China would be very powerful at the end of the war, and that, even if she were, European states would not wish her to be an enforcement agency for themselves. In these comments Stalin's realism showed to advantage, though in the last it was blended with racialism. As the conversation developed, it became apparent that his own preoccupation was very much more with the future of Germany than with that of the whole human race.

The last of Roosevelt's private talks with Stalin during the Teheran conference was on 1 December, when the President explained, with remarkable cynicism, why he had to show some solicitude for the people of Poland and the Baltic states. If the war was still in progress in 1944, he would feel obliged to run for a fourth term, and in that event would not wish to lose the votes of the six or seven million Polish-Americans, or of the smaller, though not negligible, number of voters of Lithuanian, Latvian, and Estonian origin. But, he added with a smile, the United States would not go to war with Russia over the issue.

Stalin on this occasion seems to have said little or nothing about Poland, but he did point out that the Baltic states had not been independent under the Tsar—surely a revealing comment. In general he advised Roosevelt to sedate the affected ethnic minorities with the right sort of "propaganda."

At the plenary business sessions of the conference Roosevelt was invited to take the chair. This, according to his aide and speech-writer Samuel I. Rosenman, was not because he alone of the three was a head of state as well as a head of government, but because the United States "was the leader of the world in so many ways—military, productive, *moral and spiritual*—that it was automatically assumed . . . that the head of the table was the logical place for the representative of the United States" (J.G.'s italics). No remark of the period more sublimely expresses America's mood of imperial self-confidence, which reached its amplitude during the Second World War.

Opening the first session, Roosevelt welcomed Stalin to the "family circle"—a phrase which must have echoed ironically in Churchill's ears. There followed a general discussion of global strategy, in which Roosevelt gave a report on America's private war in the Pacific and referred to the operations which were being planned for South-east Asia. But he also emphasised that Europe was the most important theatre and assured Stalin that the date for OVERLORD would be 1 May 1944.

Stalin in return gave Roosevelt the assurance he most wanted—that the Soviet Union would enter the war against Japan after Germany was beaten. Until then, he could only maintain a defensive front in Siberia.

Churchill endorsed the President's OVERLORD pledge, though he also said that there might be delays in launching the operation if there was a shortage of landing-craft, and that meanwhile Allied forces should not remain idle. He dwelt at tedious length upon the desirability of bringing Turkey into the war.

On this question Stalin was categorical. Turkey would not become a belligerent, and it was a mistake to scatter forces in the eastern Mediterranean. OVERLORD was the operation that mattered, and he even doubted the wisdom of trying to capture Rome. Ten divisions might be left to hold the existing line, and the rest of the Allied Army in Italy used for an invasion of southern France to coincide with OVERLORD.

Churchill was not a lone voice in proposing some move towards the Balkans. Indeed, it was Roosevelt who suggested a move across the Adriatic to join forces with Tito's partisans and then advance into Roumania to meet the Russians. Churchill supported the suggestion, but it appealed as little to the American Chiefs of Staff as it did to Stalin.

The second full session began with Churchill's presentation, on behalf of King George VI, of the "Sword of Stalingrad," which was received on behalf of that city by the man after whom it was renamed. Before being taken to Teheran, it had been exhibited in state in Westminster Abbey—a "symbolic" gesture of which Evelyn Waugh was later able to make good literary use.

Amid absolute silence Stalin kissed the scabbard, and then handed the sword to Voroshilov. As he did so (Churchill's detective tells us), he "let the blade fall from the scabbard" but "managed to retrieve it quickly." The ceremony has been described as impressive, but it cannot have been free from embarrassment.

Certainly it did nothing to blur the ruthless clarity of Stalin's mind, because when the assembled company reverted to normal business he soon asked the searching question: "Who will command OVER-LORD?" This was particularly awkward for the Western leaders, because it was a matter which had not yet been settled. Churchill had accepted the necessity of an American supreme commander, and was content that the job should go to Marshall. But in order to satisfy American public opinion that Marshall was not being demoted, Roosevelt wanted him to be commander not only of OVERLORD but of all Allied operations in Europe, including the Mediterranean, while at the same time remaining titular U.S. Chief of Staff, with a deputy to do his work in Washington.

This was not acceptable to Churchill, because it had been understood that, in return for the command of OVERLORD going to an American, command in the Mediterranean would go to a British officer. It was also unacceptable to the British Chiefs of Staff, who felt that Marshall's ambiguous status would make for confusion, since it would be difficult for the Combined Chiefs to control a field commander who was, at any rate nominally, one of them. The result of these conflicting pressures was that no decision had been taken, though most people in the know still assumed that the OVERLORD commander would be Marshall.

Stalin made it clear that he could not regard the OVERLORD commitment as serious until the man who would command the operation was named. Roosevelt managed to get through the meeting and the whole conference without naming anybody, but before he left Teheran he promised that the choice would be made within a few days.

The record shows that Churchill made an unfortunate speech during the discussion that followed the Stalingrad sword ceremony. It was long and rambling, and appeared to sum up the tasks before the conference in such a way as to put OVERLORD at the bottom rather than at the top of the list. His earlier assurances seemed to be in doubt. Stalin reacted sharply, asking if the British really believed in OVERLORD, which was the only thing that mattered to *him*. Churchill did his best to retrieve the situation, but the meeting ended in an atmosphere of tension.

At the last of the plenary sessions, the talk was mainly of Germany, and the Western leaders put forward alternative proposals for redrawing the map of that country. Roosevelt suggested that it should be divided into five autonomous states, one of which would be a reduced Prussia. Churchill agreed that Prussia should be detached from the rest, but proposed that the southern states become part of a Danubian confederation. Stalin did not think much of either plan, though he pretended to think Roosevelt's the better of the two. To him, there seemed little difference between one part of Germany and another. "All Germans, with the possible exception of the Austrians, fought like the devil."

As well as business meetings there were lunches and dinners at which the leaders talked politics in a supposedly more relaxed, and often more revealing, manner. During the evening of 28 November, Stalin disconcertingly questioned the policy of unconditional surrender. In his view, it "merely served to unite the German people, whereas to draw up specific terms, no matter how harsh, [would] hasten the day of German capitulation."

After Roosevelt had gone to bed, Churchill tackled Stalin on the question of Polish frontiers, and when he said that he was determined to hold the territory up to the Curzon Line, but that Poland should be compensated by German lands up to the Oder, Churchill appeared to concur. He failed to persuade Stalin that the Big Three should try to work out a general understanding on Poland, but when Eden asked, with some boldness, how much the Russians intended to "eat," Stalin replied that they "did not want anything belonging to other people, although they might have a bite at Germany."

Dinner on the twenty-ninth was a very unpleasant occasion for Churchill. Stalin kept needling him about his reluctance to be really nasty to the Germans. Strong measures, he said, would be needed to keep them under control after the war, and Churchill's resentment was aroused when "the Marshal entered in a genial manner upon a serious and even deadly aspect of the punishment to be inflicted" upon them. At least fifty thousand officers and technicians should be liquidated. Only thus would German military power be brought to an end.

Churchill might have commented that Stalin's comprehensive pre-war purge of the Red Army's officer corps had not destroyed Russian military power, and he might also have suggested that if this were to be one of the specific terms imposed by the Allies an early German capitulation was hardly to be expected. But he was too angry to be subtle or sarcastic. He replied with noble indignation.

According to himself, he said: "I would rather be taken out into the garden here and now and be shot myself than sully my own and my country's honour by such infamy." According to Harriman, his words were a little different, but in the same spirit: "The British Parliament and people will never tolerate mass executions. Even if in war passion they allowed them to begin, they would turn violently against those responsible after the first butchery had taken place. The Soviets must be under no delusion on this point."

Roosevelt tried to restore amity with a joke in bad taste. As a "compromise" he would propose that not 50,000 should be shot, but only 49,000. His son Elliott then made matters far worse by saying that he cordially agreed with Stalin's plan and that he was sure the U.S. Army would support it. At this, Churchill walked off into the next room, which was, appropriately, in semi-darkness.

Stalin and Molotov came after him, "both grinning broadly, and eagerly declaring that they were only playing." Without being convinced of their sincerity, Churchill agreed to rejoin the party. Later, Stalin tried to make it up to him by saying that he would personally like to see the British Empire expanded, particularly in the area around Gibraltar. When Churchill then asked him about Russia's territorial ambitions, he replied: "There is no need to speak at the present time about any Soviet desires; but when the time comes, we will speak."

Before Churchill went to bed that night, his doctor took his pulse and found it was up to 100. He seemed in a state of gloom bordering on despair. "Stupendous issues are unfolding before our eyes," he said, "and we are only specks of dust that have settled in the night on the map of the world." Moran, anxious for him, hung around for a few minutes and then asked if he should put out the light. But there was no answer. Churchill was already asleep.

The next day was his sixty-ninth birthday, and it was his turn to give a dinner party. There were presents and a birthday cake, and when the guests were seated Churchill announced that toasts would be drunk in the Russian fashion. Accordingly, he left his seat and went over to Stalin, touched glasses, and said: "I sometimes call you Joe and you can call me Winston if you like, and I like to think of you as my very good friend." He also said that the British were turning politically pink. Then he gave the toast: "Stalin the Great."

Incidentally, at lunch that day Churchill had volunteered the suggestion that Russia should be given access to warm-water ports after the war. When Stalin asked if this meant that Britain would agree to relaxing the provisions of the Montreux Convention, so that Russian ships could pass freely through the Dardanelles, Churchill replied that Britain hoped to see Russian ships, both naval and merchant, sailing all the seas. If Stalin had tried to mollify him the night before, he was now going out of his way to mollify Stalin.

There were many other toasts at the dinner, including two proposed by Stalin to Churchill's valet, Frank Sawyers. At one point a waiter tripped and emptied a large ice-pudding over the head of Pavlov, Stalin's interpreter, who was in the middle of translating for his master. Though dripping from head to foot, he would not allow the waiter to mop him up until the translation was completed.

When Churchill raised his glass to give the last toast, Stalin cut in with a request that the privilege should be his. He then drank to the President and people of the United States. Replying, Roosevelt said that the diversity of political complexions round the table reminded him of the rainbow, which to Americans was a symbol of good fortune and hope. As they left Teheran, they could see, for the first time (he said), that symbol in the sky.

There can be no doubt that Roosevelt meant what he said. For all his hard realism where American interests were concerned, he had infinite faith in his own capacity to charm people, however alien, into doing what he wished. Since the concessions that he made were largely at others' expense, his diplomatic campaign at Teheran cost him little more than the effort, such as it may have been, of showing affability to a tyrant and some disloyalty to a fellow-democrat.

Churchill's position was confused. He, too, wanted to get along with Stalin and fancied his own ability to establish rapport across the immense ideological gulf that divided them. But he lacked Roosevelt's easy throwaway manner, and above all he lacked Roosevelt's power. He could not afford to quarrel with either of his confederates, and when he made a demonstration of fury it had to be short-lived. Though a greater man than Roosevelt, and an immeasurably better man than Stalin, he was, in effect, patronised by both.

As for Stalin, he was almost as free from illusion as from scruple. He alone of the three had definite aims and a clear idea how they could be realised. Indeed, by the end of 1943 he was well on the way to achieving that hegemony in the eastern half of Europe which was his paramount postwar aim. The Anglo-Americans had already missed their chance of occupying non-Soviet Europe before he could evict the Germans from his own territory. It was obvious that by the end of the war he would be present in strength in those areas that he intended to control.

Brooke saw him as the dominant figure at the conference: "I rapidly grew to appreciate the fact that he had a military brain of the very highest calibre. Never once in any of his statements did he make any strategic error, nor did he ever fail to appreciate all the implications of a situation with a quick and unerring eye. In this respect he stood out compared with his two colleagues. Roosevelt never made any great pretence of being a strategist and left either Marshall or Leahy to talk for him. Winston, on the other hand, was more erratic, brilliant at times, but too impulsive and inclined to favour unsuitable plans without giving them the preliminary deep thought they required."

Of course it seemed to Brooke that Stalin's discouragement of any move by his Western allies towards the Balkans, and his suggestion that the attempt to capture Rome might be abandoned in favour of a landing in the South of France to precede OVERLORD by a month, were not bona fide military opinions but politically motivated. He was secretly hoping, Brooke thought, that the Americans would start OVERLORD "on the wrong leg."

This may be true, but many would now agree that the idea of penetrating the Balkans from the south or south-west was wildly over-ambitious, and that the protracted struggle in the Italian peninsula was a waste of resources. It would also be admitted that the case for a landing in the South of France *before* D-Day was a good deal stronger than for the landing nearly ten weeks after it which eventually occurred. Moreover, there is surely no reason to doubt that Stalin was still interested in the success of OVERLORD, all the more so as it was no longer likely to threaten his own occupation of Eastern Europe.

Sherwood naturally felt, like Samuel Rosenman, that Roosevelt was the star at Teheran. He "sat in the middle, by common consent the moderator, arbitrator and final authority." The evidence does not support this bland view, though it certainly indicates that the postwar division of the world between American and Russian spheres of interest was prefigured at Teheran. In *Antony and Cleopatra* Menas speaks of "These three world-sharers, these competitors." There may have appeared to be three at Teheran, but in fact there were only two.

Sartorially, Roosevelt was outstanding: he alone wore civilian clothes. Stalin, having transformed himself from "Premier" into Marshal, wore a mustard-coloured uniform with thick epaulettes embroidered with gold lace and white stars, and trousers perfectly creased, with a broad red stripe. The whole outfit seemed to one observer to have been specially designed for the occasion and never worn before. Churchill, who always took a rather childish delight in fancy dress, wore the uniform of an air commodore, in which he was photographed with the somewhat irregular addition of a Persian astrakhan hat—a birthday present from the press.

At the Congress of Vienna Talleyrand was impressed by the sobriety of Castlereagh's dress compared with the ostentatious finery that others sported. He would have been similarly impressed by Roosevelt at Teheran.

The declaration issued at the end of the conference was ludicrous and shameless, even by the standards of such documents. "We shall seek the cooperation and the active participation of all nations, large and small, whose peoples in heart and mind are dedicated, as are our own peoples, to the elimination of tyranny and slavery, oppression and intolerance. We will welcome them, as they may choose to come, into a world family of democratic nations . . . We leave here friends in fact, in spirit and in purpose."

At the second conference in Cairo, which immediately followed the Teheran conference, various decisions were taken in the light of what had been said to, and by, Stalin. One casualty was the amphibious operation across the Bay of Bengal to the Andaman Islands (code-named BUCCANEER), which had been promised to Chiang Kai-Shek at the earlier Cairo meeting.

The British had always been opposed to this, because they thought it would involve an unwarrantable diversion of landing-craft from the European theatre, and in any case, they were not particularly interested in South-east Asia now that India was safe. The reconquest of Burma and other British possessions in the Orient could, so far as they were concerned, wait.

Roosevelt, for his part, no longer cared so much about meeting Chiang Kai-Shek's demands, since Stalin had promised that he would enter the war against Japan as soon as the European war was over. This meant, in effect, that winning the war in Europe would be the quickest way to set up a winning combination against Japan. So BUCCANEER was scrapped, Chiang was told (though not in so many words) that the recent promise to him was cancelled, and Mountbatten was instructed to do as well as he could with his existing resources.

There was much discussion of future operations in the Mediterranean, and between 4 and 6 December the Turkish President was in Cairo for talks with Roosevelt and Churchill, while his Foreign Minister conferred with Eden and Hopkins. (Hull was absent from Teheran and Cairo, as from Casablanca.) The Turks reaffirmed their unwilling-ness to come into the war unless and until they could be sure of doing so with relative impunity—which meant that they would require Allied support on a scale that could not, in the circumstances, be contemplated.

This was a cruel disappointment to Churchill, who had remained incurably hopeful of persuading the Turks to come in long after even Brooke—who had originally promoted the idea—had ceased to re-gard it as realistic. To the Americans the Turks' refusal was not only understandable but welcome. Roosevelt said in President Inönü's presence that he quite appreciated that the Turks did not wish to be "caught with their pants down," and Marshall was saying privately that Turkish entry into the war would "burn up our logistics right down the line."

The Combined Chiefs agreed at Cairo that operations in the Aegean, including the capture of Rhodes, were desirable, but only if they could be mounted without detriment to OVERLORD and the South of France landing, which was code-named ANVIL. The eastern Mediterranean was thus given a low priority in the planning for 1944.

Churchill's false optimism about the Turks did not make him an out-and-out exponent of Balkan strategy. The only Allied leader who believed that the main effort should be in the eastern Mediterranean, rather than in Italy or France, was Field Marshal Smuts; and Church-ill rejected his view. But he hated to see troops without anything positive to do, and would really have liked things to be happening more or less everywhere. Because he advocated, at one time or an-other, so many different lines of strategy, it is easy to represent him —either for praise or blame—as one who sought victory through Allied intervention in south-east Europe. But at Teheran it was Roosevelt who raised the idea of an Allied move across the Adriatic and into the Balkans.

At any rate, the supreme tasks for 1944, confirmed at Cairo, were OVERLORD and ANVIL, and it was agreed that they should be carried out in May. It was also agreed that the COSSAC plan for OVERLORD allowed too small a margin for the initial assault, and that everything practicable would have to be done to increase its strength.

But perhaps the most important decision to be taken at Cairo—a decision that was long overdue—concerned the choice of a supreme commander for OVERLORD. It was taken by Roosevelt alone, without further discussion with Churchill, and against the known wishes and expectations of most of his advisers. On 5 December, "near lunchtime," he called Marshall to his villa and settled the matter in a characteristically roundabout way, knowing that the Chief of Staff was not the man to press his own claim. Marshall later gave this account of the interview:

As I recall, [the President] . . . asked me after a great deal of beating about the bush just what I wanted to do. Evidently it was left up to me. Well . . . I just repeated again in as convincing language as I could that I wanted him to feel free to act in whatever way he felt was to the best interest of the country and to his satisfaction and not in any way to consider my feelings. I would cheerfully go whatever way he wanted me to go and I didn't express any desire one way or the other . . . Then he evidently assumed that concluded the affair and that I would not command in Europe. Because he said, "Well I didn't feel I could sleep at ease if you were out of Washington."

With Marshall eliminated, the more or less inevitable choice was Eisenhower. And so it was. Marshall himself wrote out an order for the President to sign: "The immediate appointment of General Eisenhower to command of OVERLORD operation has been decided on." The order was sent to Ike by radio, but Marshall retrieved the handwritten draft, with Roosevelt's signature, and sent it to Ike as a souvenir.

The President's decision was due, in fact, not to any feeling that he would be lost without Marshall as Chief of Staff—though he certainly rated his services very highly—but rather to pressure from the British and from his own public opinion. As we have seen, the British did not at all object to Marshall's appointment as such. If the OVERLORD commander had to be an American, they were content that it be Marshall. But they did object to the only formula that would have made the appointment wholly acceptable in the United States—that of giving Marshall overall command in the whole of Europe, north and south, while also leaving him formally in the position of U.S. Chief of Staff. Since no compromise was possible, Marshall did not get the job in either form.

If he had fought for it, perhaps Roosevelt would have defied either the British arguments or American public opinion. But Marshall would not lift a finger on his own behalf, and it may be that he had some inner doubts which reinforced his natural selflessness. He may have both longed for the opportunity and at the same time wondered if he was quite fit for it, granted that he lacked the experience, which Eisenhower now had, of commanding armies in the field.

In due course the new pattern of leadership took shape. The British General Maitland Wilson became supreme commander in the Mediterranean, with Alexander still commanding the Allied forces in Italy. For OVERLORD, Ike's deputy was to be the British airman Arthur Tedder (as in the Mediterranean), and three more Britons—Montgomery, Bertram Ramsay, and Trafford Leigh-Mallory—were to have, respectively, the land, sea, and tactical air commands for D-Day. The American Bedell Smith, however, was to remain Ike's chief of staff, an American was to command ANVIL, and it was obvious that, after D-Day, the Allied forces in France would soon become preponderantly American, if all went well.

Roosevelt gave Churchill the news that Marshall would not be commanding OVERLORD "almost casually," as they were driving out from Cairo to the Pyramids. He then said that he proposed instead to appoint Eisenhower, and Churchill replied that the British would trust their fortunes to his direction "with hearty goodwill."

On 6 December Churchill showed his "great friend" the Sphinx. The two men "gazed at her for some minutes in silence as the evening shadows fell." But she told them nothing and "maintained her inscrutable smile." The next day Roosevelt flew off, stopping on his way home to Washington at Tunis, in Malta, and in Sicily. He talked a lot to Eisenhower, who "felt complimented by the President's frankness and indications of complete confidence in him." Roosevelt warned him that in London he would be "surrounded by the majesty of the British Government and by the powerful personality of Winston Churchill."

In fact, Ike had to deal with that personality within a week, but in circumstances that suggested weakness rather than power. Churchill arrived at Tunis on the eleventh intending to stay one night with Ike before going on to Italy. But on arrival he admitted to feeling very tired and complained of a sore throat. Two days later Moran diagnosed pneumonia. In the event, he stayed at Ike's villa (again "the Man Who Came to Dinner") until after Christmas, when he moved to Marrakesh to complete his convalescence.

There was trouble with his heart as well as his chest, and he had to take digitalis. But his remarkable stamina was equal to the test and he pulled through. During the period of enforced quietness he continued to attend to war matters, though he also had *Pride and Prejudice* read to him by his daughter Sarah—surprisingly, his first reading of the book. And he later wrote: "What calm lives they had, those people! No worries about the French Revolution, or the crashing struggle of the Napoleonic wars. Only manners controlling natural passion so far as they could, together with cultured explanations of any mischances." Not a bad antidote to the after-effects of a meeting with Stalin.

At Marrakesh he must have recalled his visit there with Roosevelt at the beginning of the year. Now the President was all kindness to him from afar, agreeing to delay the departure of landing-craft from the Mediterranean, bound for OVERLORD, so that they could be used for the Anzio landing. And in a broadcast from Hyde Park he said that the "heartfelt prayers" of all Americans were with "this great citizen of the world."

In the same broadcast he spoke at greater length, and in at least equally fulsome terms, of Stalin. "He is a man who combines a tremendous, relentless determination with a stalwart good humour. I believe he is truly representative of the heart and soul of Russia; and I believe that we are going to get along very well with him and the Russian people—very well indeed."

PART THREE

QUESTIONS
AND ARGUMENTS

I. THE VICTORY THAT WAS

The Anglo-American invasion of France, promised at Teheran for 1 May 1944, eventually took place on 6 June. Nearly a year then passed before Germany surrendered, in May 1945. But after the Germans were defeated it was only another four months before Japan surrendered as well. In September 1945 the world war was over.

How did these events come about? Despite increased risks due to delay, the Allied landings in Normandy were on the whole a success and a firm bridgehead was swiftly established. It was wider than the COSSAC plan had envisaged, because Eisenhower and Montgomery had decided that the operation should be on a front of five rather than three divisions. Most of the landings were along the Normandy coast between the rivers Orne and Vire, but there was also an airborne drop east of the Orne, and combined airborne and seaborne landings north-west of the Vire, at the base of the Cotentin peninsula.

On all but one of the beaches—the American "Omaha"—the troops got ashore and moved some distance inland without a serious check. Even on "Omaha" the crisis lasted only from dawn until the early afternoon. On the eastern flank it had been hoped that Caen would be captured on the first day, but for various reasons the British 3rd division failed to reach it, and it was more than a month until it was finally taken. Bayeux, however, was liberated on D-Day, and above all the main spearheads of the invading army—British, Canadian, and American—had by evening broken through the German coastal defences, so that the Allies had French soil as well as sand under their feet.

This vital achievement cost them about 10,000 casualties, of whom about 2,500 were killed. All casualty lists are tragic, and the price that had to be paid for breaching Hitler's Atlantic Wall should not be underrated. Yet when we compare it with the 60,000 British casualties —20,000 of them killed—on the first day of the battle of the Somme in 1916, it seems almost miraculously cheap. We should note, too, that the human cost of securing a bridgehead in France was less than that of landing at Salerno and capturing Naples.

Having secured a bridgehead, the Allies had to make sure of building up their forces inside it more rapidly than the Germans could build up and concentrate their forces against it. In this, too, the Allies were successful, thanks largely to the fact that the whole power of their bomber fleets in Britain had been diverted, during the two months before D-Day, to the destruction of road and rail communications in northern France.

No victory in the entire war was more important than this one, scored by one group of Allied officers over another. A key figure was Tedder, deputy supreme commander under Ike—an R.A.F. officer whose philosophy of air power was different from that of Portal and Harris. He believed in the closest possible cooperation of land and air forces, and had learned from experience in the Mediterranean that the movement of enemy troops could be more or less interdicted by the accurate bombing of communications.

Even so, the Allies had their problems before they were able to break out of the bridgehead, partly because of the doggedness of German resistance, and partly because a freak storm which struck in the third week of June smashed one of their two artificial harbours ("Mulberries") and brought the unloading of supplies to a temporary halt. This was a bit above the odds after the storm which had caused D-Day itself to be postponed from the fifth to the sixth, and which had nearly led to its cancellation. The second storm not only hindered the Allies but gave the Germans a much-needed respite.

Before long, however, the respite had to end, because the Allies' power was inexorable. Montgomery first launched a tremendous attack on his left flank, on 18 July, which was intended to bring about a German collapse and so enable General Miles Dempsey's Anglo-Canadian army to drive ahead towards Paris. But when the attack was held it had the effect of helping General Omar N. Bradley's American forces to break through, a fortnight later, on the Allied right flank.

Montgomery deserves much credit for adapting his tactics to the changing fortunes of war in the bridgehead, and it is fair to say that the Battle of Normandy was the greatest and best victory of his career. But he later fostered a characteristic myth that it had gone entirely according to plan. He wanted posterity to believe that his big attack on the left flank had had no other purpose than to force the enemy to concentrate there, so that the Americans would have only light opposition when they attacked on the right. In fact, nothing in war ever goes entirely according to plan, and the victory that was won at the end of July resulted from frustration in the middle of the month.

Moreover, it has to be said that Monty then showed again the weakness in exploitation of victory which was his besetting fault as a commander. Since Hitler, as usual, would not permit the strategic withdrawal that the situation of his army desperately required, the Allies had an opportunity to annihilate the Germans in northern France. But the opportunity was thrown away.

One mistake was that when the Americans broke through at Avranches on 31 July, two armoured divisions were sent into Brittany instead of thrusting southwards and eastwards to encircle the Germans. Two weeks were wasted before the Americans were far enough east to be level with the British left wing. But it was still not too late to turn the victory into an absolute triumph, because Hitler had ordered a futile counterattack which made his army more rather than less vulnerable.

Unfortunately, many of the Germans trapped in the so-called Falaise pocket were allowed to escape, mainly because Monty did not move with sufficient energy and urgency to close it from the north. All the same, a very large amount of German equipment was lost, and after Falaise Hitler's defences in the West were in total disarray. Patton's Third U.S. Army reached the Seine ahead of the retreating Germans, crossed the Meuse on 31 August, and by 5 September was beginning to cross the Moselle.

Monty was perhaps stung, as he had been in Sicily, by the rapidity

197

of Patton's advance, because he suddenly became venturesome himself. Under his orders British troops liberated Brussels on 3 September and—with the indispensable help of a coolly heroic Belgian patriot, Robert Vekemans—captured the port of Antwerp intact the following day.

At this point the war seemed as good as won, and if the Allies had kept up the momentum of their advance, it almost certainly would have been won before the end of the year. The Ruhr was almost defenceless, and the scratch collection of troops mustered to protect it consisted of policemen, sailors, sixteen-year-old boys, and convalescent wounded, as well as paratroopers and a panzer detachment with only twenty-five tanks and self-propelled guns. On the whole Western Front the Germans had barely a hundred tanks, compared with more than two thousand in the advancing Allied armies, and fewer than six hundred aircraft compared with the Allies' fourteen thousand operating in the West.

But once again a moment of supreme advantage was lost. One reason was that there had been a month of indeterminate leadership since, at the beginning of August, Monty had become commander of the Anglo-Canadian 21st Army Group, while retaining a vague operational control over Bradley's U.S. 12th Army Group. It was not until the beginning of September that Ike assumed the overall battle command which it had always been understood he would assume as the campaign developed, with American forces preponderating. During the month between the break-out from the bridgehead and his assumption of command, there had been no proper direction or coordination of the Allied advance; and it was too much to expect that he would immediately grasp the full potential of a situation that he had hitherto been watching from afar.

In any case, he had the defects of his qualities. He was a superb staff officer who also had a genius, more political than military, for handling people and making an alliance work. The Germans were given a crucial fortnight in which to improvise a defensive line along their frontier, while Ike worked out a strategy designed to reconcile the claims of Monty and Patton—in other words, an international compromise. As a result, the enemy was spared the decisive blow that might have been inflicted.

Of course, there were other factors contributing to the winter stalemate that ensued. The failure of Monty's Arnhem operation in late September was not primarily due to the dissipation of Allied resources, but had its own independent causes. The tenacity of the German defence at either side of the mouth of the Scheldt denied the Allies the use of Antwerp until early November. This meant that the problem of supply was very acute in September and October, all the more so as the demands of the British, and particularly the American, forces were heavier than they need have been.

The Germans were helped by the Allied landing in the South of France (ANVIL), which, delayed until mid-August, was too late to have any bearing upon the struggle in Normandy, but which had the undesirable effect of pushing a German army that might have been trapped in France back into Germany. The arguments about ANVIL will be discussed in the next section, but meanwhile it can hardly be denied that, occurring when it did, the operation was of more obvious strategic benefit to the enemy than to the Allies.

By the end of 1944, France's liberation was complete, and for the last stage of the war the French military contribution was equivalent, on land, to Britain's in 1939–40. Though only a token number of Frenchmen took part in the D-Day landings, an armoured division under General Philippe Leclerc landed in Normandy on 1 August and had the just privilege of entering Paris on the twenty-fourth. A French corps landed in the South of France as part of the ANVIL operation, and soon there was a French army in the Allied line. Meanwhile, the French Forces of the Interior (F.F.I.), as the Resistance was now called, had been fighting, harassing, or capturing German troops which would otherwise have been a nuisance, not to say a menace, to the Allied command.

As metropolitan France was being freed from the Germans, de Gaulle was winning his last battles with Roosevelt to ensure that the dignity and independence of France would not go by default. It was Roosevelt's decision that the country be administered by Allied military government, with Eisenhower as the ultimate (and most unwilling) arbiter; and that the money put into circulation in liberated territory should be A.M.G.O.T. currency rather than French money issued by the Liberation Committee. (As an added insult, the A.M.G.O.T. notes contained a spelling mistake.)

Just before D-Day, de Gaulle came to England from Algiers and had a stormy meeting with Churchill on his special train near Portsmouth. When de Gaulle protested at what he saw as usurpation by the Anglo-Saxons, Churchill burst out furiously: "Each time I have to choose between you and Roosevelt, I shall always choose Roosevelt!" But Ernest Bevin, who witnessed the scene, took the General aside afterwards and told him that Churchill was speaking for himself and not in the name of the British Cabinet.

It soon became apparent that administration in France would only be acceptable, or even possible, through de Gaulle and his provisional government. By early July Roosevelt had relented and was welcoming the General in Washington with every mark of favour. Even Cordell Hull had to join in the reception. But (according to de Gaulle) the President also gave his guest a charming lecture outlining his projected future world order, in which France and other countries of Western Europe would become, in effect, dependencies of the United States.

De Gaulle naturally dissented in the loftiest terms, but Roosevelt, while perforce now recognising his authority inside France, was still determined to exclude him from Allied councils. As a result, the General was not invited to the Yalta conference in February 1945, at which decisions were taken vitally affecting the future of Europe. Roosevelt tried hard at Yalta to prevent France having a zone of occupation in Germany after the war, or a seat on the Allied control commission.

On this issue, however, Churchill strongly supported France, partly because Roosevelt had said that American troops would be withdrawn from Europe after two years, and it was therefore hard to see how the Western-occupied zone could then be manned without a French presence. Moreover, it was obvious that de Gaulle would refuse to share in the occupation unless he had a share in control. Roosevelt grudgingly agreed to lift his veto, and Stalin said that he would not object, provided the French zone were carved out of the area already allotted to the Western powers. At the same time, it was also agreed that France should be one of the five founding members of the United Nations.

Before returning to their own homeland, French troops had fought with great distinction in Italy, where 1944 was on the whole another frustrating year for the Allies. In the final battle for Rome, General Alphonse Juin's men scaled and stormed the supposedly impregnable peak called Petrella, while the ruins of Monte Cassino were eventually occupied by the Poles. But after the capture of Rome on 4 June, soon in any case overshadowed by the news of D-Day, the Germans were able to withdraw to a succession of strong lines, at the last of which —running from north of Florence to north of Rimini—they held the Allies throughout the winter 1944–5.

In April 1945 Alexander attacked again. By now Germany was collapsing, and for some time negotiations had been going on in Switzerland with a view to ending the war on the Italian Front. (For the Allies, the secret negotiator was the later well-known Allen W. Dulles.) Partisans rose against the Fascist puppet regime in north Italy, and on 28 April Mussolini and his mistress were killed by a band of them. Allied forces were meanwhile crossing the Po valley, and had reached Trieste by 2 May, when the Germans in Italy surrendered unconditionally—six days ahead of the main German surrender.

The last phase of the war on the Western Front began with the Germans' winter counter-offensive in the Ardennes, which achieved surprise and some temporary success, but was checked before it could threaten the Allies with anything like disaster. Its failure left the enemy with no reserves and no prospects. When Eisenhower resumed the offensive in February, there was little to be done to stop it.

Early in March a Rhine bridge was captured. By mid-April the Ruhr was surrounded, and soon all the Germans there surrendered. At about the same time the Russians entered Vienna. In the last week of April Berlin was isolated, Russian and American forces met on the Elbe, and even Hitler could see that the game was up. On the thirtieth he committed suicide in his Berlin bunker, with Eva Braun, whom he had just formally married. In his will he designated Grand Admiral Dönitz as his successor.

On 8 May the war in Europe came to an end in accordance with a surrender document, covering all German forces, signed the previous day at Eisenhower's headquarters. Roosevelt was not alive to witness the fulfilment of his "beat Hitler first" policy. He had died on 12 April, at Warm Springs, Georgia.

Japan was defeated by a combination of sea and air power; specifically, by the sea and air power of the United States. Military forces had the tough but subsidiary role of securing island bases for the ships —particularly submarines—and for the aircraft, whose joint role was decisive.

Like Britain, Japan was dependent for survival upon seaborne raw materials. But, unlike Britain even before American entry into the war, she did not have the help and backing of a country which was both a major source of raw materials and a major industrial power. On the contrary, that country was her enemy.

Once it was clear that the United States had not been shocked by Pearl Harbor into withdrawal from the western Pacific, the outcome of the war could hardly be in doubt. Once American naval superiority there was established, it was a foregone conclusion. The Japanese were beaten by the same method that had provoked them into war— economic strangulation.

When they attacked at the end of 1941, their merchant marine, which was their life-line, was less than one-third the size of Britain's in 1939. But whereas Britain was helped by America to fight the U-boats and to replace lost tonnage, the Japanese had no such assistance. They had to rely on their own efforts. By the end of 1944, their merchant fleet was virtually eliminated, and it could only be a matter of time before they were compelled either to surrender or to commit collective hara-kiri.

On the face of it, their collapse was brought about by area bombing, culminating in the supreme act of area bombing—the destruction of Hiroshima and Nagasaki by atom bombs. But their vulnerability to air attack was merely a symptom of the true cause of their defeat, which was their lack of the means to live and fight. In 1945 American Superfortresses could raid Japan more or less with impunity, because the Japanese no longer had enough oil to train pilots.

Before the atom bombs were dropped, the Japanese war economy had almost ceased to function. Oil-refining had declined by 83 per cent, aircraft-engine production by 75 per cent, airframe production by 60 per cent, production of electronics equipment by 70 per cent. In such circumstances, terror bombing was redundant as well as odious; but unfortunately it was practised with a vengeance.

Again before the atomic raids, the devastation and loss of life from "conventional" bombing were on a horrifying scale. A single Superfortress raid on Tokyo—on 9 March 1945—caused 185,000 civilian casualties and destroyed nearly 270,000 dwellings. The absence of defence may be judged from the fact that only fourteen of the attacking aircraft were lost.

As early as February the Japanese were trying to sue for peace, but they made the mistake of using Russia's "good offices" as a neutral to make their desire known to the Allies. Stalin, of course, had no interest in peace until he had had time to declare war on the Japanese, so he did not pass their messages on. It was three months before the Americans had any idea that the Japanese wanted peace, but then there was a further delay, partly because of the unconditional surrender formula, and partly—it must be said—because important people in the United States wished to drop the atom bomb.

Hiroshima was struck on 6 August. On the eighth Russia declared war and invaded Manchuria. Emperor Hirohito favoured peace at any price, but his Cabinet would not agree to surrender unless his sovereignty was respected. This was all the more remarkable, since the Cabinet was wholly committed to peace. The war government of General Tojo had fallen in July of the previous year, to be replaced by a more moderate one under General Kuniaki Koiso; but this in turn had given way, in April 1945, to an even more peace-orientated government under Admiral Suzuki.

Even when their position was utterly hopeless, and after they had had two atom bombs dropped on them, the Japanese would not surrender unconditionally. They were determined to maintain the monarchy, which was the key to their national identity and philosophy of life. Repugnant though such an attitude must have been to the Americans, they had to accept it. The alternative would have been a fight to the finish, in which the victors as well would have had to pay a heavy price.

On 2 September Japanese representatives signed an instrument of surrender on the United States battleship *Missouri* in Tokyo Bay. In effect, it was a conditional surrender, because the essential condition had been agreed to in advance. On 12 September Mountbatten received, at Singapore, the capitulation of all Japanese forces in Southeast Asia. (In the last stages of the war Burma had been reconquered

—from the British point of view a Pyrrhic victory, because that country soon became independent and left the Commonwealth.)

So the world war ended, and at least there could be no question who had *lost* it. Hitler and Mussolini were dead, and their regimes obliterated. The Japanese Emperor survived and continued to reign, but the Japanese empire was reduced to the islands of Japan, and even there some sacrifice of territory was exacted by the Russians. The Allies had, therefore, won the war in the sense that their enemies had been comprehensively defeated.

But had they won in a more positive sense? The British had preserved their liberty, but not much else. In most respects they emerged from the war weakened and diminished. The same was far more obviously true of France, but because it was more obvious it may, in the long run, have been less demoralising. Britain's prestige concealed a grave loss of power and fortune, and concealed it most disastrously from the British themselves.

No country, victor or vanquished, suffered greater material or human losses than the Soviet Union. Yet at the end of the war it was more advantageously placed than at any time since the Revolution. Many traditional aims of Russian foreign policy were either realised or on the way to being realised. The Red Army was flushed with triumph and in that state less likely than ever to turn against the regime. The Russian people were still slaves, but—like the Germans in 1940—slaves on the winning side.

Of all the belligerents, the Americans seemed to have done best out of the war. It had brought them from isolation to a state of world ascendancy, which was imperial in character if not in intent. Their economy was booming, and so was their self-confidence. They could see that the British era had passed and that their own had begun.

Yet even for them victory was soon to prove disillusioning. While seeking an enhancement of their own country's position, they had genuinely sought to liberate and improve the lot of others. But what had happened, in Europe at any rate? In the words of Chester Wilmot, "The Western democracies, for all their sacrifices, had succeeded in rolling back the tide of totalitarianism only from the Rhine to the Elbe."

II. THE WILMOT THESIS

The book by Chester Wilmot, from which the above words are quoted, is *The Struggle for Europe,* one of the outstanding works on the Second World War. It was published in 1952, both influenced by, and an influence on, the Cold War. Apart from its admirable narrative (Wilmot was an ace war correspondent) it expounds a controversial thesis, which seems, more than a quarter of a century later, to be partly sound but also partly misleading.

The book is in three parts. In the first, entitled "The Way Back," Wilmot considers the period from Dunkirk to D-Day, looking at the argument about a Second Front, "not merely in the light of its influence on the defeat of Germany, but also as a political issue the outcome of which was that Anglo-American military power was employed in Western Europe, not in the Balkans." So far as 1943 is concerned, the argument is not very fully or satisfactorily developed. Much is taken for granted that should be examined with rigour.

The second part, "The Battle of Normandy," consists largely of straight military history, but the third, "The Road to Berlin," is highly polemical and contains the core of the Wilmot thesis. The American insistence on operation ANVIL is subjected to a powerful critique, and much is made of the opportunities that were, allegedly, missed as a result of that insistence. The author also maintains that Berlin, Prague, and Vienna could, and should, have been captured by the Western Allies rather than by the Russians. Had they been, the outcome of the war would, in his belief, have been very much more favourable to the cause of democracy.

The case against ANVIL, as and when the operation was eventually carried out, is indeed strong. The original idea had been that it should be mounted either before, or to coincide with, OVERLORD. This was a good idea, which was abandoned for a variety of bad reasons. One was the late appointment of the supreme commander for OVERLORD; another that Ike was reluctant to disappoint Alexander, with whom he had been working closely in the Mediterranean theatre. But the main reason was that there were not enough landing-craft in Europe for the simultaneous launching of ANVIL and OVERLORD (on the wider front required by Ike and

Monty). As a result, ANVIL was postponed, at first indefinitely.

This encouraged Alexander, Churchill, and others to assume that it was off, and to plan for ambitious use of the existing forces in Italy. But Marshall was dead against such plans, and after the landing in France Ike felt the need for Marseilles as a port of access while the Atlantic and Channel ports were unserviceable. Moreover, de Gaulle was adamant that the four French divisions in Italy must be sent to France.

On the other hand, landing in the South of France on 15 August was unsound in relation to the general course of operations, and definitely harmful in its strategic effects. On balance, it may have been inescapable, but it was most unfortunate that ANVIL did not occur at the time originally planned, when its benefits would have been far greater and the countervailing drawbacks absent.

In Wilmot's view, however, the most serious drawback was that Alexander was denied the chance to launch another big offensive in Italy, in the hope not only of breaking through to the Po valley but of then pressing on through the Ljubljana Gap into Austria. This seems now, as it seemed to many at the time, optimistic to the point of fantasy. The record of Allied progress in Italy, before seven divisions were switched to the South of France, does not suggest that, even with his strength undiminished, Alexander would have broken the German mountain defences in the "thigh" of Italy with anything like the speed that he anticipated; still less that he would have been able to win the war by a mortal thrust at Germany from the south.

The objections to this strategy were military, not political. After all, Roosevelt had put forward a rather similar idea at Teheran, but it never had any support from his service advisers and would probably have been scotched by them even if Stalin had welcomed it. Incidentally, Wilmot somewhat exaggerates Churchill's political motive for espousing such a strategy at the time. He was still more interested in winning the actual war than in taking up positions of advantage for what would become the Cold War.

Beating the Russians to Berlin, Prague, and Vienna would have been possible in 1945—of that there can be no serious doubt. Ike clearly saw that he would be able to reach Berlin first, but reported that he would not do so without explicit orders from on high. It was not a worth-while military objective, but if its capture was thought desirable on political grounds, then the politicians must decide.

Churchill certainly favoured taking Berlin, because he felt that allowing the Russians to occupy it would give them a psychological advantage. But was he right? Would it really have made any difference if the Allies had got there first? What was the magic of capital cities, when the control of countries had already been virtually settled at Yalta, and was anyway determined by the plain facts of power?

Inescapably the Russians *had* a psychological advantage. Long before the Western Allies had opened a comparable front in Europe, they had held the Germans and started to drive them back. Their sacrifices were on a scale that made those of Britain and America seem paltry. Huge tracts of their country had been overrun and devastated. Seven and a half million of their soldiers, and about fifteen million civilians, had been killed. It was only natural to sympathise with their craving for security, and to interpret as such Stalin's demand for physical control in Eastern Europe.

Nor was this interpretation quite so false as it was later made out to be, in the cruder anti-Soviet demonology of the Cold War. Stalin was a savage tyrant whose conversion to Western liberal values only the most naïve could hope for. But his foreign policy had never been reckless. He was not, like Hitler, a gambler or an adventurer.

Stalin's prime concern during the last stages of the war was, no doubt, to protect his immense, stricken, and still largely undeveloped empire against any future threats. But when he found that the Western leaders were rather muddled and not exactly of one mind about the postwar world—more especially about postwar Europe—he did not forbear to exploit the situation. Above all, when Roosevelt said that American forces would be unlikely to stay in Europe for more than two years after the war, it must have seemed to Stalin that he was being given a licence to dominate the Continent.

Churchill saw the impending dangers more clearly than Roosevelt, but his opposition to Stalin was less principled and resolute than many later came to believe. He did not stand firmly on national self-determination or on democratic right. He favoured the division of Germany, though on rather absurd lines, and with a view of the German problem that was less shrewd than Stalin's. He also admitted the necessity for Great Power spheres of influence.

What distressed him most at Teheran and Yalta was that his own power was not as great as he would have liked it to be, and that Roosevelt was playing the Western hand, often without reference to him. But he, too, believed in doing business with, and in making substantial concessions to, Stalin. During the period that Wilmot considers, the difference between him and Roosevelt as appeasers of Russia was only one of degree.

Western public opinion at the time was so pro-Russian that politicians would have had to take account of it, even if they had not also to a greater or lesser extent shared it. Russian gallantry was so admired, and had been so relentlessly extolled, while the nature of the Soviet regime and of Russian state policy had been so played down, that it would have been quite impossible to introduce the "Iron Curtain" motif suddenly before the end of the war. Faced with such a volte-face in propaganda, people would have been at first bewildered, then indignant.

It is illogical to assume that the Russians' hegemony in Eastern Europe, and in Czechoslovakia, derives simply from their prior occupation of the various capitals in 1945. After all, they voluntarily withdrew from Vienna ten years later, when Austria became an independent, though neutral, state. The politics of the Cold War have been more complicated than anyone could deduce from reading Cold War polemics. This is not the place to discuss the Cold War, but it has to be said that judgments on what Western statesmen did, and did not do, to check the Russians in 1944–5 are necessarily distorted if they are made in the light of postwar changes in policy and propaganda.

By no means all of Wilmot's criticisms are anachronistic in this sense. He is surely right to deplore the policy of unconditional surrender, which was gratuitously thrown out by Roosevelt in one of what Marshall called his "cigarette-holder gestures." There was no compelling need for it, and Churchill was never really happy about it, though he made too little effort to prevent its ill-considered proclamation at Casablanca.

Admittedly, it did not deter anti-Hitler officers from trying to kill the Führer in July 1944, and it may well be that after the failure of their assassination attempt no further move against him was possible. His survival seemed an act of Providence, justifying his mystical claim to loyalty and obedience from the German people. Moreover, his aroused suspicions led to an intensification of the terror by which he was able to maintain his rule. All the same, his enemies would almost certainly have been far more numerous in 1943 and 1944 but for the sense of isolation and hopelessness that the unconditional surrender demand induced. It was most dangerous to give the Germans, of all people, apparently no choice save that between a fight to the death and national dishonour.

Yet Wilmot is on weaker ground in arguing that, without "unconditional surrender," Hitler would not have made what turned out to be his last gamble—the Ardennes offensive—against the West. Even if this operation did, in fact, enable the Russians to advance from the Vistula to the Oder, it must be obvious that the Western Allies could never have offered terms to Hitler. And, for all his powers of self-delusion, it is hard to believe that even he could have imagined that they would have been prepared to negotiate with *him*.

The fundamental flaw in the Wilmot thesis is that it deals mainly with the last year of the war in Europe, when the Russians had already progressed so far that—quite apart from political and psychological factors—the Western Allies' chances of meeting them, say, on the Vistula rather than on the Elbe left no margin for error. Though it is certainly very arguable that there were errors of strategy after the break-out from Normandy, without which the war might have been won before the end of 1944, it is a truism that in war such errors are always liable to occur.

The only way that the Western Allies could have given themselves a good chance of occupying Europe ahead of the Russians, allowing for the normal quota of mistakes, and without having to act with indecent haste, was by landing in France in 1943 rather than in 1944. But Wilmot does not address himself to that question. Like others before and since, he takes the case against 1943 for granted.

It should be said at once that the case *for* it does not rest primarily upon *ex post facto* Cold War considerations. There are strong military arguments in its favour, relating to the war that was actually being fought. But above all, it must now seem that an earlier end to the war would have been a godsend on elementary human grounds. War is at all times such a ghastly process, and what happened in Europe during the last phase of the Second World War so peculiarly ghastly, that victory a year or more earlier would have been an immeasurable good in itself.

III. "IMPOSSIBLE TO LAND IN 1943"

But would it have been possible to carry out a cross-Channel invasion in 1943? Few historical questions have been answered more generally or more confidently in the negative. Even Basil Liddell Hart, least conventional of military historians, has on this issue endorsed the conventional wisdom. Recording, in his account of the Second World War, the view of the British Chiefs of Staff that any attempt at a direct attack across the Channel in 1943 would end in disaster or futility, he adds that their estimate "will hardly be questioned in historical retrospect."

So far, indeed, it hardly *has* been questioned. But why, it is not very easy to understand. Although there has been a good deal of peripheral revisionism about the war, the central strategic issue has mysteriously escaped re-examination. Those responsible for what may be termed the Casablanca strategy have had things almost entirely their own way.

The chief reason for this may be that most people in the West were broadly satisfied with the outcome of the war, and felt that it had been conducted with less disregard for human life than the monstrous struggle on the Western Front in 1914–18. There will always be recriminations in defeat, and there may also be recriminations when victory seems to have been obtained at too heavy a price. But in Britain and the United States there has been a general acceptance of the view that the West's victory in Europe in the Second World War was relatively economical.

So it was, by comparison with the First World War—at any rate for the troops. But it does not follow that a quicker victory would have been any less economical; it might well have been more so. And of course it would have saved an incalculable number of civilian lives on the Continent, where every month added to the war was a cruel affliction.

It might have been thought that the Americans, who were such strong exponents of an earlier cross-Channel strategy during the war, would have kept the argument alive subsequently. But, in fact, they have tended to be somewhat muted on the issue, complaining of British obsession with the Mediterranean without putting forward a coherent alternative. This reflects the fatalism that overtook Marshall himself after he had lost the battle for a cross-Channel operation in 1942 and had reluctantly agreed to TORCH.

American writers on the war have been rather too prone to accept Marshall's view that TORCH started a process that was irreversible. The six months' campaign against the Germans in Tunisia (whose position there was hopeless anyway), and the eventual decision to fight in Italy, were not necessary consequences of the landings in North Africa. The objections to becoming too deeply committed in the Mediterranean were not pressed home at the time, and have since been only half-heartedly stated by historians.

The truth is that, after TORCH, many leading Americans had a vested interest in the Mediterranean—including Eisenhower, until he was appointed to OVERLORD. It was not only the British who saw gleaming opportunities in that theatre, or who tried to get resources deflected to it. By 1943, therefore, the original difference between Americans and British on the basic issue of European strategy had become considerably blurred. And it has remained blurred ever since.

It is also true that interpretations of the war such as Chester Wilmot's have not been without influence in the United States. The rather facile and spurious connection between more far-reaching campaigns in the Mediterranean and more effective resistance to the Soviet Union has appealed to Cold Warriors in America as elsewhere. Some who now condemn Roosevelt's foreign policy during the war, and impute superior wisdom to Churchill, are apt to make similar judgments about strategy.

In fact, Churchill's views on political and strategic issues have been much over-simplified, particularly his views on the question of a cross-Channel attack. He was, to be sure, immovably (and rightly) opposed to any large-scale operation of the kind *in 1942*. This would have had to be carried out mainly by British troops, since the Americans could not be ready in sufficient numbers, and Churchill was determined not to squander British lives in an enterprise which, he believed, had no conceivable chance of success.

But his original attitude towards landing in 1943 was, as we have seen, very different. He more or less promised Stalin at their last meeting in Moscow the previous August that a Second Front (as

Stalin understood the term) would be opened in 1943. Throughout the autumn and early winter of 1942, he continued to press the British Chiefs of Staff to prepare for a cross-Channel attack in 1943, and on the eve of the Casablanca conference he was still talking of a "preliminary" invasion that year.

Unfortunately, he wanted to do exciting things in the Mediterranean as well, and was therefore outmanoeuvred by Brooke, whose aims were less diffuse. Brooke's mind was set against any cross-Channel operation in 1943, and in favour of unlimited activity in the Mediterranean. He persuaded Churchill before the conference that the immediate priorities should be clearing the whole North African shore and capturing Sicily. Though Churchill did not realise it at the time, this meant—and Brooke meant it to mean—that there would be no cross-Channel attack until 1944 at the earliest.

By degrees Churchill came to share Brooke's Mediterranean infatuation, including his belief that Turkey could be brought into the war. And, being Churchill, he was able to make a bad strategy more plausible than it would otherwise have been, to posterity as well as to contemporaries, by giving it the benefit of his eloquence and imagination. TORCH was a brilliant (though perilous) concept, and it was unquestionably his own. Most later Mediterranean plans were his only at one remove, and their brilliance consisted in his advocacy rather than in the plans themselves.

The postwar belief that a potentially war-winning—and peace-winning—Churchillian strategy in the Mediterranean was frustrated by American blindness and obstinacy was flattering to British self-esteem at a time when more substantial grounds for it were being undermined. But in fact such a strategy could never have won the war, could never have changed the face of Europe after the war, and was not in origin Churchillian.

Both for winning the war, and for being well placed after the war, there was *far* more to be said for landing in north-west Europe than on any part of the Continent's southern littoral. Geography and logistics alike favoured the north rather than the south. The Mediterranean coast of Europe is naturally "hard"; its northern coast, from France to Denmark, naturally "soft." Fighting in the Mediterranean involved for the Allies extremely long communications, for the Germans much shorter ones. On the other hand, a landing in France would, anyway at first, have stretched the Germans more than it would have stretched the Allies.

Above all, it offered the prospect of liberating the largest and most important of enemy-occupied countries, at whose side Britain had entered the war. It would have denied to the Germans the territory from which they had been inflicting, and could still inflict, most damage on Britain—particularly by their U-boats based in French ports—while at the same time bringing a great democratic nation back into the war. It would have enabled the Western Allies to win decisive victory by the shortest route, in the shortest time, and over the widest area of Europe.

For a successful landing in France there were four vital pre-conditions. There had to be overwhelming air superiority for the Allies. (Naval supremacy in the Channel could be taken for granted.) There had to be enough Allied troops in Britain to establish a bridgehead and for the subsequent build-up. There had to be the technical means to transport them. Finally, the enemy had to be prevented from concentrating his forces against the bridgehead before the Allied position there could be secured. All these pre-conditions either existed, or could have been made to exist, in 1943.

The Allies already had the potential of total command of the air over northern France. Despite the incorrect and wasteful use to which Allied air power was actually being put, and the failure to achieve the right balance in aircraft production, the means could undoubtedly have been found for the required alternative strategy. In other words, it should have been possible in 1943, as in 1944, for Allied aircraft based in Britain to smash enemy communications in northern France before D-Day, to provide a tremendous bombardment of enemy positions just before the landings, and thereafter to dominate the sky above the battle zone, destroying any German aircraft that tried to interfere.

By 1943 there was no shortage of Allied troops, trained and ready for combat. While the bulk of the German Army was committed in the desperate struggle on the Eastern Front, British and American forces in the West were bound to outnumber whatever German forces could be spared to oppose them. The American Army alone had grown from a strength of 1,686,000 men (37 divisions and 67 air combat groups) at the end of 1941, to 5,397,000 men (73 divisions and

167 air combat groups) at the end of 1942. As for the British, in March 1943 there were 16 divisions in the United Kingdom, ostensibly being got ready for a cross-Channel attack in August, and 11 other home-based divisions. In the rest of the world there was a total of 38 divisions under British command.

Eisenhower's eventual revision of the COSSAC plan for OVER-LORD required the landing of eight divisions by sea and air on D-Day itself, and a build-up to reach thirty divisions by $D+35$, with more reinforcements to follow. If the available Allied troops had been properly distributed, or rather concentrated, in 1943, there should certainly have been enough of them in Britain to carry out the invasion, without detriment to necessary tasks, as distinct from superfluous "sideshows," elsewhere.

Of course it is true that some of the ingenious technical aids to landing and supplying the invasion force were not produced until 1944. But there is every reason to suppose that they could and would have been produced a year earlier if the Allied leaders had decided that the invasion was to take place then, putting all their authority behind it and instilling into all concerned a due sense of urgency. Instead, the Casablanca decisions, without explicitly excluding cross-Channel action in 1943, excluded it in effect by giving it only a low and dubious status in the year's agenda.

So the opening of a true Second Front, rightly delayed in 1942, was (it would seem) wrongly delayed in 1943, with many tragic results and at the risk of disaster to the Allied cause. A whole mythology has been evolved to justify the delay, and the more prominent myths will now be examined in detail.

IV. "ATLANTIC WALL TOO STRONG"

One favourite argument is that Hitler's system of coastal defence in northern Europe—the so-called Atlantic Wall—was so formidable that any attempt to breach it before 1944 would have been suicidal lunacy. In support of this view it is often alleged that the Dieppe raid in August 1942 proved the impossibility of landing an army on the north coast of France the following year.

In fact, it proved nothing of the sort. Crazy operations prove only that crazy operations should be avoided. The Dieppe raid was an isolated fiasco, which had about as much general significance as the Charge of the Light Brigade.

Before it, there had been a number of successful commando raids on the coast of France, among which those on Saint-Nazaire and Bruneval stand out. But the Dieppe raid attempted the impossible. It was planned as a reconnaissance in force, to see if an enemy port could be captured and held for a limited time. The planning was confused by changes of command and based on defective intelligence. In its final form, the operation was doomed to failure, and nearly half of the five thousand Canadians who took part in it did not return. The total German casualties were six hundred.

Dieppe was far more than a commando raid, though commandos were involved. At first the responsibility of Combined Operations, it was transferred to Home Forces, and this resulted in a most unfortunate change of plan. Mountbatten (who, as we have seen, was sent by Churchill on a mission to America at a crucial stage in the planning) intended that Dieppe should be taken by a pincer movement on either side of the town, rather than by frontal assault. Home Forces decided that it should be attacked frontally, with tanks landing on a beach of loose shingle—where their tracks could not gain a hold, and where in the event they were all knocked out.

To complete the folly, it was decided that there should be no preliminary bombardment. The wonder is, not that the raid failed, but that any of the attackers survived it. Lord Lovat, a distinguished participant, has written this post-mortem comment:

In battle, the right things often happen for the wrong reasons—but not when a plan is basically unsound. Was Dieppe a worthwhile effort? It is difficult to think so. There were no military objectives to justify landing a division in France, and why use tanks and why attack in daylight? Heavy bombers could have destroyed the batteries, harbour facilities and most of the shipping, and hit the radar stations and airfields behind the town. These were the only targets of any significance . . .

He concludes: "It was a bad plan, and it had no chance of success."

The practical lessons learned from Dieppe were that it would be unwise to try to seize a harbour on D-Day, prudent to develop a ready-made harbour in case no captured harbour could be put in working order for some time after D-Day, preferable to land on open beaches than in a built-up area, necessary to have good intelligence of the area where the landings were to take place, and essential to precede the attack with a heavy bombardment. These lessons could have been learned at much less cost, and could have been applied no less effectively in 1943 than in 1944.

Dieppe was a particularly well-fortified point in the Atlantic Wall, but there can be little doubt that it would have been captured if there had been some softening-up of the defences in advance, and if the method of attack had been indirect rather than head-on. Commandos who landed a few miles west of the town were able to get ashore and carry out their mission successfully. The raid in no way proved that the Atlantic Wall was impenetrable in 1942, and of course it can tell us nothing about the Wall's relative strength in 1943 and 1944.

As a matter of fact, the Wall was much stronger when the invasion occurred than it was the year before. In October 1943 Field Marshal Karl von Rundstedt, German commander-in-chief in the West, reported to Hitler that "the so-called Wall" had "no depth and little surface." It was no more than a weak cord, as it were, connecting a succession of knots, which were the fortresses. But even the fortresses were of "insignificant" value, because they were unable to defend themselves against a land attack. (The same—he might have mentioned, if he knew it—had been true of Singapore.)

In the first half of January 1944 General Alfred Jodl, chief of the German Operations Staff, visited the area between the Scheldt and the Seine, and reported on the state of the defences. One consequence of his visit was that the most important harbours on the Channel and Atlantic coasts were provided with concrete fortifications on the land-ward side. As a result, many of these places were able to hold out for months after the invasion in 1944, and very seriously complicated the Allies' supply problem. If the invasion had occurred in 1943, they would have been far more vulnerable and would, in all probability, have been captured more quickly.

But what of the "cord" between the "knots"? In Rundstedt's view, there was no hope of preventing an Allied landing or the establishment of a bridgehead. With two thousand miles of coastline to defend, it was impossible to man and fortify every part of it to a degree of solidity that would resist the impact of the Allies' initial assault at their chosen spot. The only chance of defeating them was to have a sufficiently powerful reserve which could be thrown against the bridgehead before they had time to expand it.

This, however, was not at all the view of Rommel, to whom, in the winter of 1943–4, Hitler turned to make his Fortress Europe able to withstand the threatened invasion from the west. At first Rommel's post was merely that of inspector-general of fortifications, but in January 1944 he was appointed to command Army Group B, which comprised all German troops in Holland, Belgium, and France north of the Loire. Though in theory Rundstedt's subordinate, in fact he became the man responsible for preparing against, and in due course repulsing, the Allied attack.

Rommel dissented from Rundstedt's view because he was convinced—and events were soon to prove him right—that Allied air superiority was such that it would be impossible to concentrate reserve forces in time to prevent the expansion of a bridgehead once established. If the Allies were to be stopped, they had to be stopped *on the beaches.* It was, therefore, vital to put in hand a crash programme to strengthen the defences of the whole coastline. A mass of obstacles, mines, and booby-traps had to be placed along the northern coast, both on the beaches and under the water. Only thus, he believed, could the Allies be defeated.

His attitude naturally appealed to Hitler, whose instinct was always to stand firm and not to yield an inch. So Rommel had his way, and in Normandy alone he planted, along 240 kilometres of beach, about 200,000 obstacles, behind which he laid two million mines. In open areas immediately behind the coast there were posts tipped with shells that could be set off by trip-wires. Low-lying areas were flooded.

It was Rommel's aim to destroy a large proportion of Allied landing-craft before they could reach the shore, and then to destroy any forces that were able to land before they could penetrate beyond the beaches. "The highwater line," he said, "must be the main fighting line." Americans who landed on "Omaha" beach had most reason to appreciate the significance of his words.

Fortunately, the German defences, even in 1944, were not of equal density the whole length of the coast. Rommel had too little time to give effect to his ideas, and there were many competing claims upon the available labour. Moreover, the Allies were well informed about what he was doing, and had good equipment for dealing with his various devices. Yet it must be obvious that the Wall was, materially, much tougher in 1944 than in 1943.

So far as manpower was concerned, there was little difference. In the summer of 1943 the Germans had forty-nine divisions in the West (excluding Italy); on D-Day they had fifty-seven divisions. On the face of it, therefore, they had more men to face the invasion in 1944 than they would have had the year before. But this cannot be assumed, because as the war went on the strength of German divisions was progressively reduced.

Even in 1943, however, the average strength of a German division was, in reality, little more than half what it should have been. It is fair to say that the balance of manpower would have been no more unfavourable—or rather, no less favourable—to the Allies if they had landed in France a year earlier than they did.

V. "NOT ENOUGH LANDING-CRAFT"

Apologists for the delayed invasion have made much of the alleged shortage of landing-craft in 1943. It would simply not have been possible, they say, to transport such a large army to France, with all the necessary supplies and accoutrements, at any time before 1944. Only then did the Allies have the necessary number of ships.

This argument ignores one particularly awkward fact—that the armada which set sail for Sicily in July 1943 was *larger* than that which set sail for Normandy in June 1944. The trouble, surely, was not that the landing-craft did not exist in Europe but that they were in the wrong place. If the invasion of Sicily had either taken place earlier, or had been given a less high priority at Casablanca, there could have been quite enough landing-craft in Britain by the summer of 1943.

In the event, there was a landing-craft crisis even in 1944, partly because there was a muddle about moving some from the Mediterranean—this was why D-Day had to be postponed from May to June —but above all because there were too few in Europe as a whole. It was not that the Allies suffered from any general shortage of these vessels, but that a disproportionate number of them were in the Pacific theatre.

The statistics are hard to believe, when we remember that it was supposed to be Allied policy to beat Hitler first. In May 1944 the U.S. Navy had more than 31,000 landing-craft at its disposal. But of these fewer than 2,500 were allocated to OVERLORD. At the second Cairo conference it was decided that two-thirds of the landing-craft, as well as all the warships, for OVERLORD should be provided by Britain, the British Dominions, and the European Allies; and towards the end of 1943 the U.S. Navy actually transferred some landing-craft from the Mediterranean to the Pacific.

Why was this preposterous situation allowed to develop? British lack of enthusiasm for a cross-Channel attack was undoubtedly one reason, though of course not the only one. As soon as it was realised that operations in Europe in 1943 would not be of a kind to win the war against Hitler, the pull of the Pacific became irresistible. In September 1942 Dill sent a warning to London that heavy cuts were contemplated in the shipments of landing-craft to Britain, and by the end of 1942 the U.S. Army was engaged in the Pacific on a scale far exceeding anything that had been intended. Granted the nature of warfare in that theatre, big military operations there could only mean a big landing-craft requirement.

Along with the switch from Europe to the Pacific, production of landing-craft in the United States was scaled down when it became apparent that there would be no cross-Channel invasion until 1944. From having been top in the order of priorities, landing-craft dropped to twelfth place as soon as ROUND-UP was abandoned in favour of TORCH.

These facts all point to the same conclusion—that if there had been a firm resolve to invade north-west Europe in 1943, landing-craft would have been available for the operation in abundance.

VI. "TECHNICAL RESOURCES INADEQUATE"

Laymen are easily baffled by science, and in the controversy about dates for D-Day there has been much invocation of technical mysteries. But when the matter is looked into carefully, there seems to be no basis for the claim that, until 1944, the Allies would have been incapable of achieving what they eventually did achieve in the Normandy landings.

It is no argument to say that, because no "Mulberry" harbour, for instance, was produced in 1943, therefore it would have been impossible to produce such a harbour in time for an invasion that year. The only relevant questions are: (1) Had anybody thought of the idea? (2) Could the necessary development and experimentation have been carried out in time? (3) Did the means of manufacture exist? The answer to all three questions is, emphatically, yes.

A brief summary of the "Mulberry" saga should explain why. It was Churchill who first had the idea for an artificial harbour of this sort. He put it forward when advocating a plan to occupy the Frisian Islands in *July 1917*. So it can hardly be suggested that the originating spark was too recent to permit implementation of the idea by 1943.

Eisenhower reports that it first came to his notice in the spring of 1942, when Mountbatten, then head of Combined Operations, told a conference of service chiefs: "If ports are not available, we may have to construct them in pieces and tow them in." According to Ike, this remark was greeted with hoots and jeers.

But Mountbatten was not discouraged, and in the summer of 1942 a study was made under his auspices, which in turn led to small-scale experiments to find a means of reducing the height of waves within a given space. By trial and error it was found that the best way was to sink old and obsolete ships filled with concrete, to create a breakwater. Another essential ingredient of "Mulberry" was suggested to Mountbatten by Churchill, in a note dated 30 May 1942:

Piers for use on beaches.

They must float up and down with the tide. The anchor problem must be mastered. Let me have the best solution worked out. The difficulties will argue for themselves.

The best solution proved to be what came to be known as the "Spud Pier."

Things were not moving very fast, however, for the simple reason that there was no agreement among the Allied leaders to invade the Continent from Britain at an early date. Mountbatten could see that the provision of artificial harbours would not be pursued as a matter of high priority unless and until a date for invasion was agreed on and firm requirements were stated. At the Quebec conference in August 1943 such agreement was at last reached, and it was then decided that two "Mulberries" should be built, one for the British sector, one for the American.

Both were duly built in time for OVERLORD, and the British one, which was put together at Arromanches, proved of inestimable value. (The American one at "Omaha," which seems to have been less efficiently assembled, succumbed to the storm that hit the Normandy coast in the third week of June.) In all, 47,000 vehicles, 223,500 men, and nearly 544,000 tons of stores were landed by means of "Mulberry" between D-Day and the end of October.

Nobody would dispute the vital importance of this remarkable technical device. Without it, OVERLORD would almost certainly not have succeeded. But the evidence surely suggests that it was produced in 1944, not because there was any insuperable difficulty about producing it in 1943, but because there was *no pressure* to produce it then.

The same could be said of many other inventions, gadgets, and tricks that were brought into play for OVERLORD. Their development was no valid excuse for delaying the invasion, but was, on the contrary, itself held up by the delay. If the political and strategic decision had been taken sooner, the technical aids would have been evolved more swiftly.

Among many fascinating items of equipment, one should mention, perhaps, above all, the specialist tanks that were built for OVERLORD—the amphibious (DD) tank, the flail tank for detonating mines, and the tank which could lay a carpet of matting to facilitate movement over a sandy surface. These were the brain-children of a British general, Sir Percy Hobart, and a glance at his story will show that he could have produced them long before he did, if he had been given the chance.

Hobart was a pioneer of armour, whose ideas were acted on by the Germans before the war, while he himself was denied command of Britain's first armoured division. Shunted off to Egypt in 1938, he took the initiative there of forming the 7th Armoured Division, which became a famous unit in the Desert war. But in 1940 he was prematurely retired and joined the Home Guard ("Dad's Army").

He was recalled to active command the following year, apparently through Churchill's personal intervention, but it was not until March 1943 (note the date) that the division which he was commanding was turned into an experimental formation, to devise and develop specialised armour for a cross-Channel attack. He then delivered the goods, as he might have done at any previous time in the war if the assignment had been given to him.

His unique contribution to the success of D-Day was never recognised. At the end of the war he was retired again, to become a pensioner in charge of pensioners, as Lieutenant-Governor of the Royal Hospital, Chelsea. His exceptional talents had been used only for a brief period, when they were desperately needed, and that period began in March 1943.

So much for the technical "mysteries" on sea and land. In the air it was just the same: when the appropriate decisions were taken, the technical achievements followed. OVERLORD was made possible by the preliminary attack on German communications in France. This, in turn, required a decision at the highest level that the strategic bomber forces should devote themselves to the task, and a rejection of Harris's doctrine that bombing could never be accurate enough for this particular task to be carried out effectively.

In May 1943 aircraft of his own command had shown what precision could be achieved even at night, when they "busted" the Möhne and Eder dams. Obviously daylight bombing had a greater potential of accuracy, but this depended, as we have seen, upon the development of a long-range fighter. The improved Mustang was there, waiting to be mass-produced, from October 1942 onwards. In fact, the decision to mass-produce it was not taken until after the heaviest American losses in unescorted daylight bombing, in October *1943*.

During the bombing campaign before D-Day a new perfection of technique was evolved by Wing Commander Leonard Cheshire, which reduced the average bomb error from 680 yards in March 1944 to 285 yards in May. The key to this was low-level marking of targets by Mosquito bombers, and it seems likely that, given the challenge, the technique could have been evolved the year before, when Mosquitoes were already in service.

VII. AMERICAN MISTAKES

In judging the past it is always essential to remember the circumstances of the time, and not to criticise what people did or did not do by reference to facts that they could not have known or ideas that were not yet in circulation. Some would say that all retrospective judgments are unfair, dismissing them indiscriminately with the single word "hindsight." But since history itself *is* hindsight, in the most obvious sense, there can surely be nothing inherently wrong in offering judgments on the past, provided they conform to the stated rule.

There has, in any case, been plenty of retrospective comment on the Second World War, not least by men who held important positions in it, and one recurrent theme on the British side has been that the Americans were gravely at fault in pressing for a "premature" cross-Channel invasion, instead of exploiting to the full the opportunities of a Mediterranean strategy. A juster criticism, it would seem, is that they did not press strongly or persuasively enough for a cross-Channel invasion *in 1943,* or make a tough enough stand against distracting commitments in the Mediterranean.

Marshall was in principle right to insist that north-west Europe was the decisive theatre, and that the Allies should engage the enemy there at the earliest possible moment. But he was wrong to think that any large-scale cross-Channel attack was feasible in 1942. Then, indeed, it would have been premature, and Marshall's over-eager interest in SLEDGEHAMMER only served to increase British prejudice against American strategic ideas generally.

In fairness, one should not forget that SLEDGEHAMMER was designed to meet the emergency of a Russian collapse which, before Stalingrad, was bound still to be regarded as very much on the cards.

All the same, it was unfortunate that Marshall was so slow to accept the necessity for TORCH, on political no less than military grounds, and that his reluctance contributed to the postponement of that operation from October to November 1942.

As well as the delay, American caution made the plan for TORCH less bold than it might have been, and was therefore a direct cause of the Allied failure to secure at once the whole of French North Africa. This was the background to the Casablanca conference, to which the Americans came ill-prepared, and at which, on the whole, a very bad course was set for 1943. The more one considers it, the more Casablanca seems a fatal turning-point for the Western Allies.

It was there that the drift towards a purely Mediterranean strategy in 1943 was allowed to get out of hand. In their fight for an alternative strategy, the Americans were not united, lacked the fire of utter conviction, and were inhibited from using what might have been one of their best argumentative weapons. They were not united because the U.S. Navy was more interested in the Pacific than in Europe. They lacked conviction because they were not wholly impervious to British arguments about the dreadful difficulty of landing in France. (For instance, they, too, were more influenced than they should have been by the Dieppe fiasco.)

The argument that they neglected to use, because of a fundamental policy error which they would not correct, was that a successful cross-Channel invasion would bring an independent France back into the war. To Roosevelt and most other leading Americans, France was a defeated nation whose authentic representative was Pétain, and which de Gaulle did not represent at all. The consequences of this mistake were disastrous not only for the war but in a much longer perspective.

Americans failed to notice the many symptoms of French revival, although to do so required, at the beginning of 1943, no clairvoyance. Despite the powerful discouragement resulting from America's cordial recognition of Pétain, French opinion had turned overwhelmingly anti-Vichy and pro-de Gaulle. Inside France, resistance was growing, and outside, the Fighting French controlled large parts of the French empire and were already, even militarily, a far from negligible force.

At Casablanca, the Americans might—if their own attitude had been different—have compelled the British to think of the very palpable advantages of resuscitating their former ally, rather than of the more than dubious advantages of "knocking Italy out of the war" (to say nothing of the fantasy of bringing Turkey into it). They might also have questioned the strategic desirability of a protracted campaign to eliminate the German bridgehead in Tunisia, when containment might, arguably, have been just as effective in the long run, and would certainly have been less costly and constricting to the Allies.

Instead, they allowed Brooke to dominate the conference, with the result that they became committed, by degrees, to a succession of operations in the Mediterranean which in sum frustrated their basic strategic aim. Marshall had no need to come to Casablanca in a mood of fatalism. TORCH had not, as he seems to have believed, closed all options other than Mediterranean options for 1943. But his listless performance at the conference sold the pass, though of course the ultimate responsibility was Roosevelt's.

The President, as commander-in-chief, was the one man who could impose a strategy upon the American services. He was also, when he chose to be, immensely influential with Churchill, whose unwillingness to press any quarrel with him too far was demonstrated over and over again. Yet he failed to impose, with urgent and consistent purpose, a strategy to match his policy of beating Hitler first. In the end, therefore, the Japanese were beaten almost as soon as Hitler.

The "beat Hitler first" policy itself was fully justified from the point of view of America's vital interests. Germany was a much greater threat to the United States than Japan, if only because she was half the distance away. Moreover, the countries of Western Europe were more worth defending or liberating, for America's own sake, than Chiang Kai-Shek's China. Roosevelt and his professional advisers agreed, before Pearl Harbor, that Germany was the prime enemy, and they were right to maintain this view, even though it was Japan that struck the first blow.

Roosevelt willed the end, but in some respects he did not will the means. He never explained to the American people with sufficient firmness and clarity that beating Hitler first would mean only limited operations in the Pacific until the war in Europe was won. He was unduly responsive to pressure from the China and other lobbies demanding a more active war against Japan. At the same time, since he always tended to be a "soft touch" for the Navy, he allowed Admiral King far more latitude than he should have had. The result was that, in 1943, the Pacific theatre was employing a grossly excessive share of America's fighting resources.

But for this, Roosevelt would have been in a strong position to insist upon a cross-Channel invasion in 1943, and he could thus have provided the most powerful antidote to Brooke's influence on Churchill. At Casablanca the Prime Minister was still unhappy about postponing cross-Channel action to 1944, and might have been won back. A clear lead on future strategy might then have been given by the two leaders, instead of the compromises and double-talk that in fact emerged.

Roosevelt is open to severe criticism for his handling of some issues at Teheran and Yalta, but Casablanca was perhaps his unfinest hour. He came to the conference with his own system of command not properly organised, with no coherent plan for winning the war in Europe, and with a lamentable policy towards France. He had evidently given no thought to the problem of Italy, in either its military or its political aspect. His one distinctive contribution—the unconditional-surrender formula—was disgracefully casual and a bad mistake.

It was his way to work through special aides and cronies, rather than through the normal machinery of government. He kept his Secretary of State at arm's length, and his personal chief of staff, Admiral Leahy, though certainly a friend, was never made responsible for concerting the efforts of the services, even if he had had the capacity.

Under Roosevelt's leadership, America rose to the leadership of the world. Yet his knowledge of the world was defective, his sense of direction often faulty, and his administrative style often chaotic. He had charm, flair, cunning, adroitness, and, above all, courage. Unquestionably there was greatness in him, though rather less, perhaps, than appeared at the time.

VIII. BRITISH MISTAKES

There is a sad parallel between Roosevelt's failure to prevent the distortion of Allied strategy by Admiral King and Churchill's failure to prevent its distortion by General Brooke. Yet between the two cases there are differences of constitutional form as well as personality.

Churchill interfered far more than Roosevelt in the detailed running of the war. As Minister of Defence he felt that he alone was responsible for the British war machine and how it was used, while as an individual he was conscious of having unrivalled knowledge and experience in the sphere of defence. He was not, however, commander-in-chief of the armed forces—as Roosevelt was. In theory, and also to quite a large extent in practice, his authority over the services was less than the President's.

One problem was that in Britain there were three independent services, whereas in America there were only two. This meant not only that Churchill had one more fully-fledged Chief of Staff to deal with, but also that the British Chiefs of Staff Committee could be a more formidable body than the American. If the three principal members stood together, they could be daunting even to Churchill. Often they would disagree among themselves but would maintain a solid front when reporting to him.

They were the "steady" professionals, he the brilliant, but erratic, amateur. That was their view of him, and they were not conditioned, as American officers have always been, to the idea of a civilian commander-in-chief. They would humour Churchill, put up with his unsocial hours of work, defer to him in minor matters, and often pretend to defer to him on major issues. But as a rule they got their way on anything that they considered really important.

To do so, they might have to strike implied bargains among themselves, which could be very much against the general Allied interest. For instance, Brooke was opposed to the area bombing strategy, but did not make an issue of it, because he wanted Portal's support for his Mediterranean strategy. Instead of both strategies being strongly challenged and tested in argument at the highest professional level, both were accepted in what was, in effect, a secret deal between partisans.

Churchill believed that he could provide, himself, the unifying inter-service, "triphibious" view—that he could act as coordinator of the Chiefs of Staff as well as head of the government. Unlike Lloyd George in the First World War, he made a point of keeping his War Cabinet colleagues so busy with day-to-day tasks that they would not be free to think about war policy as a whole. The result was that he became very isolated and, in his dealings with the top brass, less effective than he should have been, while appearing to be omnipotent.

Though he had the title Minister of Defence, there was no Ministry of Defence as there is today. The three service departments were still autonomous, and Churchill had no institutional backing for his role of would-be coordinator. In particular, there was no independent Chief of the Defence Staff—no senior officer, emanating from one of the three services, but with the express duty of presiding over the Chiefs of Staff Committee in the interests of the whole war effort. (The same, as has been indicated, was true in the United States, though the future organisation of Defence there was foreshadowed when the Pentagon building was opened, a few weeks before the Casablanca conference.)

The case for an independent chairman of the Chiefs of Staff was stated with remarkable insight and prescience by Sir Edward Grigg, in an article that appeared in the London *Times* on 11 April 1942. Until recently, Grigg had been a member of the government at the War Office, and he would join it again, in 1944, as Minister Resident in the Middle East. His varied career included a notable record in the First World War.

In his article he wrote:

I find it hard . . . to believe that a Combined General Staff will give us what we require so long as it has no chief of its own. The Chiefs of Staff . . . have each of them their separate preoccupations and an immense amount of work to discharge . . . It is said that [they] seldom disagree. If that be indeed so, their recommendations must often be a matter of compromise, a lowest common denominator between incompatible ideas . . . the functions proper to a Chief of the Combined General Staff are not functions which a Minister is best suited to exercise, least of all a Prime Minister who must be the dominant figure in any discussions which he attends . . . The Chief of the Combined General Staff should [have] no responsibility but that of presiding over the Chiefs of Staff Committee and advising the War Cabinet on the long-range conduct of the war.

This article attracted at the time considerable attention and quite a lot of informed support. But Churchill rejected the argument out of hand. In his view, an independent chairman of the Chiefs of Staff would restrict his own authority. He maintained, therefore, the system whereby the chairman of the committee was one of the service chiefs—an interested party—and his own permanent representative on it was the charming but accommodating General Ismay.

As it happened, the committee had acquired a new chairman only a month previously, and the new chairman was Brooke. He took over from Pound in March 1942, and we can now see how much Churchill's authority was worth, on key issues, when faced with the Chiefs of Staff under Brooke's chairmanship.

There can, of course, be no proof that a different system, and a different man, would have averted the mistakes that occurred. But the influence of Brooke upon Churchill is a matter of record, and it is at least possible that if there had been an independent chairman of the Chiefs of Staff, less prejudiced than Brooke against cross-Channel action, and less starry-eyed about Mediterranean strategy, the war might have taken a more favourable course for Britain and the Western Alliance in 1943.

The fallacy of the "soft underbelly"—Churchill's phrase but Brooke's notion—and of the allegedly greater strain to Germany than to the Allies of a campaign in Italy, has been indicated in earlier chapters. Unfortunately, Churchill was so uneasy, after Singapore and Tobruk, about the morale of British troops that he was more susceptible than he would otherwise have been to arguments for delaying, at least until 1944, the direct attack on Fortress Europe.

Brooke always made out that he was not against OVERLORD. On the contrary, he claimed to be all for it—if and when the conditions were right. This qualification gave him, as it were, a permanent cover story for his Mediterranean plans, because he never ceased to argue that fighting Germany in the Mediterranean was the best way to weaken her to the point where OVERLORD could, with confidence, be undertaken.

His American colleagues tended either to doubt his sincerity or to regard him as a victim of self-deception. They suspected him of a deep and incurable reluctance to venture back across the Channel, which (they felt) many others in Britain, including the Prime Minister, shared. Their suspicion seems to be corroborated by a well-placed British witness—COSSAC himself, General Morgan—who visited America in the autumn of 1943 and wrote of that time:

> In spite of the fact that we were ourselves British, we still found it hard to interpret the true intentions of our senior compatriots. Though, looking back over the past months, there was no doubt that we had effected something, there persisted the feeling that, on the British side, concessions to our demands were made sometimes grudgingly . . . Though there were obvious and immense difficulties on the British side in putting any plan of the nature we had concocted into effect, it was not always easy to convince oneself that objections raised were quite, quite genuine.

The political effects of Britain's foot-dragging over the invasion were damaging. No doubt it helped to turn American public opinion away from Europe and towards the Pacific. (In May 1943 polls in the United States were showing more interest in beating Japan than in beating Germany and Italy.) In the longer run it contributed to the problems and tribulations of postwar Europe.

Churchill's worst political mistakes in 1943 were that he continued to bank too heavily on exclusive Anglo-American partnership, both in the war and after it; that he did not obtain, at Casablanca, a sensible (or indeed any) understanding about terms for an armistice with Italy; that he did not stop the unconditional surrender rot; that he failed to give de Gaulle solid backing against Roosevelt, but more often backed Roosevelt against the General; and that he decided to take no further constitutional initiative in India until the war was over. All had baleful consequences.

IX. RISK AND COST OF DELAY

Much was made at the time, and much has been made since, of the appalling risks of embarking on a cross-Channel invasion before 1944. But there seems to have been very little consideration, then or since, of the equally appalling risks of delaying it so long, or of the horrifying human cost.

In retrospect, the last phase of the war has been seen by many in the West as a race against the Russians. But surely it would be less anachronistic, and truer to contemporary facts which even then could have been seen as strong probabilities, to regard it as a race against time. Most of Continental Europe was in the grip of a half-crazy tyrant who was showing every sign of becoming more deranged, though no less formidable, in adversity than in success. Fighting for survival, Hitler could be expected to stop at nothing, exploiting to the full the talent, courage, patriotism, and credulity of the German people, and intensifying his persecution of those for whom his warped mind had long ago conceived implacable hatred. There was, almost literally, not a moment to lose.

Churchill had warned, in his great speech in the House of Commons on 18 June 1940, that the world might "sink into the abyss of a new dark age made more sinister, and perhaps more protracted, by the lights of perverted science." Should those lights not have been more present to his imagination in 1943, giving him a sense of desperate urgency? How could he be sure that Hitler would not be able to use a further year of immunity to develop some wonder-weapon, by which civilisation might be destroyed and his monstrous regime saved?

On 8 November 1942 Hitler referred in a speech to secret weapons which would strike his enemies dumb. We now know that he had in mind, particularly, the V-1 flying bomb and the V-2 rocket. Fortunately, work on these weapons was spotted at an early stage, with the result that their production and installation were hard hit by bombing. All the same, they eventually killed nine thousand people and caused much destruction in southern England.

Far more serious—indeed, mortal—was the danger that Germany might be the first to produce an atomic bomb. This was no empty

231

threat. Though Hitler was denied, by poetic justice, the aid of what he called "Jewish physics," nuclear research was nevertheless going on in Germany, and in June 1942 a leading German physicist, Werner Heisenberg, was able to report to his masters that an amount of uranium no larger than a pineapple would be enough to destroy a city.

Not very much was known to Allied Intelligence of the progress of German nuclear research, though there was no doubt of its existence or, of course, of its power to revolutionise the fortunes of war. But the Germans' interest in Norwegian heavy water was noticed, and the attack by six Norwegian commandos on the heavy water plant at Rjukan in Norway, in February 1943, ranks as one of the outstanding exploits of the war. Even so, the plant was put out of action for only a period of months, and the threat that Germany might somehow be the first to make an atom bomb remained.

Other products of advanced science which might have cheated the Allies of victory were the ME–262 jet fighter, the Schnorkel U-boats and the Walther U-boats (propelled by hydrogen peroxide, and with homing torpedoes). The Germans could also have won the war by using nerve gases, had Hitler not believed that equally lethal gases were available to the Allies.

Finally, mention should be made of guided missiles, in which Germany had a potentially decisive lead. Professor R. V. Jones tells us that, had the war lasted much longer, "guided missiles, both from the air and from the ground, would have come into service, for in this respect—pressed by the need for new forms of defence—the Germans were well ahead of us all."

So far as the scientific war was concerned, the Allies won the race against time—but only just, and apparently as much by luck as by good management. Until the Continent was occupied there could be no assurance of safety, and delaying the invasion until 1944 involved risks which, on balance, hardly seem warrantable.

When we turn from science to the fate of hundreds of thousands of human beings, we cannot, alas, say that the race was won. Even an invasion in 1943 would have been too late to save millions of Hitler's victims, but many could probably still have been saved.

Despite the mass-murder of Jews in 1941, 1942, and 1943, astonishingly many were still alive in Hitler's Europe even in 1944. Between May and November of that year no fewer than 600,000 of them were brought to the slaughterhouse at Auschwitz. For Hungarian Jews, indeed, 1944 was the most terrible year, because it was during that summer that at least a quarter of a million of them were killed.

Though the full enormity of Nazi genocide could not be known to the Allies until Germany was defeated, they had no excuse for not realising that a delayed invasion would be likely to cost many European Jews their lives. In addition, it must have been obvious that delay would be fatal to many brave people in resistance movements, who had already been waiting long enough for the dawn of liberation.

No incident in 1944 was more tragic than the Warsaw uprising of August-October, in which at least ten thousand members of the Polish underground army were killed, and nearly all survivors wounded. Stalin's cold-blooded refusal to help those who were, from his point of view, the wrong sort of Poles, has aroused fervent moral indignation. But if the Western Allies had been approaching Warsaw from the west they could have done what the Russians, approaching it from the east, deliberately failed to do. Practical assistance on the ground would, of course, have meant infinitely more to the embattled Polish patriots than sympathy from afar.

By not invading until 1944 the Western Allies prolonged Europe's agony and condemned a multitude of heroes and innocents to death.

X. THE VICTORY THAT MIGHT HAVE BEEN

The purpose of this book has been to show that, in 1943, Allied grand strategy went sadly astray; also to question, if not refute, arguments commonly used to pooh-pooh any suggestion that it was then, rather than a year later, that the Allies should have crossed the Channel. Granted, however, that a fundamentally different strategy should have been attempted, how might it have worked?

We have to suppose the Western Allies agreed, in 1942, that their big operation for 1943 would be an invasion of north-west Europe. We must also suppose them agreed that it was far more important to bring France back into the war than to knock Italy out of it, and that de Gaulle was the French leader most deserving of confidence.

TORCH would then have been undertaken on the strict understanding that it would lead to no further commitments in the Mediterranean prejudicial to the main plan for 1943. It is arguable that
American support for de Gaulle would have been TORCH's undoing,
because Darlan would have refused his indispensable cooperation to
any backers of de Gaulle. But, in fact, it took a good deal of arm-
twisting to make him cooperate, in any case, and he was never the man
to allow principle to prevail over expediency. The fluke was that he
happened to be in Algiers at the critical moment, and since he was
there, it is likely that he would, in the end, have agreed to cooperate.

If the Americans had not vetoed the bolder plan of landing as far
east as Bône, Tunis might well have fallen within weeks. But for our
present purposes it is best to assume the German bridgehead established in Tunisia, with the Allies having decided, however, to contain
it rather than to waste men and time in a full-scale effort to reduce
it.

The vital thing would have been for Roosevelt and Churchill, and
their staffs, to come to Casablanca utterly resolved that there should
be no Mediterranean operations in 1943 on a scale to impair the
prospects for OVERLORD (as it was later called). It would still have
been possible to retain very substantial Allied sea, land, and air forces
in the Mediterranean, but all plans there would have been made on
the assumption that it was a subordinate theatre.

At Casablanca the chief item on the agenda would have been the
cross-Channel invasion, for which the command structure would have
been set up there and then, if it had not been set up already. There
would also have been extensive political discussion between Roosevelt
and Churchill, more especially on the subject of armistice terms for
Italy. It would have been agreed that overtures from the Italians
would be entertained with the minimum of pre-conditions, which
would, however, necessarily have included the overthrown of Mussolini, the evacuation of occupied territory, the release of prisoners,
and the surrender of the fleet.

With or without an Italian armistice, the two leaders would have
envisaged keeping the enemy in a constant state of uncertainty and
nervousness in the Mediterranean. If the Italians had stayed in the

war, they would have been an increasing burden to the Germans, who would have had to divert ever larger numbers of troops to support them. At the same time, the scope for successful local uprisings would have been greater if the occupying army had been at least partly Italian than when it was wholly German.

Britain's Middle Eastern forces alone would have been enough, together with Allied sea and air power, to compel the enemy to hold many divisions in southern Europe against the threat of Allied landings. (Churchill later inadvertently conceded this point, by implication, when he used against ANVIL the argument that the mere threat of a landing in the South of France would be enough to force the Germans to keep their troops there.)

It might or might not have been possible to capture Sardinia or Sicily in 1943, consistently with launching the invasion of north-west Europe. OVERLORD had to be the over-riding priority. Anything else had to be treated as optional and expendable.

Roosevelt and Churchill would have made sure, at Casablanca, that the Allied air forces in Britain were properly concerted both with each other and with the forces preparing to invade. They would have given clear instructions that bombing had to be concentrated upon key targets in the German war economy, and upon road and rail communications in northern France. Area bombing would have been ruled out for the future, as would unescorted daylight bombing. The leaders would have given a directive for the rapid production of Mustangs.

The manifest and agreed supremacy of OVERLORD in Allied plans for 1943 would, in itself, have prevented the diversion of American resources to the Pacific, and would therefore have guaranteed that the American share in the invasion would have been at least as great as it was a year later. In the provision of landing-craft, indeed, it could well have been more generous. At Casablanca the leaders would have considered all the technical requirements, and fixed the right priorities.

In one respect the line of battle on D-Day would have been different, if the Anglo-Saxons had shown more imagination. France would have been represented, in the initial landings, by at least a division. The men were available, their ardour for the task could be taken for granted, and their arrival in strength on the first day of liberation would have been inspiring to them and to their compatriots.

There would never have been any nonsense about imposing A.M.G.O.T. on liberated French territory. From the first, de Gaulle's organisation would have been recognised as the valid provisional government, and would have been asked to make all the necessary preparations in advance. De Gaulle himself would have been consulted about invasion plans, and would have been encouraged to land in France as soon as possible after D-Day. (It was humbug to say that the Fighting French could not be trusted with secrets. This was only an excuse for excluding them from Anglo-Saxon councils.)

Inside metropolitan France the invasion was expected in 1943—by the famous "Colonel Rémy," for instance, and by countless others. Their faith would have been doubly rewarded if the invasion had not only come then, but come with a large force of Frenchmen in the leading wave.

But would it have succeeded? There is every reason to believe that it would. The Germans had no more men to withstand it than they had a year later, and the defences of the Atlantic Wall were, as we have seen, much less elaborate. Allied air superiority was already crushing, and it would have been far easier to destroy the Luftwaffe over Normandy than over Germany.

The enemy would have been much worse placed than in 1944 to fight the war on two fronts, because the two fronts would have been so much farther apart. In July 1943 the Eastern Front was still deep inside Russia, with the Germans still holding Smolensk, Orel, Kharkov, and Taganrog. A year later the front was, in the north, either close to, or across, the Polish border, and in the south at the approaches to Roumania, with Odessa in Russian hands. By December 1944 the Red Army had occupied the Baltic States, Roumania, and Bulgaria, was at the gates of Warsaw, and had captured Budapest.

Clearly the Germans' east-west communications would have been far more stretched if the Western Allies had landed in 1943, and if —as in 1944—there had been a winter campaign, the enemy's interior lines would probably have been too extended to allow, for instance, Sepp Dietrich's 6th S.S. Panzer Army to move, undetected, from Austria to a position threatening the Ardennes. The overall strategic dispositions would have favoured the Allies more, the Germans less, than a year later.

If, say, at the beginning of August 1943, the invading forces had broken out of the bridgehead and had been swiftly liberating the rest of France, the moment would have been suitable for an Allied summit meeting, to be held in London and to be attended by de Gaulle as well as Roosevelt and Churchill. It would have been appropriate for the British to have a chance to welcome their American benefactor, and for the President himself to receive their homage. Stalin, of course, would have been invited to attend, but would presumably have refused to travel to London.

At the conference the terms for a German armistice would have been discussed, and a determined effort made to reach agreement among the major Western Allies on the future of Europe. This would have been a most helpful preliminary to the meeting with Stalin at the end of the year.

How different the Teheran conference would then have been from the Teheran conference that actually occurred! Even assuming that the Western Allies had, as yet, liberated only France and Belgium, and were temporarily held at the approaches to Germany (on the analogy of the following year), we can see how vastly more advantageous the Western position would have been.

The Russians would not yet have emerged from their own country and would have had a long way to go even to the main centres of *Eastern* Europe. It would, therefore, have been obvious to Stalin that the Western Allies were likely to end the war occupying most of the Continent, and in Stalin's eyes possession was certainly nine points of the law.

Apart from having less of a physical advantage than the following year, the Russians would also have had a less marked psychological advantage, because the Western Allies would not have been open to the charge of having let the Red Army do all the serious fighting on land before opening a true Second Front. Though the balance of casualties would still have been overwhelmingly in the Russians' "favour," the balance of achievement would have been more even.

Roosevelt would still have been very anxious to make friends with Stalin, particularly with a view to persuading him to join in the war against Japan. But Churchill's position would have been much stronger, with the invasion successfully accomplished, and without the appearance that he lacked enthusiasm for it, which suggested weakness.

It would also have been good for the interests of Britain, and of Western Europe, if he had asserted France's right to be represented at Teheran. With that country liberated, and de Gaulle universally accepted as its authentic spokesman, the claim would have been justified. And de Gaulle's presence at Teheran would certainly have been an aid to clarity on the Western side.

Another gesture of enlightened self-interest that Churchill might have made during 1943 would have been towards Indian nationalism. If he had freed the Congress leaders and negotiated a settlement with them, granting virtual self-government to a united India, he might in return have obtained a close partnership between India and Britain, including a military alliance. It would, in any case, have been a condition of the settlement that India should stay in the war against Japan.

The Muslim League was not yet as powerful as it later became, thanks to the vacuum created by the Congress leaders' incarceration (and some encouragement from the British authorities). There was still a real chance of breaking the constitutional deadlock in India without splitting the country. But it was the last chance.

If Churchill had decided to seek a political solution, and to appoint a Viceroy equal to the task—rather than one expressly chosen to be non-political—he might have put Britain's connection with India, on which her status as a world power largely depended, on a new and viable basis. In not even trying to turn the British Raj into a working partnership, he "threw a pearl away richer than all his tribe."

Had India not been one of his supreme blind spots, he might have responded, when Roosevelt invited Chiang Kai-Shek to Cairo, by himself inviting Nehru. India's contribution to the war was at least as impressive as China's, and India, like China, was an emerging Asian giant. It would have been a masterstroke for Churchill to produce Nehru as Britain's answer to the American obsession with China, and as living proof that the old imperialism was being voluntarily abandoned.

By the time of Yalta the war in Europe would have been over, probably many months over. And it is likely that the Western Allies would have met the Russians not on the Elbe but on the Vistula, or even further east. There would still have been any number of knotty problems, more especially those of Germany and Poland. But at least the Western Allies would have been able to negotiate from a position of strength.

No victory is won without painful effort, and of course there was no easy way of beating the Germans in the Second World War. Invasion in 1943 could not have provided a cheap victory. But it might, surely, have helped to bring the war to an end both sooner, and at a lower cost in lives—military and, above all, civilian—than the strategy which delayed invasion until 1944.

The Normandy landings themselves might have been rather less costly, for reasons that have been explained. A different use of British and American bombers would manifestly have saved the lives of many Allied airmen, as well as very many German civilians. Avoidance of large-scale offensive action in Tunisia and Italy would also have saved many lives that seem to have been needlessly sacrificed.

But the most poignant thought of all is that an earlier end to the war might have saved literally hundreds of thousands of European Jews from massacre, as well as exacting a less heavy toll from the liberating forces. An unnecessary year of life for the Nazi regime was a deadly price to pay for the advantage, anyway most dubious, of a less risky crossing of the Channel.

Churchill's title for the last volume of his history of the Second World War was *Triumph and Tragedy.* There is usually a mixture of both at the end of any war. Even the supposed winners are likely to have much to lament as well as to celebrate. But there are differences of degree, and it is the contention of this book that, if the British and Americans had landed in France in 1943, their triumph might have been greater and the accompanying tragedy less.

Select Bibliography*

This list includes a number of major sources, whether or not quoted in the text, as well as any books that have been quoted, whether or not they are also major sources for the subject as a whole.

Arnold, H. H. *Global Mission*.

Arnold-Foster, Mark. *The World at War*.

Barnett, Corelli. *The Desert Generals*.

Bradley, Omar N. *A Soldier's Story*.

Bryant, Arthur. *The Turn of the Tide, 1939–1943* and *Triumph in the West, 1943–1946*. (Two volumes based on the diaries and autobiographical notes of Field Marshal Lord Alanbrooke.)

Bullock, Alan. *Hitler: A Study in Tyranny*.

Butcher, Harry C. *Three Years with Eisenhower*.

Butler, J. R. M. *Grand Strategy*, Volume III, Part 2 (June 1941–August 1942).

Cadogan, Sir Alexander. *Diaries* (edited by David Dilks).

Chalfont, Alun. *Montgomery of Alamein*.

Churchill, Winston S. *The Second World War* (6 vols).

Clark, Mark. *Calculated Risk*.

Cooper, Matthew. *The German Army, 1933–1945*.

Crozier, Brian. *De Gaulle*.

Cunningham of Hyndhope, Lord. *A Sailor's Odyssey*.

Davis, Kenneth S. *The American Experience of War, 1939–1945*.

de Gaulle, Charles. *Mémoires de Guerre* (3 vols.).

de Guingand, Sir Francis. *Operation Victory*.

* Like the text of the book, this bibliography is unchanged from the original edition. Obviously, it would have been misleading to add titles that have appeared since the book was written.

Eden, Anthony. *The Reckoning*.

Ehrman, John. *Grand Strategy,* Volume V (August 1943–September 1944).

Eisenhower, Dwight D. *Crusade in Europe*.

Eisenhower Foundation. *D-Day: The Normandy Invasion in Retrospect*.

Feis, Herbert. *Churchill, Roosevelt, Stalin*.

Foot, M. R. D. *SOE in France* (in the *British History of the Second World War)*.

———. *Resistance*.

Gilbert, Martin. *Winston S. Churchill*, Vol. III.

Gunther, John. *Roosevelt in Retrospect*.

Gwyer, J. M. A. *Grand Strategy*, Volume III, Part I (June 1941– August 1942).

Harriman, W. Averell, and Abel, Elie. *Special Envoy to Churchill and Stalin, 1941–1946*.

Harris, Sir Arthur. *Bomber Offensive*.

Harrisson, Tom. *Living Through the Blitz*.

Harvey, Oliver. *War Diaries, 1941–1945* (edited by John Harvey).

Hilberg, R. *Destruction of the European Jews*.

Howard, Michael. *Grand Strategy*, Volume IV (August 1942–September 1943).

Jackson, W. G. F. *Overlord Normandy, 1944*.

Jones, R. V. *Most Secret War: British Scientific Intelligence, 1939– 1945*.

Kedward, H. R. *Resistance in Vichy France*.

Kennedy, Sir John, and Fergusson, Bernard. *The Business of War*.

King, E. J., and Whitehall, W. M. *Fleet Admiral King*.

Kolko, Gabriel. *The Politics of War: The World and United States Foreign Policy, 1943–1945*.

Lash, Joseph P. *Roosevelt & Churchill, 1939–1941*.

Leasor, James, and Hollis, Sir Leslie. *War at the Top*.

Lewin, Ronald. *Ultra Goes to War: The Secret Story*.

Liddell Hart, Basil. *History of the Second World War*.

Lovat, Lord. *March Past*.

Macmillan, Harold. *The Blast of War*.

Montgomery of Alamein, Lord. *Memoirs*.

Moorehead, Alan. *Eclipse*.

Moran, Lord. *Winston Churchill: The Struggle for Survival*.

Morgan, Sir Frederick. *Overture to Overlord*.

Murphy, Robert. *Diplomat Among Warriors*.

Nicolson, Nigel. *Alex*.

Origo, Iris. *War in Val D'Orcia*.

Parkinson, Roger. *A Day's March Nearer Home*.

Patton, George S., Jr. *War As I Knew It*.

Pogue, Forrest C. *George C. Marshall: Ordeal and Hope, 1939–1942*.

———. *George C. Marshall: Organizer of Victory, 1943–1945*.

Reitlinger, Gerald. *The Final Solution*.

"Rémy, Colonel." *Memoirs*, Vol. I.

Richards, Denis George. *Portal of Hungerford*.

Roosevelt, Elliott. *As He Saw It*.

Roosevelt, Elliott, and Brough, James. *A Rendezvous with Destiny*.

Rosenman, Samuel I. *Working with Roosevelt*.

Shepperd, G. A. *The Italian Campaign*.

Sherwood, Robert E. *The White House Papers of Harry L. Hopkins*, Vol. I, September 1939–January 1942; Vol. II, January 1942–July 1945.

Snyder, Louis L. *The War: A Concise History, 1939–1945*.

Speer, Albert. *Inside the Third Reich*.

———. *Spandau: The Secret Diaries*.

Taylor, A. J. P. *English History, 1914–1945* (in the Oxford History of England series).

———. *The Second World War*.

Tedder, Lord. *With Prejudice*.

Thompson, W. H. *I Was Churchill's Shadow*.

Thorne, Christopher. *Allies of a Kind: The United States, Britain, and the War Against Japan, 1941–1945*.

Wavell, Lord. *The Viceroy's Journal* (edited by Penderel Moon).

Webster, Sir Charles, and Frankland, Noble. *The Strategy of Air Offensive Against Germany, 1939–1945*.

Wedemeyer, Albert C. *Wedemeyer Reports!*

Wheeler-Bennett, J. W. (ed.). *Action This Day: Working with Churchill*.

Wilmot, Chester. *The Struggle for Europe*.

Young, Kenneth. *Churchill and Beaverbrook*.

Zuckerman, Solly. *From Apes to Warlords*.

Index

Acheson, Dean, 66, 125
aircraft, British superiority in Middle
  East, 49; Liberators, 117; Flying
  Fortresses, 138; Mustangs, 140, 155,
  222, 235; Mosquitoes, 145, 173, 223;
  Lancasters, 145; Superfortresses, 202;
  ME-262 jet fighter, 232
Alamein, El, 32, 49, 95, 116
Alam Halfa, 48
Alexander, General Sir Harold (later
  Field Marshal Earl), 45, 48, 49, 70,
  73, 81, 95, 96, 104–5, 206
Algiers, 42, 43, 51, 53, 86, 92, 102, 103,
  107; de Gaulle moves to, 165
A.M.G.O.T. (Allied Military
  Government), 110–11, 114, 236; for
  France, 199
ANVIL, Operation, 189, 199, 205–6,
  235
ARCADIA, 14, 15, 17, 20, 21
Ardennes, 201, 209, 236
Arnhem, 199
Arnim, General Jürgen von, 55, 80–3
Arnold, General Henry H. ("Hap"),
  65–6
Arnold-Foster, Mark, 33
Atlantic, Battle of the, 13, 32–3; won,
  116–17
Atlantic Wall, 196, 214–18, 236
atom bombs, 202, 203, 231–2
Auchinleck, General (later Field
  Marshal) Sir Claude, 32, 45, 46

Australia, 27, 29, 55, 119
Australian Army, 27–8
AVALANCHE, Operation, 98, 101,
  102, 196
Avranches, 197
Azov, Sea of, 24

Badoglio, Marshal Pietro, 100, 101,
  103, 113, 125
Balkans, 20, 63, 64, 83, 85, 92, 93, 98,
  100, 108, 110, 182, 187
Baltic States, 180–1, 236
Bari, 105
Bataan, 27, 29, 174
Beaverbrook, Lord, 25, 34, 86
Belgium, 20, 63, 162, 198, 199, 217,
  237
Bell, Bishop George, 152–3
Berlin, 138, 146, 147, 156, 201, 205–7
Bir Hacheim, 168
Bizerta, 81
BOLERO, Operation, 21
Bomber Command, see Royal Air
  Force
bombing policy, 19, 44, 72, 227;
  Portal's aim to bomb S. Germany,
  70; Casablanca bombing directive,
  136, 144–5; POINTBLANK, 136–7,
  147, 148; R.A.F. night-bombing
  policy, 136, 155, 156; U.S. Air Force
  day-bombing policy, 136, 139, 155,
  156; Churchill and, 142–4, 148–9,

Index

bombing policy (*Cont.*)
151–2; terror-bombing explicit, 144;
policy discussed, 149–57; oil
directive, 148; effects of oil offensive,
155; before D-Day, 148, 196, 222,
235; precision bombing, 222–3
Bône, 42, 43
Borkum, 85
Bottomley, Air Marshal Sir Norman,
147
Bradley, General Omar N., 67, 197, 198
Bremen, 144
Brest, 33, 69
Brindisi, 105
British Army, 235; disasters in Far
East, 28–30; 8th Army retreats, 31;
checks Rommel, 32; changes of
command in Middle East, 45–6;
victory of Alam Halfa, 48;
superiority before second El Alamein
battle, 48–9; in fight for Tunisia,
80–1; in Sicily, 96–7; in Italy, 104–6;
in Normandy, 195–7; after break-out,
198–9; strength, 214; specialist tanks
for, 221–2
British Chiefs of Staff, 38–9, 62, 64–6,
70–1, 145; relations with Churchill,
18, 28; independent chairman
suggested, 34, 228–9; interpretation
of TORCH commitment, 40; plan for
TORCH bolder than Americans', 43;
united front at Casablanca, 70;
pledge against terror bombing, 150;
chairmanship of, 228–9
British Commonwealth and Empire, 11,
23, 122, 165, 219; affected by fall of
Malaya and Singapore, 76, 117–18;
Churchill praises contribution to war,
119; Churchill's view of, 122–5; war
casualties, 170
British merchant marine, Arctic
convoys, 25
British Special Operations Executive
(S.O.E.), 169, 170, 172
Brooke, Field Marshal Sir Alan (later
Viscount Alanbrooke), 4, 67, 70–2,
73, 78, 82, 83, 111, 170, 189, 227;
alarmed by TORCH, 39; with
Churchill in Russia, 44–5; converts
Churchill to Mediterranean strategy,
62–5, 134, 212; personality, 68–9;

compact with Portal, 70; with
Churchill to Turkey, 83–4; at
TRIDENT, 86–8; and
AVALANCHE, 102; denied
command of OVERLORD, 108; on
Stalin, 186–7; chairman of British
Chiefs of Staff, 229; U.S. suspicion
of, 230
Brooke, Sir Basil, 69
Bruneval, 215
Bryant, Sir Arthur, 50
BUCCANEER, proposed operation,
188
Bufton, Air Commodore S.O., 146–7
Bullock, Alan (Lord), 150–1
Bulolo, H.M.S., 76
Burma, 9, 29, 30, 64, 73, 177
Butcher, Captain Harry C., 91, 114–15

Cadogan, Sir Alexander, 126
Caen, 172
Cairo, 68, 106, 219, 238; Churchill
visits, 43–4, 45–7; Allied conferences
at, 175, 177–8, 188–91
Çakmak, Marshal, 84
Canadian Army, and Dieppe raid, 39,
215; and HUSKY, 94; in Normandy,
195–7; after break-out, 198–9
Caroline Islands, 73
Casablanca, 43, 55, 80, 82, 83, 85–8,
98, 106, 116, 138, 163, 208, 210, 214,
218, 223–5, 230, 234, 235; Allied
conference at, Jan. 1943, 59–78;
bombing directive, 136
Castellano, General Giuseppe, 102
Caucasus, 24–5, 55
Ceylon, 31
Chalfont, Alun (Lord), 49–50
Chamberlain, Neville, 131, 150, 167
Chennault, General Claire, 87
Chequers, 145
Cheshire, Wing Commander Leonard,
222–3
Chiang Kai-shek, Generalissimo, 238;
at Cairo, 176–7; pledge to cancelled,
188, 225
Chiang Kai-shek, Madame, 176
China, 9, 11, 87, 118, 177, 180, 225,
238
Churchill, Clementine S., 106
Churchill, Mary, 106

Churchill, Randolph S., 124; at
  Casablanca, 61
Churchill, Sarah, 177, 192
Churchill, Winston S. (later Sir), 4, 11,
  24, 26, 28, 29, 30, 35–6, 38, 46–8, 72,
  73, 74, 85, 89–90, 95, 116–18, 128–9,
  135, 160, 167, 171–2, 175, 211, 222,
  237, 238, 239; reaction to Pearl
  Harbor, 12–14; travels to U.S., 14;
  relationship with F.D.R. and two
  men compared, 14–18; three papers
  on future Allied strategy, 18–20;
  reaction to fall of Singapore and
  Tobruk, 32; political insecurity in
  1942, 33–6; tells Molotov not to
  expect Second Front in 1942, 37;.
  visits Washington, June 1942, 39;
  travels to Cairo and Moscow, 43–7;
  meetings with Stalin, 44–5; accepts
  Darlan deal, 54; at Casablanca
  conference, 59–78; converted to
  Mediterranean strategy by Brooke,
  62–5, 134; and Unconditional
  Surrender, 75–7, 100; with F.D.R. at
  Marrakesh, 78–9; mission to Turkey,
  83–4; and HUSKY, 85–9; and
  AVALANCHE, 98; at
  QUADRANT, 106, 109–10; and
  Stimson, 107; disappoints Brooke,
  108; at Hyde Park, 106, 108, 118;
  and capture of Rome, 114; at
  Quebec, 118–19; Harvard speech,
  119–21; discussed, 121–5; anxiety
  about Stalin, 125–7; and India, in
  1943, 129–34; and bombing policy,
  142–4, 148–9, 151–2; and de Gaulle,
  161, 163–6, 199–200; leaves for Cairo
  and Teheran, 176; at first Cairo
  conference, 176–8; at Teheran,
  178–88; and future of Germany, 183;
  at second Cairo conference, 188–91;
  ill on return journey, 191–2; and
  ANVIL, 206, 235; favours taking
  Berlin, 207; attitude to Stalin, 207–8;
  and "Mulberry" harbours, 220; and
  Chiefs of Staff, 227–9; worst political
  mistakes in 1943, 230; and German
  science, 231
Clark, General Mark, 51, 67, 104–6
Clyde River, 51
Cold War, 4, 205–9

Cologne, 144
Colombo, 31
Combined Bomber Offensive, *see*
  bombing policy
Combined Chiefs of Staff Committee,
  80, 97, 124, 145, 176, 179, 182; set
  up, 21; routine at Casablanca, 62;
  outstanding figures on, 65; final
  agreement at Casablanca, 72–3; and
  HUSKY, 85, 87; on future
  Mediterranean operations, 88; target
  date of invading France agreed, 88;
  agreement at Cairo, 189–90
Coral Sea, Battle of, 27
Corregidor, 27, 29
Corsica, 110, 111
COSSAC (Chief of Staff to Supreme
  Allied Commander designate), 109,
  173, 195, 214, 229
Cotentin peninsula, 195
Coventry, 142
Crete, 83
Cripps, Sir Stafford, 30, 34–5, 130
Cunningham, Admiral of the Fleet Sir
  Andrew (later Viscount), 73, 102,
  105
Czechoslovakia, 208

D-Day, 155, 195–6, 213, 216, 218–22,
  235, 236; Allied casualties, 196
Dakar, 19, 41, 55
Daladier, Edouard, 160, 169
Dardanelles, 85, 185
Darlan, Admiral, 53, 54, 55, 74, 77,
  100, 112
Dempsey, General Miles, 197
Denmark, 20, 63
Dieppe raid, 39, 214–16, 224
Dietrich, General Sepp, 236
Dill, Field Marshal Sir John, 21, 65,
  219
Dodecanese Islands, 83, 110; British
  evicted from, 176–7
Dönitz, Admiral, 117, 201
Douglas, Lewis, 68
Dresden, 149
Duke of York, H.M.S., 14
Dulles, Allen W., 201
Dunkirk, 68, 95, 108, 205
Dutch East Indies, *see* Nether-
  lands

Eaker, General Ira C., 136
Eastern (Russian) Front, 23–6, 64;
  evident that Russians will win on,
  126–7; position of in 1943, 236
Eden, Anthony (later Earl of Avon),
  93, 165, 175, 188; unwilling to lead
  cabal against Churchill, 35; and
  Mussolini, 76; not at TRIDENT, 86;
  at Algiers, 90; at Quebec, 126; and
  Indian Viceroyalty, 130–2; and
  F.D.R.'s "Wallonia" scheme, 162;
  paper on U.S. policy towards France,
  166
Egypt, 19, 20, 31–2, 39, 43, 96, 176,
  178
Eisenhower, General Dwight D., 51,
  60, 67, 71, 80–1, 88, 114–15, 199,
  201, 220; appointed to command
  TORCH, 40, 42; endorses Darlan
  deal, 54; calls off attempt to reach
  Tunis till spring 1943, 55; and new
  command structure in N. Africa, 73;
  and HUSKY plans, 86–7; Churchill
  visits at Algiers, 90–2; and launching
  of HUSKY, 94; fails to exploit, 96–7;
  and Short Terms for Italian
  surrender, 101, 103–4; appointed
  OVERLORD commander, 190–1;
  Churchill stays with, 191–2; and
  invasion, 195; assumes overall battle
  command, 198
Elbe River, 204, 209, 239
English Channel, 33, 107
Essen, 144
EUREKA, code name for Teheran
  conference, *see* Teheran

Falaise, 197
Foot, M. R. D., 169–70, 172
Free French or Fighting French, 19,
  224, 236; excluded from TORCH, 41;
  de Gaulle proclaims, 159; equivocal
  British support, 161; U.S. hostility,
  162
French Army, in N. Africa at time of
  TORCH, 41; in action, 54; troops
  inside France taken by surprise, 54;
  at Bir Hacheim, 168; after TORCH,
  168–9; in 1940, 170; losses, 170; in
  Italy, 200–1
French Empire, 4, 9, 10, 19, 41, 74,

159, 224; F.D.R.'s hostility to, 162,
  166
French Equatorial Africa, 159
French Indo-China, 10; discussed at
  Teheran, 180
French National Committee, 199; de
  Gaulle chairman of, 165; Allied
  recognition of, 166, 169
French Navy, 53; in N. Africa, 41;
  scuttled, 54
French North Africa, 19, 20, 21, 50,
  71, 211, 224; Allied plans for landing
  in (TORCH), 39–40; rival plans for
  landing in, 42–3; Allied landings in,
  51–5
French Resistance, 167–8, 171, 172;
  French Forces of the Interior
  (F.F.I.), 199
French Vichy regime, 9, 19, 42, 54, 55,
  74, 161, 165, 167, 168, 179; in
  Hitler's shadow, 41; cordial U.S.
  recognition, 41; denounced by de
  Gaulle, 159; sentences him to death,
  161
French West Africa, 19, 55, 159
Franco, Generalissimo Francisco, 42,
  50, 84

Gandhi, M. K. (Mahatma), 30–1,
  130
Gaulle, General Charles de (later
  President), 19, 164, 234, 236, 237,
  238; French opinion turns towards,
  41, 168, 169, 224; U.S. hostility to,
  41–2, 161, 224; given no prior notice
  of TORCH, 51; at Casablanca, 74–5,
  163–4; personality, 159–61; proclaims
  Free France, 159; British official
  attitude to, 160–1; Churchill and,
  161, 164–5, 230; F.D.R. and, 162–3,
  230; moves to Algiers, 165; chairman
  of French National Committee,
  165–6; conflict with "Anglo-Saxons"
  when France invaded, 199–200; in
  the U.S., 200
George VI, King, 118, 182
German Air Force (Luftwaffe), 140,
  173, 236; able to fight at short range,
  137; weakened over Germany, 148;
  forced to concentrate on fighter
  production, 154

German Army, 19, 20, 23, 44, 71, 87, 215, 236–7; casualties in Russia, winter 1941–2, 24; 4th Panzer Army switched, 24; moves into Unoccupied France, 54; checks Allies in Tunisia, 54–5; loses battle for Stalingrad, 55; fight for Tunisia and losses there, 80–1; but strategic benefit of, 82–3; able to reinforce Eastern front, despite Allies' N. African campaign, 93–4; gets away from Sicily, 95–7; redeployed in Italy, 100–1; in Italian campaign, 104–6; relative strengths in Italy and Balkans, 111–12; prowess of, 152; and French Resistance, 172; in Normandy, 196–7

German war production, 156; and Allied bombing, 136, 138–9, 153; oil production hit, 155

Gibraltar, 42, 51, 185

Gilbert, Martin, 84

Giran, Olivier, 168

Giraud, General Henri, 42, 51, 53, 165, 170; at Casablanca, 74–5; superseded by de Gaulle, 165

Gneisenau, 33

Goebbels, Dr Joseph, 77

Gott, General William ("Strafer"), 45, 135

Grant, President Ulysses S., 75, 76, 78

Greece, 83, 99, 100, 108

Grew, Joseph C., 10

Grigg, Sir Edward, 228–9

Guadalcanal, 28, 174

Gunther, John, 16

Halifax, Earl of, 12, 13, 90

Hamburg, 146, 156

Hanover, 138

HARLEQUIN, invasion exercise, 174

Harriman, W. Averell, 61, 93, 118, 125–6, 179, 180, 184; on F.D.R., 79

Harris, Air Chief Marshal Sir Arthur T. (later Marshal of the R.A.F.), 4, 136, 146, 147, 154, 155, 172, 173, 196; interprets Casablanca directive his own way, 144–5; personality, 145; backed by Portal, 145

Harrisson, Tom, 142

Harvey, Oliver (later Lord), 32

Heisenberg, Werner, 232

Hirohito, Emperor, 78, 203–4

Hiroshima, 202

Hitler, Adolf, 18, 20, 23, 25, 63, 64, 70, 72, 82, 83, 100, 117, 124, 150, 158, 161, 171, 204, 208–9, 219; declares war on U.S., 9, 13–14; assumes personal command against Russia, 24; insists on no retreat in Tunisia, 81; Mussolini a burden to, 98–9; orders no retreat in Normandy, 197; suicide, 201; contrasted with Stalin, 207; approves Rommel's strategy in the West, 217; and secret weapons, 231–2

Hobart, General Sir Percy, 221–2

Hong Kong, 29

Hoover, President Herbert, 107

Hopkins, Harry L., 61, 76, 79, 90, 127–8, 163, 177; Marshall and, 68

Horton, Admiral Sir Max, 117

Howard, Professor Michael, 53, 77, 98

Hull, Cordell, 175, 226; not at Casablanca, 61; and Free French, 162, 165; absent from Teheran and Cairo, 188–9

HUSKY, Operation, 98, 101, 105, 113, 135; agreed at Casablanca, 72; command structure for, 73; planning for, 85–9, 92; launched, 94; qualified success of, 95–7

Iceland, 20, 59

Illustrious, H.M.S., 38

India, 29–30, 31, 90, 188, 230, 238; Japanese held at approaches to, 55; Churchill and, in 1943, 129–34; F.D.R. discusses with Stalin, 180

Indian National Congress, 30, 238; "Quit India" campaign, 30–1, 130

Inönü, President Ismet, 84, 188

Intelligence, Allied, 169–70; U.S. superior to Japanese, 27; French network, 159

Iowa, U.S.S., 176

Ismay, General Sir Hastings ("Pug"), 66, 86

Italy, 19, 63–4, 71, 77–8, 92, 97, 108, 169, 189, 191, 206, 211, 230, 234, 239; Pact with Germany and Japan, 10; reels under impact of defeat, 55; policy of "knocking Italy out of the

Index

Italy (*Cont.*)
war," 65, 72, 91, 98–100, 110, 115, 166, 225, 233; Unconditional Surrender demanded, 75; Churchill tries to make exception of, 76; military disaster in Sicily, 95; surrender of, 102–4; attitude to surrender, 113–14; Soviet reaction to, 125–6; war casualties, 170

Jacob, Brigadier (later General Sir) Ian, 69, 73

Japan, 19, 20, 24, 39, 64, 89, 225, 230, 237; attacks U.S. at Pearl Harbor, 9, 12–14; Pact with Germany and Italy, 10; Non-Aggression Pact with Russia, 10; U.S. attitude to, 9–11; land victories, 27, 29–30; tide of naval war turns against, 27; Unconditional Surrender demanded, 75; in the event, conditional, 77–8, 203; U.S. wants Russian intervention against, 128; how defeated, 177, 201–4; Stalin pledges intervention against, 181

Japanese Navy, 29, 31
Jean Bart, 42
Jews, 232–3, 239
Jodl, General Alfred, 216
Johnson, President Lyndon B., 15
Jones, Professor R. V., 168, 232
Juin, General Alphonse, 201

Kayser, Jacques, 169
Kedward, H. R., 167
Kesselring, Field Marshal Albert, 97, 101
Kharkov, 127, 236
Khartoum, 59, 68
Kiel, 138
King, Fleet Admiral Ernest J., 39, 226, 227; at Casablanca, 65; gives priority to Pacific, 67; anti-British, 67–8; conflict of interest with Marshall, 70; satisfied by Casablanca, 73; at TRIDENT, 87
King, W. L. Mackenzie, 118–19, 178
Knox, Frank, 107
Kohan, Albert, 169
Koiso, General Kuniaki, 203
Konoye, Prince Fumimaro, 10
Kursk salient, 126–7

Lampedusa, Island of, 94
Lampson, Sir Miles (later Lord Killearn), 130
Landing-craft, 71, 181, 205, 218–19, 235; pre-empted for Pacific, 67, 219; diverted from Britain for HUSKY, 86
Laval, Pierre, 41, 53, 167
Leahy, Admiral William D., 41, 66, 162, 186, 226
Leathers, Lord, 61, 86
Leclerc, General Philippe, 199
Lee, General Robert E., 76, 89
Leigh-Mallory, Air Marshal Sir T., 191
Leningrad, 23
Liddell Hart, Sir Basil, 81–2, 127, 160, 210
Lincoln, President Abraham, 26
Linlithgow, Marquess of, 130
Ljubljana Gap, 206
Lloyd George, David (Earl), 15, 134, 228
Loire River, 217
London, 97, 107, 169, 174, 191, 237; air attacks on, 142
Lovat, Lord, 215–16
Luftwaffe, *see* German Air Force

MacArthur, General Douglas, 20–1, 27, 87
Macmillan, Harold, 60–1, 101
"Magic," code-breaking process, 11
Malaya, conquest of, 29
Malta, 44, 103
Mareth Line, 81
Marrakesh, 78–9, 83, 192
Marshall, General George C., 11, 64, 65, 171, 186, 189, 208, 211, 223; disagrees with Churchill's strategy, 20–1; relationship with Dill, 21; dreads "sideshow," 37; agrees to aid for British in Middle East, 39; tries to stop TORCH, 39–40; personality, 66–7; F.D.R. and, 68; and King, 70; fails to question priority for capture of Tunis, 71–2, 83; sent to Algiers with Churchill, 89, 90–1; on postwar threat in Europe, 93; suggests AVALANCHE, 98, 101; Stimson proposes as commander for OVERLORD, 108; U.S. formula for

his appointment to OVERLORD command, 182–3, 190; denied OVERLORD command, 190–1

Marshall Islands, 73

"Mass Observation," 142

Mediterranean strategy, 44–5, 84–5, 90–2, 110, 114, 176, 188–9, 210–12, 223, 227, 229–30, 234–5; future course of, 85–6; "hardness" of Mediterranean coast of Europe, 99; F.D.R. and, 106–9; Stalin on, 181–2

Mers-el-Kébir, 41, 53

Messina, 96–7, 101, 104

Middle East, 31–2, 70, 99, 174, 228, 235; U.S. aid for British in, 39; Churchill concerned by number of troops idle in, 91

Midway, Battle of, 27

Missouri, U.S.S., 203

Möhne and Eder dams, 146, 222

Molotov, Vyacheslav, 37, 40, 175–6, 184

Montagu, Ewen, 92

Montgomery, General Bernard L. (later Field Marshal Viscount), 4, 36, 104–5, 134–5; appointed 8th Army commander, 45; qualities assessed, 46; wins battle of Alam Halfa, 48; El Alamein, 49; but fails to exploit, 49–50, 71, 80; enters Tunisia, 81; in Sicily, 96–7; appointed OVERLORD land commander, 191; and invasion, 195–9

Moran, Lord, 32, 47, 61, 91, 119, 163–4; finds Churchill has pneumonia, 192

Morgan, General Sir Frederick, 109, 173–4, 230

Morocco, 42, 51–3, 59–79, 82, 176

Moulin, Jean, 168, 171–2

Mountbatten, Admiral Lord Louis (later Earl), 66, 188, 203; mission to F.D.R., 38; Allied commander in S.E. Asia, 132; Churchill on, 132–3; comment, 133; at Cairo, 176; and Dieppe raid, 215; and "Mulberry" harbours, 220–1

"Mulberry" harbours, 196, 220–1

Murphy, Robert, 60–1, 101

Muslim League, 31, 238

Mussolini, Benito, 82, 112–13, 204, 234; declares war on U.S., 9; liability to Hitler, 98–9; fall of, 100; killed, 201

Nagasaki, 202

Naples, 98, 101–2, 104, 110, 196; falls to Allies, 105

Nehru, Jawaharlal, 29–30, 238

Netherlands, 20, 63, 217

Netherlands East Indies, 9, 11, 29

New Britain, 73

Newfoundland, 16, 90, 162

New Guinea, 27–8

New Zealand, 28, 119

Nicolson, Nigel, 96

Nile River, 45, 55, 91, 99

Nimitz, Admiral Chester W., 87

Normandy, 173, 209, 217, 218, 236, 239; campaign in, 195–7, 199

North-west Europe, invasion of, 85, 86, 92, 210, 211, 219, 223, 235, 239; Marshall favours, 21, 25; Churchill's opposition to, in 1942, 37–8; Mountbatten dissuades F.D.R. from, in 1942, 37–9; Churchill initially favours, in 1943, 63–5, 84–5, 212; Casablanca decisions on, 72–3; Germans able to discount in 1943, 93; F.D.R. insists on at QUADRANT, 106–9; STARKEY exercise, 173–4; invasion launched, 195; bridgehead established, 195–6; France's liberation complete, 199; preconditions for successful invasion, 213

Norway, 20, 63, 69, 109, 232

Nuremberg, 146

Oder River, 184, 209

"Omaha" beach, 195, 217, 221

Oran, 42, 53, 102, 161, 167

Origo, Iris, 113

OVERLORD, Operation, 67, 94, 126, 133, 135, 172, 176, 187, 192, 205, 211, 214, 221, 222, 234, 235; named, and target date fixed, 88; claims for asserted at QUADRANT, 106–10; Americans determined on absolute priority for, 177; date pledged at Teheran, 181; Stalin wishes to know who will command, 182–3; plan for criticised, 189; Ike appointed to

OVERLORD (*Cont.*)
command, 190; command structure, 191; Brooke and, 229–30

Pacific Ocean theatre, 10, 11, 18–20, 26–7, 177, 202, 235; switch of U.S. resources to, 62, 67, 73, 226; U.S. desire for Russian intervention in, 128
Palermo, 96
Pantellaria, Island of, 94
Patton, General George S., 51, 67, 96–7, 197–8
Pearl Harbor, 9, 10, 12, 13, 20, 26, 31, 63, 83, 162, 202, 225
Percival, General A. E., 29
Pershing, General John J., 66
Persia, 45
Persia, Shah of, 178
Pétain, Marshal Philippe, 41, 51, 55, 160, 161, 162, 179, 224
Philippines, 26–7, 29
Ploesti, 83
Pogue, Forrest C., 69
POINTBLANK, Operation, *see* bombing policy
Poland, 239; discussed at Teheran, 180–1, 184; Poles occupy Monte Cassino, 201; Warsaw rising, 233
Poletti, Colonel Charles, 110–11
Portal, Marshal of the R.A.F. Sir Charles (later Viscount), 4, 69–70, 157, 172, 196, 227; at Casablanca, 65; strategic direction of POINTBLANK, 136–7, 147; sceptical of daylight bombings, and developing long-range fighter, 139; exchanges with Churchill on bombing policy, 142–3, 149; Trenchard's favourite, 145; belief in terror bombing, 147–8; slow to restrain Harris, 148
Portugal, 169
Pound, Admiral Sir Dudley, 65, 229
Prague, 205–7
Prince of Wales, H.M.S., 29, 33
Prinz Eugen, 33

QUADRANT, conference, 101, 116, 118, 127, 132, 176; Churchill travels

to, 106; unfortunate timing of, 109–10
Quebec, first Allied conference at, *see* QUADRANT

Rabaul, 73, 177
Ramsay, Admiral Sir Bertram, 191
Rangoon, 30
Red Army, 184; holds Germans, 23–4; set to win outright, 126–7; generals younger in, 133; triumph, 204; position in 1943, 236, 237
Renown, H.M.S., 176
Repulse, H.M.S., 29, 33
Reynaud, Paul, 160
Rhine River, 201, 204
Rjukan, 232
Ritchie, General Neil, 31
rockets, V-1 and V-2, 231; guided missiles, 232
Roma, 103
Rome, 102, 103, 107; agreed Allied objective, 110; Churchill over-optimistic about, 114, 176; Stalin doubts wisdom of trying to capture, 181, 187; final battle for, 201
Rommel, General (later Marshal) Erwin, 45, 46, 218; counterattacks in Middle East, 31; storms Tobruk, 31; halted by Auchinleck, 32; defeated at Alam Halfa and second El Alamein, 48–9; gets his army away, 50, 71; in Tunisia, 80–2; seizes Alpine passes, 100–1; and French at Bir Hacheim, 168; and how to stop Allied invasion, 217
Roosevelt, Eleanor, 118
Roosevelt, Elliott, 61, 74; at Cairo, 177; at Teheran, 184
Roosevelt, Franklin, Jr., 61
Roosevelt, President Franklin D., 4, 10, 12, 33, 66, 67, 72, 73, 74, 89, 125, 132, 134, 211, 226, 227, 234, 235, 237, 238; relationship with Churchill, and two men compared, 14–18; favours N. African landing, 20–1; "beat Hitler first" policy, 20, 27, 87, 225; visited by Mountbatten, 37–9; approves Darlan deal, 54; at Casablanca conference, 59–78; with King and Marshall, 68; and French

leaders at Casablanca, 74–5; and Unconditional Surrender, 75–8; accompanies Churchill to Marrakesh, 78–9; and HUSKY, 85; insists on return to Continent in 1944, 87; takes Churchill to "Shangri-La," 89–90; wants conference at Quebec rather than London, 106; and Stimson, 107–8; OVERLORD politically desirable to, 109; at Quebec, 118; and Churchill's Harvard speech, 120; attitude to British Empire, 124; attitude to Russia, 127–9; and terror bombing, 149; and de Gaulle, 162–3, 166, 224, 230; agrees reluctantly to go to Teheran, 175; at first Cairo conference, 176–8; moves into Russian embassy in Teheran, 178; conversations with Stalin, 179–81; takes chair at meetings, 181; suggests move across Adriatic, 182; and future of Germany, 183; joke about shooting German officers, 184; his diplomacy at Teheran, 186–7; at second Cairo conference, 188–91; appoints Ike to command OVERLORD, 190; broadcast, 192; and government for liberated France, 199–200; death, 201; and Stalin, 207–8

Rosenman, Samuel I., 181, 187
Roumania, 70, 83, 108, 155, 182, 236
ROUNDUP, Operation, 21, 40, 64, 219
Royal Air Force, 49, 173; bombers transferred from Coastal Command, 33; Bomber Command under Harris, 136; night bombing policy, 136, 138; Fighter Command, 139; Army Co-operation Command, 139; terror bombing campaign, 144–6; Pathfinder force, 145; losses, 146; bombing policy challenged, 146–7; change of policy before D-Day, 148, 196, 222; limited attacks on oil targets, 148
Royal Navy, 25, 29
Ruhr, 142, 146, 156, 201
Rundstedt, Field Marshal Karl von, 216–17

St. Nazaire, 69, 215
St. Pierre and Miquelon, 162
Salerno operation, *see* AVALANCHE
Sardinia, 66, 91, 92, 98, 110, 111
Scharnhorst, 33
Scheldt River, 199, 216
Schweinfurt, 138–9, 140, 146, 147, 153
Seine River, 197, 216
Sherwood, Robert E., 120, 187; quotes assessment of Russia postwar, 127; assessment of U.S. policy towards China, 177
Sicily, 63, 71, 85–7, 90–2, 100–1, 103, 106, 109–12, 197, 212, 218; Allies agree to invade, 72; invaded, 94; conquered, 95–7;
Singapore, 37, 144, 152, 174, 203, 216, 229; fall of, 29; significance of fall, 29–30; Churchill's reaction, 32
SLEDGEHAMMER, Operation, 21, 37, 223; scrapped, 39–40
Smith, General Walter Bedell, 60, 191
Smolensk, 236
Smuts, Field Marshal J. C., 92, 189
S.O.E., *see* British Special Operations Executive
Solomon Islands, 28
South Africa, 119
South-east Asia, 19, 133, 176, 188, 203; new command, 108, 132
Spaatz, General Carl A., 148
Spain, 26, 42, 50, 169
Speer, Albert, 138, 139, 153–4, 155, 156
Spezia, 103
Stalin, Joseph (Marshal), 24, 25, 33, 70, 77, 87, 134, 163–4, 166, 171, 188, 203, 208, 233, 237; visited by Churchill, 43–5; and Darlan deal, 54; declines to attend Casablanca conference, 59; and Casablanca decisions, 92–3; reacts to Western deal with Badoglio, 125–6; agrees to meet F.D.R. and Churchill at Teheran, 175–6; persuades F.D.R. to stay at Soviet embassy, 178; conversations with F.D.R., 178–81; promises intervention against Japan, 181; wishes to know who will command OVERLORD, 182–3; and shooting German officers, 184; toasted by Churchill, 185; most

Stalin (*Cont.*)
clear-headed of the Three, 186–7;
F.D.R.'s fulsome tribute to, 192;
contrasted with Hitler, 207
Stalingrad, 24–5, 223; Germans lose
battle for, 55, 94; Sword of, 182
Stark, Admiral Harold R., 11
STARKEY, invasion exercise, 173–4
Stilwell, General Joseph W., 87
Stimson, Henry L., 107–8
Suzuki, Admiral, 203

tanks, 39, 48–9, 221–2
Taranto, 105
Taylor, A. J. P., 49
Tedder, Marshal of the Royal Air
Force Sir Arthur (later Lord), 73,
110–11, 191, 196
Teheran, 44, 106, 207, 237, 238; Allied
conference at (EUREKA), 175–88
Tito, Marshal, 182
Tobruk, fall of, 31, 144, 152, 174, 228;
Churchill's reaction, 32; U.S.
reaction, 39
Tocqueville, Alexis de, 117
Tojo, General Hideki, 10, 203
Tokyo, 203
TORCH, Operation, 49, 50, 61–4, 70–1,
106, 116, 164, 168, 211–2, 219,
224–5, 234; agreement on plans for,
40; hazards of, 40–3; date postponed,
43; Churchill expounds to Stalin,
44–5; crucial test for Allies, 47;
carried out, 51–5
Toulon, 54
Trenchard, Marshal of the R.A.F.
Lord, 141, 145
TRIDENT, Washington conference in
May 1943, 85–9, 100, 109, 110, 137,
165; compromise at, 88
Trieste, 201
Trincomalee, 31
Tripoli, 46, 50, 80, 102
Truman, President Harry S., 15
Tsushima, battle of, 29
Tunis, 86, 92, 94, 191; Allies near, 54;
attempt to reach postponed, 1943, 55;
priority for capture of, 71–2, 80–2;
fall of, 81
Turkey, 19, 86, 99, 177, 211, 225, 239;
policy of bringing into war, 65, 72;

more afraid of Russians than
Germans, 83; Churchill's mission to,
83–4; discussed at Teheran, 181;
leaders at Cairo, 188–9

U-boats, 72, 202; losses due to, 32–3;
improved models, 232
"Ultra" code-breaking process, 48, 82
Unconditional Surrender, 113;
declaration at Casablanca, and merits
of policy, 75–8; edited out of Italian
surrender, 104; not strictly applied to
Japanese, 203; Wilmot's criticism of,
208
United States Army, in Philippines, 27;
in New Guinea, 27–8; in N. Africa,
51–5, 59, 80–1; in Sicily, 96–7; in
Italy, 104–6, 114; in Normandy,
195–7; after break-out, 198–9;
expansion of, 213–14; in Pacific, 219
United States Army Air Forces,
Doolittle raid, 27; Arnold
commanding, 65; 8th Air Force
under Gen. Eaker, 136; raids in
1943, 138–9; slow to order Mustangs,
140
United States Chiefs of Staff, 38–9, 228;
abandon SLEDGEHAMMER and
agree to TORCH, 40, 42; not united
at Casablanca, 67, 70; ill-prepared for
conference, 71
United States Congress, 11–13, 17, 59;
influence of mid-term elections on
strategy, 20; Marshall and, 68;
support for MacArthur in, 87;
Churchill addresses, 90
United States Navy, 224; attacked at
Pearl Harbor, 9, 12, 26; political
influence of, 20; battles in Pacific,
27–8; and convoy system, 32–3;
assumes responsibility for S. Atlantic,
117; superiority in Pacific, 202; huge
concentration of landing-craft there,
219

Vekemans, Robert, 198
Vichy French, *see* French Vichy regime
Victor Emmanuel III, King, 102, 103,
113
Vienna, 201, 205–7, 208
Vishinsky, Andrei, 179

Vistula River, 209, 239
Volga River, 24
Voroshilov, Marshal Kliment, 179

"Wallonia," 162
Warsaw rising, 233, 236
Wavell, Field-Marshal Sir Archibald
   (later Earl), 86, 130–2
Wehrmacht, see German Army
Wilmot, Chester, 4, 204, 205–9

Wilson, General Sir H. Maitland (later
   Field Marshal Lord), 172, 191
Wilson, President Woodrow, 16;
   "Fourteen Points," 78

Yalta conference, 106, 200, 207, 238
Yugoslavs, 99

Zuckerman, Solly (Lord), 111

READ MORE IN PENGUIN

READ MORE IN PENGUIN

HISTORY

A History of Twentieth-Century Russia Robert Service

'A remarkable work of scholarship and synthesis . . . [it] demands to be read' *Spectator*. 'A fine book . . . It is a dizzying tale and Service tells it well; he has none of the ideological baggage that has so often bedevilled Western histories of Russia . . . A balanced, dispassionate and painstaking account' *Sunday Times*

A Monarchy Transformed: Britain 1603–1714 Mark Kishlansky

'Kishlansky's century saw one king executed, another exiled, the House of Lords abolished, and the Church of England reconstructed along Presbyterian lines . . . A masterly narrative, shot through with the shrewdness that comes from profound scholarship' *Spectator*

American Frontiers Gregory H. Nobles

'At last someone has written a narrative of America's frontier experience with sensitivity and insight. This is a book which will appeal to both the specialist and the novice' James M. McPherson, Princeton University

The Pleasures of the Past David Cannadine

'This is almost everything you ever wanted to know about the past but were too scared to ask . . . A fascinating book and one to strike up arguments in the pub' *Daily Mail*. 'He is erudite and rigorous, yet always fun. I can imagine no better introduction to historical study than this collection' *Observer*

Prague in Black and Gold Peter Demetz

'A dramatic and compelling history of a city Demetz admits to loving and hating . . . He embraces myth, economics, sociology, linguistics and cultural history . . . His reflections on visiting Prague after almost a half-century are a moving elegy on a world lost through revolutions, velvet or otherwise' *Literary Review*

READ MORE IN PENGUIN

HISTORY

The Vikings   Else Roesdahl

Far from being just 'wild, barbaric, axe-wielding pirates', the Vikings created complex social institutions, oversaw the coming of Christianity to Scandinavia and made a major impact on European history through trade, travel and far-flung colonization. This study is a rich and compelling picture of an extraordinary civilization.

A Short History of Byzantium   John Julius Norwich

In this abridgement of his celebrated trilogy, John Julius Norwich has created a definitive overview of 'the strange, savage, yet endlessly fascinating world of Byzantium'. 'A real life epic of love and war, accessible to anyone' *Independent on Sunday*

The Eastern Front 1914–1917   Norman Stone

'Without question one of the classics of post-war historical scholarship' Niall Ferguson. 'Fills an enormous gap in our knowledge and understanding of the Great War' *Sunday Telegraph*

The Idea of India   Sunil Khilnani

'Many books about India will be published this year; I doubt if any will be wiser and more illuminating about its modern condition than this' *Observer*. 'Sunil Khilnani's meditation on India since Independence is a *tour de force*' *Sunday Telegraph*

The Penguin History of Europe   J. M. Roberts

'J. M. Roberts has managed to tell the rich and remarkable tale of European history in fewer than 700 fascinating, well-written pages ... few would ever be able to match this achievement' *The New York Times Book Review*. 'The best single-volume history of Europe' *The Times Literary Supplement*

READ MORE IN PENGUIN

HISTORY

Hope and Glory: Britain 1900–1990   Peter Clarke

'Splendid ... If you want a text book for the century, this is it' *Independent*. 'Clarke has written one of the classic works of modern history. His erudition is encyclopaedic, yet lightly and wittily borne. He writes memorably, with an eye for the telling detail, an ear for aphorism, and an instinct for irony' *Sunday Telegraph*

Instruments of Darkness: Witchcraft in England 1550–1750
James Sharpe

'Learned and enthralling ... Time and again, as I read this scrupulously balanced work of scholarship, I was reminded of contemporary parallels' Jan Morris, *Independent*

A Social History of England   Asa Briggs

Asa Briggs's magnificent exploration of English society has been totally revised and brought right up to the present day. 'A treasure house of scholarly knowledge ... beautifully written, and full of the author's love of his country, its people and its landscape' *Sunday Times*

Hatchepsut: The Female Pharaoh   Joyce Tyldesley

Queen – or, as she would prefer to be remembered king – Hatchepsut was an astonishing woman. Defying tradition, she became the female embodiment of a male role, dressing in men's clothes and even wearing a false beard. Joyce Tyldesley's dazzling piece of detection strips away the myths and restores the female pharaoh to her rightful place.

Fifty Years of Europe: An Album   Jan Morris

'A highly insightful kaleidoscopic encyclopedia of European life ... Jan Morris writes beautifully ... Like a good vintage wine [*Fifty Years*] has to be sipped and savoured rather than gulped. Then it will keep warming your soul for many years to come' *Observer*